LONDON AT WAR

1939–1945

Published by IWM, Lambeth Road, London SE1 6HZ
iwm.org.uk

ISBN 978-1-904897-33-0

A catalogue record for this book is available from the British Library.
Printed and bound by Gomer Press Limited
Colour reproduction by DL Imaging

Every effort has been made to contact all copyright holders. The publishers will be glad to make good in future editions any error or omissions brought to their attention.

Front cover image: © IWM (HU 36220) *see page 50–51*
Back cover image: © IWM (HU 131433) *see page 231*

LONDON AT WAR

1939–1945

A Nation's Capital Survives

ALAN JEFFREYS

Edited by Mark Hawkins-Dady

Dedicated to the memory of my father-in-law, Derek Brook,
a Londoner who lived through this period.

CONTENTS

PREFACE

In the Second World War, London, as the capital of not only a country but of an Empire and Commonwealth, came to stand as a defiant symbol of the resistance against Hitler's surging conquests across Europe. The most celebrated manifestation of that phase of the war was the eight months of 1940–1 during which London was bombed relentlessly from the air and the war was brought to the very homes of civilian men, women and children who paid the price in their thousands. For a while, this 'Blitz', which wrought destruction on other British towns and cities too, *was* the front line: British soldiers were dying in far fewer numbers over this period than were the civilians at home.

London's experience resonated deeply and widely, for this was also the period when Britain and its Empire were the last man standing after the Nazi victories of 1939–40. London's fate, and Londoners' lives and experience, were scrutinised with fascination, by Britain's political masters but also abroad, not least in the United States. After all, there had never been such a prolonged campaign of aerial bombing against a single target in history. Would the bomber 'always get through', as the gloom-merchants of the 1930s had asserted? Would the beleaguered city and country – what one US journalist called 'Churchill's island' – make it through? Would the people put up with the punishment dealt out, or would they demand that their government come to terms and stop their suffering? Would democracy itself survive?

In words and pictures, *London at War 1939–1945* begins by taking the reader from the build-up to the Blitz – from 1939 through the aerial combat of the Battle of Britain – to Hitler's strategic decision to target London. But it also follows the city's story right through to 1945, for the conclusion of the Blitz was by no means the end of London's, nor of Londoners', plight. The prominence of the Blitz, and its myth of an unquestioned 'Blitz spirit', has tended to obscure these later stages, but, without the benefit of hindsight, Londoners could never rest easy. The whole of their lives was conditioned by the circumstances and everyday details of war, from rationing to the blackout, from evacuation to sheltering in the Underground, from the civil defence services into which so many men – and women – volunteered or were drafted, to the constant effort to prevent the city's infrastructure collapsing. And when Germany's latest wonder weapon in the shape of supersonic missiles started falling in deathly silence, from September 1944, Londoners appreciated a new kind of fear: no anti-aircraft gun or RAF fighter could stop that sort of attack hitting home.

Using the matchless collections of images, artwork, letters, diaries, interviews and other original materials in London's Imperial War Museum, this book seeks to place the lives of ordinary Londoners at the heart of that experience. A large number of these materials – such as photos from the Press and Censorship Bureau (which was responsible to the wartime Ministry of

Information) – have never been published before. In particular, readers will find here a cast of Londoners who kept diaries and wrote letters throughout the war, and through whom we can track the unfolding responses and emotions of people who could never know whether things were about to get better or worse. Here are the intimate thoughts, reactions and commentaries of the time, by men and women such as Gwladys Cox, Vivienne Hall, Vere Hodgson and George Britton. As with the best of diaries and letters, they demonstrate that it is impossible to observe the daily life of the individual in isolation; the context of the wider war is apparent in all of them. These individuals are joined in *London at War 1939–1945* by Mollie Panter-Downes, a middle-class semi-professional writer, who, from 1939 to 1945, kept Americans eloquently informed about London's trials and tribulations in her column 'Letter from London', published in the *New Yorker* magazine. Living in the capital during the week, she would escape to her Surrey pig farm at weekends to work up her copy.

Today, as the war itself recedes in history and the numbers of those who can personally remember it dwindles and will soon vanish, London's war experience still endures. It continues to spread out from history and penetrate popular culture. From coffee cups to T-shirts, the ubiquitous Blitz-era slogan 'Keep Calm and Carry On' epitomises understated grit and insouciance. Images of the dome of St Paul's Cathedral, proud against a wall of flames, have become a poster child for that spirit of defiance. Contemporary wartime documentaries such as *London Can Take It*, although made with a manifestly morale-boosting and propagandist intent, have become classics of the genre. In television drama, the series *The Halcyon* (broadcast 2017) has invented a fictional hotel and cast of characters but with clear analogies to the real habitués and incidents associated with London's top wartime hotels and nightspots, such as the Savoy or the Café de Paris. And on film, *Their Finest* (released 2017) captured the essence of wartime London and the Ministry of Information rather well. In these and other ways, London's war experience in the mid-twentieth century continues to play a part in a sense of British identity in the twenty-first century.

Prime Minister Neville Chamberlain arrives at Heston Airport following the Munich Agreement with Adolf Hitler, Benito Mussolini and French Prime Minister Edouard Daladier (30 September 1938). Brandishing an accord signed with Hitler, Chamberlain trumpeted his success in averting hostilities, and for a while he was lionised for it. The agreement did not rein in Hitler's ambitions.

PROLOGUE

FROM FRAGILE PEACE TO PHONEY WAR

'Isn't this a queer war?'

In 1939, London was the largest capital city in the world, with a population of 8,615,000. More than one in five of the people of England and Wales could account themselves a Londoner. They lived in the same place, but they lived very different lives, reflecting a country that, in many ways, was a divided society. If London was the metropolitan home to the great and the good, and to fashionable, wealthy society, it also contained some of the deepest depths of urban poverty. To an extent, these extremes were embodied in the cultural and geographic distinctions of West End and East End, between which were many gradations.

Housing was one very visible marker of difference. For those who lived in the new suburbs, or even in local authority housing estates, economic conditions had improved. But the housing situation in the East End was appalling. In 1938, in the 346 flats of Bethnal Green's Quinn Square, four families normally had to share one tap, while every two families had to share a lavatory. In this case, growing support for the Communist Party spurred a successful rent strike against greedy landlords. In another deprived borough, Stepney, a Tenants' Defence League was formed, led by an Anglo-Catholic priest, Father John Groser, with the avowedly Communist 'Tubby' Rosen as its secretary. It acquired thousands of members, as rent strikes took place in street after street – and again were mostly successful.

When Poland was invaded on 1 September 1939 and war became a reality, it was little surprise to the people of London – Hitler had already marched into Austria and Czechoslovakia, and the British policy of appeasement was in tatters; what was more uncertain was whether, under duress, the physical fabric of the city and the social fabric of such a diverse population would hold together.

At 11.15am on 3 September 1939, Prime Minister Neville Chamberlain gave the news over the wireless that Britain had declared war on Germany. Just 20 minutes later, air raid sirens were heard over London: it was a false alarm, though a prescient one. They sounded again at two in the morning. An unusually large congregation at St Paul's Cathedral, minus the boys from St Paul's School (who had already been evacuated to Truro in Cornwall), had just finished singing 'O God of love, O King of Peace/ Make wars throughout the world to cease!', whereupon the Bishop of Willesden led them down to the safety of the crypt. Across London, people were experiencing the frisson of danger as they took refuge. In a shelter in Hammersmith, West London, one observer reported everything to be 'quite orderly and no hysterics'.

A newspaper seller disseminates the day's breaking news: 'WAR – OFFICIAL' (3 September 1939). Hitler's invasion of Poland confirmed what everyone knew already: that British and French appeasement of Germany had failed, and that the 'peace for our time', which Chamberlain had declared in September 1938, was a dead dream.

Mollie Panter-Downes, a middle-class housewife living in London and Surrey, wrote a column about the city for the *New Yorker* magazine. She left an evocative description of London's changing landscape and Londoners' changing habits on this first day of war:

> On the stretch of green turf by Knightsbridge Barracks, which used to be the scampering ground for the smartest terriers in London, has appeared a row of steam shovels that bite out

mouthfuls of earth, hoist it aloft, and dump it into lorries; it is then carted away to fill sandbags. The eye has now become accustomed to sandbags everywhere, and to the balloon barrage, the trap for enemy planes, which one morning spread over the sky like some form of silvery dermatitis.

Posting a letter has acquired a new interest, too, since His Majesty's tubby, scarlet pillar boxes have been done up in squares of yellow detector paint, which changes color if there is poison gas in the air and is said to be as sensitive as a chameleon. Gas masks have suddenly become part of everyday civilian equipment and everybody is carrying the square cardboard cartons that look as though they might contain a pound of grapes for a sick friend.

Iron railings from a park are removed in May 1940. In the expectation that non-essential iron would be needed for the war effort, railings were removed across the country. The capital's squares and parks became truly open spaces.

One sign of the new circumstances was the introduction, by Act of Parliament, of full-scale conscription for men aged between 18 and 41, replacing a much more limited form of compulsory military service brought in earlier in the year. In truth though, several of the important changes that would fundamentally affect Londoners' lives had already arrived. For a start, from 1 September the city had to be plunged into darkness at night to conform to the new blackout regulations. In these early days, even lighting a match during the blackout period could result in a fine. Later, a more realistic approach emerged, as limited use of illuminated signs and 'glimmer' or 'star' lighting was permitted (except during air raids).

The blackout was undeniably resented though. At the very least, it was highly inconvenient, particularly for pedestrians. In November 1939, George and Helena Britton, residents of Walthamstow, East London, described it to their daughter Elizabeth, who lived in the United States:

> You are right about the black out being awful. Down come the blinds at 4.30 and with no street lighting it is quite an adventure to go out after dark. Just now it is full moon and it isn't so bad but when there is no moon the whole place is in such darkness that although you can hear people walking along the pavement you really can't see them except at the moment of actual passing. My own opinion is that it is carried much too far. I know that fatalities on the roads have increased very greatly since the lighting restrictions.

George Britton was quite correct. In September 1939 there were 1,130 deaths from road accidents, more than double the figure (544) in the previous September. Moreover, by January 1942, one in five people had acquired some form of injury as a direct result of the blackout. In 1939–40, matters were not helped by the coldest winter for fifty years, with snow and burst pipes exacerbating the situation.

Nellie Carver lived in West Norwood, South London, with her mother and aunt. She also kept a diary throughout the war, inspired by Samuel Pepys whom she thought 'the ideal Civil Servant who stuck to his post in Plague & Fire when many of his betters fled'. She found the blackout most trying, for example during her journey home from work in Central London:

> Once outside, I couldn't persuade myself to take a step forward. I'd never known real darkness before, our practice blackouts being only 'semi' & for the moment I was paralysed & lost all sense of direction. I stood still, panic-stricken – then said firmly over & over again to myself 'I know this street absolutely well & where it goes – don't be such an ass – it's the same street as in the daylight – it hasn't changed – walk forward quickly & you will come

Left A British Railways poster warns passengers of the very real dangers of accidents during the blackout. The statistics spoke for themselves, as deaths and injuries at night rocketed, even without the aid of the Luftwaffe's bombs.

Opposite This London Passenger Transport Board poster emphasises life carrying on as normal despite the blackout. New themes and designs in poster art sprang up on London's billboards throughout the war, combining advice, admonition, reassurance and propaganda in equal measure. **© TFL from the London Transport Museum Collection**

> into Newgate St OK. After a few seconds fight with myself I did venture along & came to Holborn safely, but when I made the train (in pitch blackness) I felt damp with perspiration & quite exhausted for a few moments.

Another Londoner, Mrs Gwladys Cox, had lived in West Hampstead for more than forty years, along with her husband Ralph, a retired barrister, and their cat, Bob. She too wrote up a diary throughout the

Steering London through

daylight & blackout - faithfully

Opposite Two young siblings, June and Tony Bryant, with their bags packed and labels attached (stating name, birth date, school and destination), wait at Clerkenwell for the train that will take them on their evacuation journey (1939). As June's label says, they are heading to Luton. For many of their age, it was an anxious, unsettling time; for others, it was the beginning of an exciting adventure.

Right A customer tries on one of the luminous flowers that could be worn instead of glow-in-the-dark armbands, for a more decorous way of being seen in the murky blackout. Other ways to stay visible included luminous buttons and badges.

war. For her, the blackout meant an intense 'darkness outside', in which 'to walk along the street and cross the road at night is a real adventure. In consequence, practically all shops are closing at, or before dusk, and the streets of West Hampstead are deserted by sunset.'

If London had less light, it also had fewer people. In order to reduce the number of possible deaths and injuries from aerial attack, the government had planned to evacuate children and certain other vulnerable groups from the densely populated cities and industrial areas and send them to the countryside. The first official evacuation scheme began on1 September 1939, in which almost 1.5 million people were moved to safety in just two days: school-age children, pregnant women, mothers with toddlers and the handicapped, accompanied by a whole army of teachers and helpers – the biggest internal mass migration in British history. Some 600,000 children left London, having first gathered at 1,589 assembly points before heading to 168 entraining stations. Two of these children were twelve-year-old Sheila Ward and her brother, who lived in Croydon, on the edge of South London. On the morning that war was declared, they were packing up their treasured books and stamp collection. Their father had written out their evacuation labels with their names, school addresses and identity numbers (Sheila's was CDE 64/5). Neither of the children had been away from home before, apart from the annual holiday to Broadstairs in Kent. In their case, they were excited about the prospect.

Some of the capital's evacuees, originally from Woodmansterne Road School in Streatham, South London, in a Welsh village hall in Carmarthenshire (1940). The older girls sew, while the younger children either read or sew. Around the country, there were efforts to maintain some educational provision for London's children in their new surroundings.

While the blackout was making London quieter, that effect was only intensified by this mass exodus. 'No one talked about it much, but everyone noticed it, and was sad,' noted the *Sunday Times* war correspondent Leonard Mosley. London bus driver Henry Penny thought it 'a pitiful sight to see so many thousands of small children, all labelled and carrying small cases and parcels. Some crying, some happy, all going to strange homes'. Some children looked back on evacuation as one of the happiest experiences of their lives, but others missed their families unbearably, especially if they were ill-treated by their new foster carers in the countryside. For the young East Ender Valerie Curtis, separated from her siblings during evacuation, things were unpleasant, as she later recalled:

> For several months we were shunted around from one billet to another and with one of these we had to share with several other evacuees. I recall that in this small house, we were made to sleep in a big double bed, top and tail with boys and girls all in together. It was not surprising

Pupils evacuated from Creek Road School in Greenwich, South London, help the blacksmith in Llandissilio, Pembrokeshire (1940). Provincial life brought unfamiliar sights, sounds and smells to London's urban children, although some unfortunate youngsters could find themselves exploited as drudges.

> that among these small children, incontinence problems were experienced and it does not leave a lot to the imagination to guess just what that environment was like, especially as quite often, the sheets were just dried by the fire and put back on to the bed.

Valerie was later billeted with a Mrs Newman in a village near Leominster, Herefordshire, where an older girl from Liverpool joined her, who, unfortunately for Valerie, quickly became Mrs Newman's favourite:

> ... it was automatically assumed that I was from the slums... at the tender age of no more than six, I was expected to help with the housework which sometimes included black-leading the kitchen range and scrubbing the stone floored passage and front door step.

A group of children, with their labels, bundles and cases, wait to board their train out of London, as a policeman checks that all is in order (1940). Evacuation was not a single event during the war: official, and unofficial, evacuations ebbed and flowed, as the dangers of London life grew or lessened.

Valerie's sister Violet, by contrast, was evacuated to St Osyth in Essex, where she was fostered by Joe and Vi Lawson who quickly became 'Uncle Joe' and 'Auntie Vi'. After that experience, her return to London came as a shock:

> I marched round the garden singing 'don't fence me in'... I had spent my formative years enjoying playing in a large garden. I had been used to the 'fairyland' of the blossoms of the cherry trees, and I knew I would miss the scent of the honeysuckle in the tree near the kitchen and living room windows.
>
> I was going to leave all this freedom and my school friends, to be confined to living in a terraced house with very little garden. I would have to get used to living with my parents and brothers and sisters.

However, it was not a one-way street, and foster carers could find the experience of coping with evacuees traumatic. Three weeks into the war, on 22 September, Gwladys Cox was on the bus heading home after shopping in Marylebone, when:

> ... a lady passenger nearly sat on & demolished my gas-mask, so we began to talk. People I find are much more talkative to strangers than they used to be. 'Isn't this a queer war?' she asked me. I agreed that it appeared to be different, so far, to what we had expected. She went on to tell me her sister had put her name down for 'war services', and had recently been sent to some country rectory 'to save the vicar's wife from going dotty'. The latter had been landed with six evacuated children and a teacher, the teacher more troublesome than the children.

The new young charges could be a challenge, especially if the foster parents were unused to having children around. Evelyn Waugh exploited such ideas in his satirical novel *Put Out More Flags* (1942), in which the main character, the 'ne'er do well' Basil Seal, takes on responsibility as billeting officer for the Connolly family: Doris, Mickey and Marlene, from London. They never stay long with any family, because of their dysfunctional ways, so Basil Seal comes up with a mercenary plan of getting people to pay him to take them away again.

Private schools were evacuated *en masse*. The boys of Dulwich College Prep School were initially evacuated to Cranbrook in Kent, but then moved on to Betws-y-Coed, North Wales, where they were billeted in the Royal Oak Hotel. One pupil, Peter Milton, seemed happy enough, describing to his mother (20 June 1940) how 'The Rooms are arranged so that friends are together as much as possible... and it is very satisfactory as far as I am concerned.' The following week he wrote again, about the new daily routines: 'From church we go direct to school, some to the garage, of which we use the grooms' old rooms above the actual stables, some to the Llugwy Tea Rooms of which we use the tea room part (the Annexe use the rest), and some to the sun-lounge at the hotel.' He and his friends had free time in the afternoon and were able to explore the countryside; many of them would affectionately remember learning how to fly fish for trout and climbing the nearby mountains.

With so many adults and children on the move, hundreds of very varied evacuation stories emerged. Some children, especially from poorer backgrounds, were associated with problems of lice, bed wetting and swearing; some found themselves turned into unpaid labour in rural communities. Certainly, the scheme drew attention to economic and social deprivation, particularly as existed in inner-city London. Gwladys

Cox put it well: 'one half of the world is learning how the other half lives, which may be all to the good'. A minority of children – 2,700 of those officially evacuated, and 11,000 of those privately evacuated by September 1940 – were sent overseas. The sons of MPs Duff Cooper (Minister of Information, or informally 'Minister of Morale') and the socialite Henry 'Chips' Channon went to the United States and, in Cooper's case, his actions in so doing drew much criticism. But international evacuation lost its appeal after the tragedy of the SS *City of Benares*, torpedoed by a German U-boat on 18 September 1939. Seventy-three children on their way to Canada lost their lives.

Businesses, civil servants and even whole government ministries also relocated to other parts of the country, leaving Central London feeling almost lifeless in the first few weeks of the war. The new Ministry of Food evacuated to Denbigh, in North Wales; the War Office went to Droitwich, the Air Ministry to Worcester. The Prudential Assurance Company migrated to Torquay, in Devon. Even works of art were evacuated. The statue of Eros in Piccadilly was moved to Egham, Surrey, while the National Gallery's collection was dispersed around the country, mostly in North Welsh houses and castles – and then later stored in the disused Manod slate quarry, near Blaenau Ffestiniog.

London's cultural life was certainly muted, following the closure of museums and galleries. But this period also marked the beginning of what would become a wartime tradition at the now pictureless National Gallery, which had been earmarked for government use. The pianist Myra Hess contacted its director, Kenneth Clark, suggesting that she play a concert there to raise morale among Londoners. Clark then proposed daily events, scheduling the first one for 10 October 1939. The idea took off, and the concerts, which cost a shilling (all proceeds to the Musicians Benevolent Fund), proved very popular. Hess managed to persuade composers, conductors and singers including Benjamin Britten, Michael Tippett, Sir Henry Wood and Kathleen Ferrier to take part, and audiences often numbered over a thousand (including, on at least one occasion, the Queen), far exceeding the two hundred allowed by the Home Office. These concerts carried on through the war, relocating to the Gallery's lower rooms when the bombs started falling.

For now, however, London remained quiet over the autumn of 1939, and even into the spring of 1940. Following the initial tension generated by the first few weeks of the war, people started to drift back into the capital. Many parents reclaimed their children from the foster carers, and the evacuated mothers with children under five were often the quickest of the evacuees to return. London's schools had not reopened, though, so children tended to run wild. Unfortunately, they were now also exposed to the danger from which the government had hoped to protect them: aerial bombing.

The 'experts', basing their calculations on the First World War experience, which saw 600 Londoners die from the bombs dropped by Zeppelin airships and Gotha bombers, believed that any future conflict was likely to involve mass casualties from gas and bombing. In this new age of aerial warfare, they concluded that in 60 days an all-out aerial bombardment could kill 600,000 people. Such fears seemed confirmed by bombing raids on cities during the Spanish Civil War, particularly the attack carried out by airmen from the Italian air force against Barcelona in 1938, on behalf of the Nationalist cause. Six years before, in the House of Commons, Stanley Baldwin had already accepted that – in his words – the 'bomber will always get through'. Thus, there was a general consensus before the Second World War that the bombing of London and other British cities would be devastating. A certain fatalism descended. As George Britton told his daughter, 'In the matter of air-raids there is the certainty that the bomber will always get through with more or less success....'

Such fears permeated London and British society, and penetrated the culture too, for example in H G Wells's novel *The Shape of Things to Come* (1933), which was turned into the film *Things to Come* in 1936. In West Norwood, Nellie Carver stayed up all night reading Philip Gibbs's *Broken Pledges*, which – in her description – 'dwells on the horrors of Air Bombardment of London such a huge target & so difficult to defend'. She acknowledged that perhaps it was 'not the best thing to read late at night!' before admitting: 'I wanted to stop but the subject had a morbid fascination for me & I finished the book. Have always had a horror (since the last war) of heavy things falling on me so don't pretend to be at all brave about it!' Vivienne Hall, who lived with her mother in Putney and worked as a typist in Moorgate, doubtless spoke for many when she summarised her feelings in her diary for 1 September 1939:

> We were either in or born during the last war and for the last 20 years I and all of the rest of us have heard nothing but the fact that the next war will be the destruction of civilisation and of all we hold dear, that we shall all be blown to bits, or reduced to such a sorry state that we shall wish we had been, that war was inevitable sometime and that nothing we could do would stop it.

Concert pianist Myra Hess performs at one of the famous lunchtime concerts given at the National Gallery (1940). Other musical luminaries also took part in this series of performances, which became a durable feature of London's cultural life amid the vicissitudes of war.

A response to what therefore seemed an unavoidable and grave threat to the nation was the civil defence organisation named Air Raid Precautions (ARP). By September 1939, some 1.5 million people, more than half of them part-time volunteers, had joined the service.

However, the bombs did not fall – not yet. As a result, ARP Wardens and workers were already beginning to be resented since they seemed to be doing very little other than being officious and insisting on blackout precautions. In fact, although the landscape had changed and London was now full of uniforms, the essentials of daytime life during the winter of 1939–40 were little different to what they had been before the war. People lived on in their undamaged homes, and most did the same jobs they were doing before September 1939. George Britton was sanguine enough to inform his daughter in the United States:

> It is very nice of the people to be so sympathetic to us, but really here in London nothing is happening. I read in the paper this

A London stallholder invokes a popular musical lyric to express a simple truth: that war means shortages (1940). Indeed, what would later become the world's favourite fruit effectively disappeared from the capital's shelves, as war destroyed the normal patterns of international trade.

> morning that the German wireless was talking of a terrible air raid over London, the machines flying within a few feet of the house tops. Well, I can assure you we knew nothing about it till the Germans told us.

It was, in one witty nickname, the 'Bore War', though this phase of relative inactivity (except at sea) became better known by the Americanism 'Phoney War'. For Vivienne Hall though, writing on 8 December 1939, all the incremental changes were adding up:

> A night at home again sitting by the fire and knitting I suppose – what a life!! It is amazing to think how this war doesn't seem to have affected us much yet when we think about it seriously we find that its fingers have pulled all our normal activities to bits and every little thing we used to have or do is now altered in some way. Speaking personally I find that little things are 1/2d. or 1d. more in the shops,

> that small intimate things are difficult to get; that my various clubs and societies have had to close down and I, therefore, don't see the people I used to; I only travel when I have to and visits which ordinarily caused me no bother and I made as a matter of course are now fraught with troubles and not all easy; that friends I saw frequently have disappeared and that, in fact, my whole life is quite different – yet casually we say the war hasn't started yet!

For those that could afford it – and prices were indeed rising – restaurants in London still served up sumptuous meals, where often the dining experience was accompanied by the sound of small orchestras. The high life went on, so that when Henry 'Chips' Channon lunched at the Ritz on 22 September 1939 ('which has become fantastically fashionable'), he could observe 'all the great, the gay, the Government; we knew 95% of everyone there'. Five days later, the Chancellor of the Exchequer, Sir John Simon, introduced the first wartime budget, which raised income tax by two shillings in the pound to seven shillings and sixpence. Duties were also raised on beer, spirits, sugar and tobacco. Gwladys Cox thought the budget was 'a bitter pill and it remains to be seen what its effect will be on the life (and the soul) of the nation'. This Bore War was proving expensive.

In another sign of the times, despite the onset of Christmas the buying of gifts was not what it usually was. In the West End, Gwladys Cox was able to find the 'usual Christmas display' in Marshall & Snelgrove's, 'but with so many having left London, the shop was empty and it was quite pathetic to see all the assistants standing about idle and anxious to serve me'.

There were certainly fewer cats and dogs around. For them, the outbreak of war had proved a catastrophe. The National Air Raid Precautions Animal Committee had recommended the killing of cats and dogs that could not be relocated to the country. In the first four days of the war, 400, 000 of them – just over one in four of London's pets – were put down. Such a vast culling brought consequences, as cat owner Gwladys Cox described: 'There has been a perfect holocaust of cats in London, and, as a result, some districts according to the papers are threatened with a plague of vermin. So, now, the authorities are begging people to keep their pets, if possible.' She had saved her own cat from the butchery.

Some days after Christmas, on 4 January 1940, Vivienne Hall was with her fellow typists in the City, pondering the meaning of a war that still seemed strangely abstract:

> A violent discussion with one or two girls at the office about the war – what was it for etc. I think it is clear this war is a fight between Robotism and Humanity – no-one has suggested this but it seems so obvious to me that we and all the 'human' nations are fighting furiously for existence against the relentless 'robot' nations and the world will be peopled in future (if there is a future) by either one or other of these classes – Please God it is human, for I should hate to think all the bright youngsters about today will be forced to live as numbers and cogs in some gigantic de-humanised factory of a world! I'm only a typist so I expect this idea is absurd but it's quite plain to me that this is the case.

As the weeks went on, the lack of action was bringing its own anxieties. For Gwladys Cox, it was 'a time of great tension, waiting for something to happen; wondering why nothing had happened'. And, she observed, 'more and more people were leaving town – removal vans in the streets, in fact, were the order of the day, while more and more "To Let" or "For Sale" boards were appearing on houses'. An eerie sleepiness was descending: 'The streets were emptying of traffic and silence outside, at night, that of a country village. Few, if any, children were to be seen.'

As it turned out, there was not much longer to wait, as suddenly events moved in rapid succession.

This celebrated German image shows a Heinkel He111 bomber looming over the Thames and the Isle of Dogs, in London's East End, on 'Black Saturday' – 7 September 1940, the start of the Blitz. For Londoners, months of attacks lay ahead.

CHAPTER ONE
THE ADVENT OF THE BLITZ

'Such heroism everywhere'

Winston Churchill, now prime minister, emerges triumphant on the doorstep of No. 10 Downing Street (10 May 1940). The reluctance on the part of Foreign Secretary Lord Halifax to press his own claim to the highest office delivered to Churchill what he had yearned for: overarching power to direct the war effort.

On 9 April 1940, Hitler's forces invaded and quickly overwhelmed Denmark, which surrendered within the day; at the same time, neutral Norway was attacked. Despite intense British naval actions in the North Sea, and an Anglo-French attempt to land troops, by May Norway was largely lost. In London, Prime Minister Neville Chamberlain came under sustained criticism for the Norway failings. Possession of Norway not only gave Germany access to much needed iron ore, it provided new airbases with which the Luftwaffe could threaten Britain.

Worse was soon to come. On 10 May, Germany launched its westward invasions of the Netherlands, Belgium and France. On the same day, Chamberlain, unable to retain support of the House of Commons, resigned – and Winston Churchill assumed the prime ministership. Within days, it became clear that the fighting on the Continent would be no repeat of the stagnating Western Front of the First World War. By 20 May 1940, German troops had reached the Channel coast, cutting the Allied forces in two. Plans were hastily made to withdraw the British

A long-shutter-speed photograph (1940) reveals the light streaks from car headlamps as vehicles drive around what, outside wartime, would have been London's brashest night-time scene: the advertising glitz of Piccadilly Circus. The statue of Eros had already been removed, its base now sandbagged and boarded up.

Expeditionary Force, resulting in the 'miracle of Dunkirk' in which, from 27 May to 4 June, a brilliantly improvised naval operation extracted more than 338,000 men, 118,000 of whom were French, from the Dunkirk beaches and brought them safely back to England. Some 850 vessels, including channel steamers and fishing boats, took part in Operation 'Dynamo'. Both sides interpreted Dunkirk as a victory, though Churchill felt obliged to point out to the British public that 'Wars are not won by evacuations.' While that operation was under way, another ally fell away, as the King of the Belgians surrendered his army to the enemy.

By contrast with the turmoil across the Channel, May in London was one of the balmiest for many a year, with sunshine day after day. Even as news of Dunkirk crept in, West Hampstead diarist Gwladys Cox noted that 'in spite of the eventful happenings of the past month, it is curiously calm in London'. This was not to say that things weren't changing in other ways, for, as she continued:

"Let 'em all come"
MEN
41-55
HOME DEFENCE
BATTALIONS
Apply at any Army Recruiting Centre Now

Opposite A poster drums up support among an older age group for the new home defence volunteers, who would be the last line of defence against any German invasion. The age range for the Home Guard became quite elastic, so indeed it was a matter of 'Let 'em all come'.

> In the West End, the theatres partly on account of the black-out, partly through fear of air-raids, are not booming as in the last war – that was a Soldiers' war; this, we know, is a Civilians' as well. Piccadilly presents a strange appearance without its familiar Eros statue, now stored away for safety. Its base boarded up with a gay frieze of Pearly Queen flower sellers and 'Bobbies' gives us a cheerful touch. King Charles' statue in Whitehall is now hidden by sand-bags and corrugated iron; and before Government offices, entrenched behind barbed wire, sentries with fixed bayonets march up and down.

At home, she was 'trying to live as normally and cheerfully as possible, but there is little social life, as so many of our friends have left town'.

The reality unfolding in Britain over these spring weeks was the palpable threat of a German invasion. All the security measures previously put in place seemed justified, and new ones became necessary. Had enemy troops landed in the spring of 1940, they would have found beaches lined with barbed wire, roads obstructed, hastily improvised blockades, signposts and street names removed, and unattended cars immobilised. Hydrogen-filled barrage balloons hovered over London to discourage dive-bombers and low-level attacks. A fear of Fifth Columnists gave rise to all manner of government warnings about the danger of 'careless talk'. Anxiety about an enemy within was increased by the Berlin broadcasts of Nazi-sympathiser William Joyce, dubbed 'Lord Haw-Haw', who had commanded a wide audience since the beginning of the war. German nationals and other 'Aliens' living in Britain, as well as those with suspect loyalties such as the British Union of Fascists (BUF), all represented a potential threat to security. On 23 May 1940, the BUF leader Oswald Mosley was arrested, and within the week the BUF had been dissolved, all its publications banned, and many of its party members rounded up and imprisoned. Under the Emergency Powers (Defence) Act, some 30,000 people deemed to comprise such 'threats' were interned or deported. Ironically, many of these people had themselves earlier sought refuge in Britain from the Nazis.

In these altered realities, there was a role for everyone. On 14 May 1940, War Secretary Anthony Eden broadcast a call to arms for the new home militia force: the Local Defence Volunteers. Although it was intended principally for men too old for conscription, and particularly for those who had served during the First World War, it was actually open to a wide age range (17–65). Two months later, its name would be changed to the Home Guard. Even after the possibility of invasion had diminished, the Home Guard would undertake important roles such as guarding bomb sites and other installations, as well as aircraft spotting. And, along with the other voluntary organisations, it would give civilians a real sense of involvement in the war effort. Mr Brinton-Lee, who lived in North-West London until October 1940 (when he moved out to Buckinghamshire), was just one of the 1.5 million volunteers who joined the force by the end of June 1940. His wife summarised his unit in terms that might have stood for many of the Home Guard's personnel:

Opposite A now homeless South London woman surveys the wreckage of her bombed-out terraced house, while being comforted by a female ARP Warden (29 August 1940). For this Londoner, her loss came with the added indignity of it being an error – Luftwaffe raids against the capital were, at this stage, not yet German policy.

> They were most of them elderly, with kind, careworn faces. I thought how nice they were, neither bombastic or craven, like the Germans I had met. They had done their job in the last war, as their ribbons showed; they had worked and worried and raised their families. The things they were interested in were good things, – their work, their hobbies, their children and their sport. They had no inferiority complex, they had never gone hysterical or wished to take away anybody's freedom. Their only crime was that, being unable to believe that the rest of the world was crazy, they had been rather inclined to let things slide. They did not know how to spell Czechoslovakia, or where it was, and they had been only too willing to believe that Europe was no concern of theirs. Now, when they found everything had come unstuck, they turned up quite cheerfully, and offered themselves and their services again. They were tough and uncomplaining. I was sure they would fight like tigers when it came to the point, and meanwhile they practised their drill and shooting in the friendliest way, and went home to be with their families through the night's hell, till it was time to go to work in the morning.

On 22 June 1940, France's defeat was formalised in a humiliating armistice. The invasion of Britain was surely a matter of time, and London had to be squarely in the enemy's sights. For many Londoners, and not just children, leaving the capital now seemed an advisable move – if they had not left already. But Hitler was well aware that before Germany could launch its seaborne invasion – codenamed Operation 'Sealion' – control of the skies over England was needed, and the Royal Air Force had to be destroyed. This gave Londoners some reprieve. Throughout the summer of 1940, the Luftwaffe attacked shipping in the English Channel and mounted an all-out assault on the RAF's fighter bases, in the great and sustained aerial conflict known as the Battle of Britain. Almost daily, between July and September 1940, fleets of Luftwaffe bombers, protected by

fighter planes, took off from airstrips in Occupied Europe, in search of targets; and in response, the RAF's thinly stretched squadrons of Fighter Command did everything they could to stop the bombers getting through.

If the metropolis proper was not yet itself a target, the outskirts of London were not immune. For one thing, even if German aircrews failed to locate their targets, they had to release their bombs somewhere and turn around in time to have sufficient fuel, and a light enough aircraft, for getting home safely. To live anywhere in the flight path of a German bomber was dangerous, and the Luftwaffe was now expanding its targets to include radar stations. South-East England bore the brunt of it. Diarist Viola Bawtree, living in Carshalton Beeches near Croydon, wrote eloquently of the unbearable tension:

> This waiting for danger is the very devil! Train accidents, explosions, cars mounting the pavement, all these things in normal life happen suddenly, unexpectedly, & the victims have only to face up to what has happened & be looked after. Whereas this is all waiting – waiting for a siren's ghastly wail, then waiting for what may come – day after day, night after night, with a sickening lurch of the heart at each ominous sound.

She had been told 'that 17 planes had been brought down' in a raid on Croydon Airport – London's major civil airport between the wars – and that 'not one enemy raider survived', something of an exaggeration since seven Messerschmitt Me110s had actually been downed. In fact, on that day, 15 August, the largest German bomber force to date – numbering around 600 aircraft – had crossed the Channel, among which was a group of more than 60 planes trying to target the RAF's Kenley and Biggin Hill bases. Croydon Airport was hit by mistake, as were residential properties nearby. Nellie Carver – who worked at the Central Telegraph Office near St Paul's Cathedral and spent her spare time knitting for the forces – could 'understand the Huns going for Croydon, but to bomb these purely residential districts is beastly unsporting'. However, for the Luftwaffe, this 'Black Thursday' saw them lose 75 aircraft all across Britain, from Newcastle down to Dover.

Five days later during this desperate battle, on 20 August 1940, Churchill singled out the young, brave (and increasingly barely trained) fighter pilots and other airmen for praise, proclaiming that 'Never was so much owed by so many to so few'. It was a sentiment echoed by Gwladys Cox that same day, who correctly observed: 'surely these words will live on as long as Britain lives'. Four days later, Londoners got a true flavour of the battle when German bombers on a night raid strayed too far off course, and ended up releasing bombs on the capital, mainly on Bethnal Green and West Ham. Like the raid on Croydon, it was an error, breaching the Luftwaffe's ban on targeting London; but it was an error with drastic consequences.

Sometimes forgotten amid the stories of Britain's defensive air struggle is the fact that the RAF was, at the same time, sending its own bombers across the Channel to hit the enemy. On 25 August, in retaliation for the damage to London and the civilian deaths, the RAF attacked Berlin. Hitler was outraged. Henceforth, the rules of engagement changed. On 7 September 1940, and partly in retribution for the raid on Berlin, Hitler sent Germany's bombers to the British capital. Now, just as London had been spared in the preceding months by the attacks on RAF assets, the RAF's Fighter Command was saved as London moved into the frame instead. This was not immediately obvious, though. Reichsmarschall Hermann Goering, at the head of the Luftwaffe, hoped to lure Fighter Command to its final destruction in trying to defend London.

Accordingly, from the late afternoon of 7 September around 1,000 German aircraft – bombers outnumbered by their fighter escorts – breached the skies over England, many of them to target London, as Fighter Command scrambled every available aircraft to try and intercept them. At night, 247 enemy aircraft continued to inflict punishment on the capital. The East End and parts of the City were pummelled and aflame. When Londoners were not sheltering in any way they could, they were able to look up and see Luftwaffe and RAF fighters locked in combat, and RAF planes trying to down the enemy bombers.

Goering was exultant at the result, proclaiming to the nation that 7 September represented an 'historic' moment. He had good reason – a small percentage of his armada of aircraft, around 40, had been shot down. RAF losses, though under 30, were relatively more damaging. Parts of the East End were ravaged, and more than 400 Londoners were dead, with four times that number injured.

The next day saw attacks during the day and at night. On 9 September, raiders crossed the coast in the early evening, most of them getting as far as the residential districts of South London, which bore the brunt of that day's bombs, though some planes made it to Central London

Left Two Dornier Do217 bombers over the eastern end of the vast Royal Arsenal site bordering the Thames at Woolwich, East London, on 7 September 1940. The area comprised sewer works and railways, but was also used for the manufacture and testing of weapons.

Below Obliterated small shops in Bermondsey's Lower Road, South London, testify to the ravages of the first couple of days of the Blitz (8 September 1940). To the rear, the Town Hall's tower is visible above the rooftops, though the censor has marked it for cutting, so as not to give the location away.

too. The casualty figures were almost as high as on 7 September. But a change was underway. After the initial shock of 'Black Saturday', Fighter Command was beginning to get the measure of the evolving attacks, at least when its pilots could see the enemy – before night fell. At the same time, along the French Channel coast, thousands of enemy barges were nearing final preparation to carry an invasion force, based on the belief that this final showdown with the RAF over London would win the Luftwaffe air superiority. As the Luftwaffe pounded London, day and night, RAF bombers tried to destroy the burgeoning invasion vessels, but with modest results. On 13 September, Luftwaffe aircraft got through to bomb Whitehall and – not for the first time – Buckingham Palace.

On Sunday 15 September, London and its inhabitants were threatened by the largest aerial onslaught since 7 September. In two attacks, in the morning and afternoon, the engines of 600 enemy aircraft roared towards the city, and 181 German bombers were counted over London. But a resurgent Fighter Command, recovering from the weeks of attritional attacks on its bases, was able to launch around 250 fighter planes to meet these threats – numbers that astonished the enemy pilots. That day, one week into Germany's targeting of London, was to have a decisive effect on both the city's war experience and the German war plan. The following morning, an excitable *Daily Express* ran the headline '175 SHOT DOWN'; in fact, the tally was nearer 60, but still the biggest German loss to date in the Battle of Britain, while the RAF had suffered 13 pilot losses. Faced with the reality that Britain's air defences were strengthening, not weakening, Goering turned once more to ordering attacks on RAF bases and aircraft factories, but it proved too late. On 17 September, Hitler postponed Operation 'Sealion' again, this time indefinitely, as British bombs continued to hit the vessels assembled on the French coast. By October, the invasion plan was effectively dead.

It appeared the country was saved. But London was to be punished. For London, 7 September 1940, 'Black Saturday', would prove to be the start of the Blitz – named after the *Blitzkrieg* ('lightning war') tactics that the German air and ground forces had used to such effect to subdue the Continent. For the next eight months, London – and other British towns and cities – were attacked with everything from incendiaries and high-explosive (HE) bombs to 'parachute mines' – sea mines on parachutes, which could blow a person a quarter of a mile away. If air superiority could not be won, and an invasion could not be launched, the German strategy was rationalised as one of demoralising – or terrorising – the British people into surrender by ravaging their cities, industries and population centres from the air.

In Clive Upton's oil painting *Bomb Disposal: Listening for Ticking* (1942), an officer of the Royal Engineers applies his stethoscope to detect if the large unexploded bomb is active. Some bombs dropped by the Luftwaffe carried time-delay fuses, adding to the dangers of this hazardous job.

In this new battle, civilians were to be on the front line. And every major raid would leave its trail of ruin and misery. There were the dead to be buried, the injured to be cared for and the trapped to be dug out. People who had lost their homes had to be fed, clothed and rehoused. Water, gas and electricity breakdowns had to be repaired, the streets cleared of unexploded bombs, and road, rail and telephone communications maintained. The noise of air raid sirens – unfondly known as 'Wailing Winnie' or 'Moaning Minnie' – and planes, of bombs and anti-aircraft fire, as well as the sight of air raid victims and the destruction of so many familiar places: all had a huge impact on those affected. For Londoners, sleep became a precious commodity, and lack of it caused nerves to fray. Three weeks into the Blitz, sleep-deprived diarist Viola Bawtree was surely not alone in 'behaving like a fractious, irritable child' and then feeling 'sick with shame & horror' at herself for making a fuss.

Yet a quality that would come to be so powerfully associated with the Blitz – the resilience of Londoners – was already becoming apparent. Mrs Hilda Neal, who lived in Kennington, South London, and ran a typist agency on the Strand, wrote in her diary in September 1940:

> Bruton Street, Bond Street, and Park Lane all bombed yesterday; much damage to the two former, but people are carrying on as usual. Milkman delivers slowly, pushing his tricycle during raid; the paper comes, and so on and so forth. Wonderful stoicism.
>
> Three women Legion officers have been killed in East End; Mrs Noel and Misses Cooper; yesterday, while running a mobile canteen. Several firemen too; and two were blown over a building on an escape ladder, which was broken in half. One is just stunned to read of these happenings which often are beyond belief. Such heroism everywhere in all classes.

IN FOCUS

SHELTERING LONDON'S PEOPLE

According to government figures, by the start of the Blitz around 17.5 million of the 27.5 million people living in urban and industrial areas of Britain had been provided with some sort of domestic or public shelter from aerial bombing, at public expense; and a further 5 million people had access to shelters at work. This was a dramatic improvement since the start of the war, when construction of the famous 'Anderson' shelters had got under way.

Named after Sir John Anderson, who became Minister of Home Security on the outbreak of war, the Anderson shelter was a 6-foot high, 4-foot 6-inch-wide and 6-foot-long (1.8 x 1.4 x 1.8 metre) structure of curved corrugated steel, designed to be erected in the householder's garden, and accommodating between four and six people. Such family-sized shelters reflected a government policy to disperse, rather than concentrate, a population in hiding, so as to prevent large numbers of casualties from a direct hit. But the construction programme was much behind schedule in September 1939, with only 60,000 Anderson shelters delivered: a shortfall of almost a million. Moreover, unless you earned less than £250 per annum, you were expected to pay £6 14s for your shelter. Fewer than a thousand had been sold. When the price rose, they became increasingly unobtainable. They also had a tendency to flood. Nevertheless, Anderson shelters became valued for their effectiveness against all but a direct hit.

By the summer of 1940, more than 2 million Anderson shelters had been distributed by the government, the majority of them free of charge due to the war's outbreak. These shelters were probably all right for short periods at a time, but when the alerts went on all night, the family tension and exhaustion could be awful. As soon as the 'all clear' sounded, people often went inside their homes to catch up on sleep before going to work or school.

Some people embellished their shelters. In Walthamstow, the Britton family, for example, were not alone in lining theirs with cement so that they would 'have a dry funk-hole to creep into if we have to take refuge during an air raid'. George Britton told his US-domiciled daughter on 30 October 1940:

It seems to me that the shelter will have to be the place where we spend our nights during the winter and we had better take what means we can to ensure some degree of comfort. The record time up to the present for a night 'alarm' is a few minutes under 13 hours and with the period of darkness ever increasing that may well be exceeded. The record number of times for the 'alert' in 24 hours is, I think, nine. I can't be quite sure for we have all ceased to bother about daytime warnings. They come and go and we are gravely in doubt whether the last siren was the 'warning' or the 'all clear'. I think I can say that that is the case with the majority of people.

Opposite The enterprising Mrs Alice Prendergast, a resident of Balham, South London, combines self-sufficiency and self-preservation by planting lettuce, beetroot and marrows over the top of her Anderson shelter (July 1940). The Anderson shelter was designed to be partly buried in the ground.

Accordingly, he decided he would 'erect a better roof over the entrance to the shelter so that we shall have more secure protection against wintry storms'. He added that 'A man called from the Council this week and asked if we would like "bunks" fitted in the shelter. There will be two tiers of three so that will obviate anyone sleeping on the floor, which will get very cold in the winter.'

While George Britton was contemplating his Anderson makeover, many other people were abandoning their own Anderson shelters, preferring to remain at home, under staircases or sleeping in lower rooms and cellars. Welfare worker Vere Hodgson, who kept a diary throughout the war, remembered sheltering under the stairs in terror at her shared Lancaster Gate house, following the first air raid siren. During the Spanish Civil War, the newspapers had remarked that stairs often remained standing after the rest of a building had collapsed, so people took note when the Blitz came. For one North Londoner, Mrs Edith Chaudoir of Tufnell Park, her Blitz experience of 'spending nearly 5 weeks in the cellar approx. 8 o'clock to 7 o'clock' was 'beginning to get very dull to say nothing of the fact that we had 20 panes of glass smashed in by a blast last week'. Nellie Carver, living in West Norwood, hid in the cupboard under the stairs; her mother had rejected the offer of an Anderson shelter. The real death knell of the Anderson shelter, though, was Britain's steel shortage, as manufacture decreased and eventually stopped altogether. Instead, surface shelters made of brick and concrete were built, though some of them lacked cement in the mortar (again, because of shortages), and for domestic protection, in due course the Morrison shelter was introduced (*see* page 79).

Of course, the principle of an Anderson shelter assumed you had sufficient outdoor space in which to put it in the first place, which created an immediate problem for inner-city dwellers and the inhabitants of London's East End. Pre-war advice had been that those without shelters should strengthen their basements and ground-floor rooms instead. In London, 5,000 communal shelters were built across the city, but mainly in areas such as the East End. Constructed by local authorities for those without access to domestic shelters, they could accommodate up to 50 people.

For 23-year-old Eugenie Chaudoir, writing to her elder sister on 19 September 1940, the 'Britannia' shelter on London's Gray's Inn Road, which she experienced as a shelter marshal, was rather more unusual: 'an old stable and divided into stalls. There are 5 of them either side of the centre gangway. Each family has a stall of its own. They have already made up their beds on the floor and have brought the [official] forms out so that they are across the entrance to their own bedroom.' Communal shelters were not popular. Ventilation was generally poor, they were cold, dark and damp, and they had a propensity to collapse owing to poor construction. Joan Veazey and her husband Christopher, the vicar of St Mary's Church, Kennington, visited a number of public shelters in September 1940. It was something of a disconcerting revelation:

It is amazing what discomfort people will put up with, some on old mattresses, others in deck chairs and some lying on cold concrete floors with a couple of blankets stretched round their tired limbs. In nearly all the shelters the atmosphere is so thick that you could cut it with a knife. And many of the places – actually – stink! I think that I would prefer to risk death in the open to asphyxiation. Mothers were breastfeeding their babies, and young couples were making love in full view of anyone who passed down the stairs.

The notorious Tilbury shelter in Stepney was the largest in London. From the official shelter, which was meant to house 3,000 people but now had 14,000 regularly sheltering there, people had broken through into a network of railway tunnels that led to warehouses. Journalist Ritchie Calder left a rich description in his 1941 book *Carry On London:*

It was the cause of the worst outcries about shelter conditions. Indeed, it was so appallingly bad that at first, although I was called in on the second day of the 'blitz', I did not dare write about it, because it was not only the most unhygienic place I have ever seen, it was then definitely unsafe. Yet numbers as high, on some estimates, as 14,000 to 16,000 people crowded into it on those dreadful nights when hell was let loose on East London. Nothing like it, I am sure, could exist in the Western World. I have seen some of the worst haunts on the water front at Marseilles which are a byword, but they were mild compared with the cesspool of humanity which welled into that shelter in those early days. People of every type and condition, every colour and creed found their way there ... When ships docked, seaman

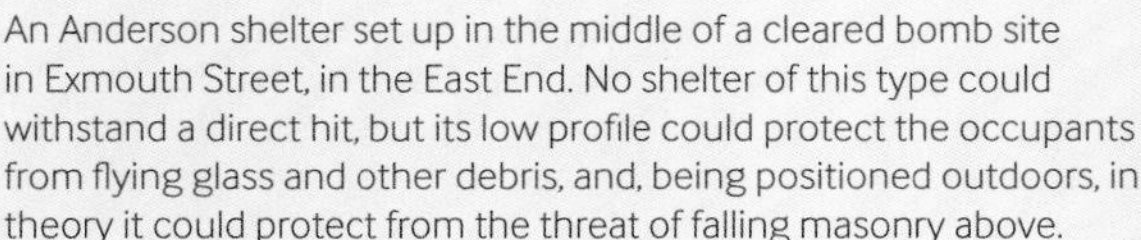
An Anderson shelter set up in the middle of a cleared bomb site in Exmouth Street, in the East End. No shelter of this type could withstand a direct hit, but its low profile could protect the occupants from flying glass and other debris, and, being positioned outdoors, in theory it could protect from the threat of falling masonry above.

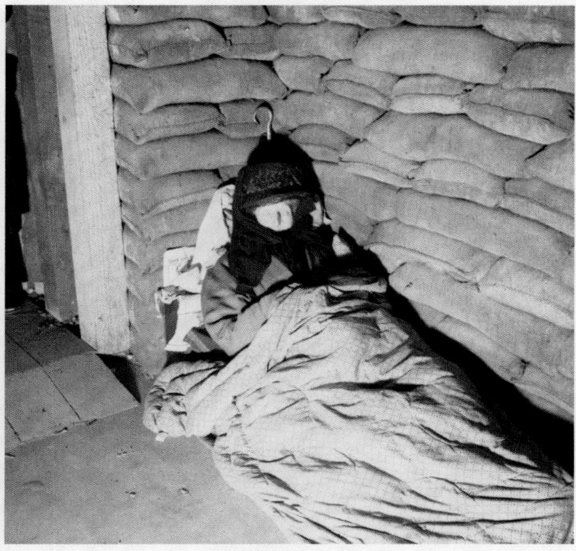
A garage in South-West London provides public shelter for one elderly Londoner, along with many others (4 November 1940). This was one of a series of photographs of shelter life taken by the leading photojournalist Bill Brandt, who was under commission to the Ministry of Information (MOI).

would come in to royster for a few hours. Scotland Yard knew where to look for criminals bombed out of Hell's Kitchen. Prostitutes paraded there. Hawkers peddled greasy, cold fried fish which cloyed the already foul atmosphere. Free fights had to be broken up by the police. Couples courted. Children slept. Soldiers, sailors and airmen spent part of their leaves there.

In September 1940, a committee was established to look into shelter conditions, with the result that shelter marshals were appointed, smoking areas were provided where possible, masks were provided to prevent infection, and there was a general drive to improve sanitation, with inspections by Health Department medical officers. When so many people crammed together, impetigo, lice and scabies were the main health hazards, with coughs and colds spreading very quickly and 'shelter throat' a common complaint.

As the Blitz progressed, and conditions worsened, provision was slowly made for better heating and lighting, as well as sanitation. It was not always the usual authorities that took the initiative. 'Mickey's shelter' in Stepney, in the East End, was designed to take around 5,000 people, but double that number used it. So Mickey Davis, a local optician, led a campaign to improve it: a shelter committee convened, and Marks & Spencer set up a canteen that used the profits to provide free milk for children. Ritchie Calder noted that when an official shelter marshal was appointed 'he could never hope to displace' Mickey 'in the confirmed affection of the people he had served throughout the grimmest days'. The shelter was even proudly displayed to the former US Republican Party presidential candidate Wendell Willkie in late 1941, as an example of democracy in action.

Addressing the 'cesspool of humanity' of Tilbury became the spearhead for a general improvement in shelters across London. Rachel Reckitt, who worked in the Citizen's Advice Bureau in the nearby Toynbee Hall, noted, following a guided tour in October 1940, that 'They have reduced the numbers in Tilbury shelter from 12,000 to about 6,000 and made some improvements'; her overall impression, however, was that 'it is still very bad and many people sleep on stones'. From December 1940, standard bunks were installed. Other improvements included first-aid posts, and small stoves or electric fires.

Food was usually provided in the larger shelters by private caterers, public bodies or the Women's Voluntary

In another of Bill Brandt's photographs for the MOI, shelterers try to grab forty winks on the platform at Elephant and Castle Underground Station, while the travelling public go about their normal routines (November 1940). Londoners, especially in poorer and more densely populated areas, badly wanted the stations to be opened up as refuges.

Service (WVS). Wardens were appointed to keep order, and a social life developed: gramophone records were played, concerts held, film shows put on, and libraries provided. People went from shelter to shelter to compare facilities, gravitating towards the ones they preferred, so that individual shelters acquired their own reputations. Some were quiet; others were noisy, catering to the after-pub crowd who brought their drinks with them. By February 1941, there were 140,000 places available for shelterers, who amounted to 1 in 5 of London's population seeking refuge. Then in March all brick shelters not made of cement were demolished at government expense and later in the year most of the dampness in the remaining shelters had been countered.

Londoners also sheltered in the trench shelters in the parks and public gardens that had been erected during the Munich Crisis of 1938. Although they proved impossible to keep waterproof, they were often more popular than the surface shelters. Alda Ravera, a London secretary, became a park regular:

After a few severe bombings, we were told we must never sleep in the house at night. So for six months, we slept in the shelter in the park. We'd come home from work and we'd each have a bowl of coffee and some French bread to dunk it in. Then we'd go in the shelter. The bunks were all full up and I can remember getting an Evening Standard, *putting it on the floor and lying on it. For six months, that was my bed.*

Local authorities could also designate buildings as public shelters. For example, shops such as Dickin & Jones in Regent Street and D.H. Evans on Oxford Street had basements that served as shelters. Stanley Parker Bird, Chief Shelter Officer for Marylebone, was tasked in 1939 with inspecting 'the main streets in Marylebone to see which basement accommodation could be made into air raid shelters. Those that I recommended were then inspected by the architects department. In due course, shelters were made in the basements of many of the big shops and church crypts.' Not all were up to scratch. 'Some places – such as Madam Tussauds – were not sufficiently well constructed to be made into shelters.' In North London though, the basement of Archway Central Hall made the grade as a designated shelter. It was run by Reverend James Mackay, the Methodist minister, who became its warden. One week into the Blitz, he wrote excitedly that 'Our air-raid shelter is the most popular thing in north London at the moment! Large crowds gather outside it every night wanting to come in. It looks like the pit entrance to a popular play, and we actually have queue artistes doing turns outside the Hall!'

Some purpose-built deep shelters in London evolved later in the war – when German bombs increased dramatically in size – but it wasn't long before London Underground stations found themselves adopted as shelters. They had been used as such during the First World War, but they were not officially shelters at the time the Blitz began – rather, they became so by default. Members of the public would buy their Tube tickets and then just stay on the platforms in many instances. The government was not keen on this behaviour, not only because they wanted to keep people and goods moving on the Underground network, but also because of safety issues such as the restricted access to platforms and the danger of flooding. Officialdom also desired to prevent a 'shelter mentality'. Nevertheless, the Tube stations gave Londoners a feeling of safety and were dry, warm, well-lit and mostly free from the noise of the air raids – and the authorities could hardly resist those who voted with their feet. For George Frankland, a South Londoner, Lambeth North was his station, where 'we used to sleep on the platform... in our pyjamas with a blanket and we'd take sandwiches and tea in a flask. We stayed down there all night and came up at dawn and walked home.'

By the end of September 1940, about 79 Tube stations were used as shelters, enough to hold 177,000 people. Queues would form from the early morning, 6am, even though people were only let in at 4pm. And popular though they were, stations were hardly salubrious. Robert Herrmann, on his way home from Pall Mall's Royal Automobile Club, on 26 September 1940, recorded in his diary his walk 'to Piccadilly Tube Station in complete silence and Stygian darkness, there being a ground mist':

Having picked my way through the thousands of people lying all over the corridors and platforms of the Tube, I gained Queens Road Station without difficulty. Every single station on the route is packed to overflowing with these unfortunate people, who spend their nights there with a few meagre possessions. The heat is unbearable until a train comes and then for a few seconds an icy blast descends upon them. What a life for the poor devils. Better to get killed in comfort, I should have thought.

The huddled masses only increased, and at the height of the Blitz, no surface was neglected, as people slept on escalators and in any other station nook or cranny they could find. And life in the stations improved. Bunks were installed, and Lambeth North was the first to get them – three-tiered metal ones, in late November 1940; by March 1941, 7,600 bunks had been installed in 76 stations. Aldwych Station, which

Aldwych Underground Station as a vast dormitory-cum-cloakroom during the Blitz (1940). The ending of train services to this particular station meant that the tracks, too, could be taken over as accommodation by those seeking a spot to lay their heads.

ceased serving a transport function at the end of September 1940, became instead an underground shelter accommodating 2,000 people, and it evolved into something of a model shelter, boasting educational lectures, theatre shows, films and other entertainments. Westminster Council donated 2,000 books from its library to the shelter, and the local vicar conducted Church of England services underground. Other stations then followed suit. At least 52 of them acquired their own libraries, while Elephant & Castle Station had a play centre for younger children. One war child, Oliver Bernard, remembered how 'The tube platforms were quite transformed. Instead of being hard, shiny circles covered in white tiles, they became lined with softness and grey brown colours. They became rather friendly and nice. People were laughing, singing and telling stories, almost like a party was going on. It was very cosy.'

Over time, the attractions of any kind of specially created shelter began to pale, as the Blitz became part of London's routine, and people preferred to stay at home, if possible. By November 1941 only about 9 per cent of Londoners were using them, while just 4 per cent of people took to the Underground, whereas in Inner London just over a quarter – 27 per cent – resorted to domestic shelters. In the suburbs, shelter use was even lower.

Henry Moore's *Women and Children in the Tube* (1940), one of 28 such drawings of Londoners sheltering underground purchased by the War Artists Advisory Committee and sent around the country. Initially aloof from attempts to co-opt him as a war artist, Moore was moved by the sights he saw in September 1940 on the Underground stations. His drawing reflects such feelings in the tender treatment of the mother–child relationships in the foreground.

No shelter could, though, inure Londoners to the unfolding daily attrition of aerial bombardment, though the pain at first seemed to be unevenly spread. For diarist and confirmed Christian pacifist Viola Bawtree, writing three days into the Blitz, the bombs held both a moral lesson and pointed up a stark social injustice:

I think that possibly God allowed such horrors, including the insecurity of shelters, so that men & women should realise to the full that this sort of thing must be abolished for all time, & that no amount of deep digging will make people immune from the peril. Only, why is not more horror & destruction allowed to happen to the homes of those in high places, who are far more responsible for allowing bombers to be created than are the poor people in the East End?

Come 19 September 1940, in her eyes a sense of shared experience was beginning to act as a social leveller: 'The West End has been badly hit but that seems only fair. We read of rich & poor sharing the same shelter & talking together.' German bombs, the Luftwaffe hoped, would deepen London's social divisions; but shelter life appeared to be doing something of the opposite.

Herbert Mason's celebrated photograph, taken on the night of 29 December 1940, in which St Paul's Cathedral appears invulnerable amid the maelstrom of flame and smoke. The building did not emerge entirely unscathed, but a combination of luck and the bravery of firemen, bomb-disposal squads and civil defence personnel saved this London icon from catastrophe.

CHAPTER TWO
THE BLITZ INTENSIFIES

'The second Great Fire of London'

Onlookers, including a mother and baby, survey the remains of a London street, six months into the Blitz (19 March 1941). To the left stands a coat-rack, an incongruous reminder of the ordinary among the extraordinary.

As the Battle of Britain began to peter out, Germany demonstrated its commitment to targeting London with the largest attack yet, on the night of 23 September 1940, comprising some 250 bombers. Indeed, for 72 consecutive nights following 'Black Saturday' of 7 September – except for two bad-weather nights in November – the Luftwaffe attacked. While some raids in the first couple of months were relatively light, others saw fleets of more than 400 aircraft roam the skies. This phase of intensive bombardment spread to provincial towns and port cities too, which suffered serious raids.

For German bombers, the darkness of night conferred an obvious level of protection, and from October 1940 the majority of raids were at night. But there was a price to be paid, by both the bombers and the civilians on the ground. Night-time made it almost impossible to bomb specific targets, and for London's inhabitants the increased randomness as to where bombs might fall added to the anxiety.

In Philip Hutton's oil painting *Destroying an Unexploded Bomb* (c.1945), a German bomb is detonated under controlled circumstances in an area where it can do no harm. For London, Hackney Marshes was the preferred site, as in the case of the unexploded St Paul's bomb of 12 September 1940.

Luftwaffe pilots, initially given specific targets, were within weeks resorting to reliance on maps that indicated broad target zones of several square miles. In London, these included the City and the docks.

Typically during the raids, the Germans would first drop incendiaries, in the hope that the fires they created would help guide aircraft carrying high-explosive (HE) bombs to their target zones. To begin with, the HE bombs were relatively light, up to 250kg, though later in the war they were ten times that size. At all sizes, they caused devastation to life and property, their destructive effects rippling back from the point of explosion, as windows far away shattered. London was, at first, ill-equipped to tackle the incendiaries. As war began, efforts were made to augment the regular fire services with small volunteer groups to respond in their locality. Thousands of stirrup pumps (for pumping water out of buckets) were distributed – one for every thirtieth house or so – and three-person teams tried to use them to put out smaller fires. It was still too little for what erupted in September 1940. That month, the first Fire Watchers Order, to maintain patrols at designated locations, was issued, but it applied only to warehouses, factories and yards.

In 1939, the Dean and Chapter of St Paul's Cathedral resurrected the St Paul's Watch, originally established during the First World War as a result of Zeppelin raids. It comprised not only cathedral staff, but also – following an appeal to the Royal Institute of British Architects for people in reserved occupations – more than sixty others, including the poet and architectural commentator John Betjeman. They patrolled the building throughout the night. On the night of Thursday 12 September 1940, in one of the largest raids that month, a 1,000kg high-explosive bomb fell very close to the south-west corner, causing a crater measured at 27 feet 6 inches (over 8 metres) deep. For the first time since the Blitz began, the dean, the Very Reverend Walter Matthews, closed the cathedral, and a bomb disposal squad led by Lieutenant Robert Davies arrived within the hour. Luckily, the bomb had a long-delay fuse; less fortunately, it also had an anti-withdrawal device. At this stage of the war, there was no advice other than to blow up unexploded bombs *in situ*, so the area was cordoned off by police. Twenty minutes later, misfortune struck Davies's team – he lost three of his men, knocked out by fumes from a broken gas main; more than that, there was an imminent danger of the gas fire creeping along the pipe towards the bomb, until a gasman blocked off the pipe.

Thereafter, it took twenty hours to actually get the steel hawsers around one end of the bomb. On the third attempt, on Sunday morning, the hawsers remained intact and two trucks managed to haul out the 8-foot-long (2.4-metre) bomb, which weighed about a ton.

Right Furniture and bedding is salvaged from the wreckage of North London tenement buildings, one week into the Blitz (15 September 1940). By the end of the war, storage depots across London were overflowing with the personal possessions of those rendered homeless by the bombs.

Below Following a raid, one Londoner thanks men of the ARP for at least saving part of her wardrobe (10 October 1940). In times of shortages and austerity, it was important to salvage whatever you could – and retrieve it before looters could take their pickings.

Left and below The gutted John Lewis department store in Central London after the raid on 17–18 September 1940. In common with other large shops and offices, the basement of the store was being used as a shelter. But at least the body parts strewn amid the debris in Oxford Street were those of mannequins rather than people.

Davies, though, was unable to defuse it. Instead, it was loaded onto one of the lorries and driven by him, with a red flag in front, at top speed through the streets of the East End to the Hackney Marshes. There, a few hours later, it was exploded, leaving a crater 100 feet (30 metres) in diameter. Gwladys Cox, for one, was suitably impressed, pronouncing it 'a wonderful story of courage in today's papers about Lieut. Davies and his N.C.Os digging up and removing a one-ton bomb buried near St. Pauls'. For his bravery, Davies was awarded the new George Cross, an honour instituted just that month by King George VI for heroism on the home front. Sapper George Wylie earned one too for the St Paul's episode – not the last that would be earned by the army's bomb disposal personnel and the fire and air raid organisations in the front line of the Blitz.

At the same time as St Paul's had a lucky escape, a different location, meant to provide safety for Londoners, instead proved to be a deathtrap. On Sunday 15 September, a sizeable public shelter in Chelsea's Beaufort Street took a direct hit. The result, as Mrs Brinton-Lee wrote in her diary, was that:

> There were no survivors, and as soon as it got light on Monday morning, the ambulance girls from the adjacent post were sent to help the rescue and demolition squad to remove the human remains. They had to put what they could collect into blue waterproof bags and take them to the mortuary. One nurse had seen a man pick up a head and put it into the sack, and another with his hand scrape a woman's scalp off the surface of a concrete block, where it had stuck when the head was smashed against it. She had seen a half-born dead baby attached to its dead mother.

Direct hits on public shelters invariably meant a high death toll.

On 17 September, the Strand was hit, as were the shops of Oxford Street. For Vivienne Hall it meant that 'the haunt of our peacetime days after office have been burned or razed to the ground – how long can this go on?' But, along with the shock of it all, 'we still keep trying to keep calm, and succeeding by some miracle in doing so too! The bouncing ability of nature is much in evidence and each smack we get sends us bouncing back to a show of normality – for which heaven or who-ever is responsible for this chaos, be praised!' Gwladys Cox's husband Ralph went into the West End ten days later. Returning home on the bus via Regent Street, he noticed 'hardly a pane of glass left, then along Oxford Street passing John Lewis, terrible wreck. D. H. Evans and Selfridges were open but most of the windows gone.'

Vivienne Hall's diary entry for the following day, 18 September, serves as a description of a typical night and day during the Blitz, with its juxtaposition of the ordinary and the extraordinary:

> What can I say? Last night, from 8 until 6 this morning heaven and earth went mad with noise. The barrage spat into the air booming and bursting shells and planes replied with whining bombs and all manner of other horrors. All night long the swish and whistle of things falling from the skies kept us on the alert, at times the whistles seemed so near that we were certain the bomb was to hit our house – but it passed over. The flashes through the curtains looked like endless lightning and the beastly planes purring overhead made a fantastic accompaniment to the crashing night chorus. We lay in bed, lucky to have beds to do this in, and listened and watched – and so the night went by. I know we're amongst the lucky ones, so many thousands are getting what rest they can in shelters or are already homeless and cared for in halls and empty houses, but its [*sic*] beastly where-ever you are. Yet everyone managed to get to work somehow, despite the fact that we had three warnings before the morning was out and during the day four more. The stairs to and from the shelter at the office, six flights of 'em, will reduce my fat I should imagine, it reduces my wind I know! A trail of smoke across the sky made me a little apprehensive as I sat in the bus at Ludgate Circus – everyone got off to look up (so sensible!) but we managed to get to the office safely. Again in the afternoon we had reports of a terrific battle overhead but we were safe in the shelter. Home early and just as I walked up the High Street the damn thing went again. The only thing to do is to ignore it and keep steadily on with one ear open for the sound of planes.

By the end of September 1940, three weeks into the Blitz, 5,730 Londoners had been killed, with just over 9,000 wounded. Indeed, even a full year later, the war had produced a higher death toll among British civilians than among British soldiers.

The suburbs did not escape. In Carshalton Beeches on 12 October, Viola Bawtree 'heard a bomb when in the cellar last night, learn that it demolished Belmont Railway Station, two boys in ticket office got under counter & had to be dug out', though fortunately the boys were not injured.

The No. 88 Bus is swallowed whole by the bomb crater on Balham High Road, following the raid of 14 October that caused the deaths of more than 60 people sheltering in the shallow Underground station beneath. Visible are the twisted tramlines, ruptured pipes and tangled cables that were so often the aftermath of the bombs.

Two days later, a much more serious disaster struck South London, when a bomb hit Balham High Road. The Underground station here constituted one of the network's more vulnerable shelters, because it lay only some 36 feet (11 metres) below street level, with sewers, water and gas pipes, and electric and telephone cables above. On the evening of 14 October, just after 8pm, a London bus on its way to Vauxhall entered Balham High Road just as the bomb fell 25 yards (23 metres) in front of it. In the driver's words:

> My bus began prancing about like a horse and the next thing I knew was that I was lying in a shop doorway. I picked myself up and was taken to Ducane Road for first aid. My conductor had been laid out. Apparently he had flung himself on the floor of the bus as I braked and so consequently was concussed... After leaving the first-aid post I decided I must go back to the bus, but as I approached it I said to myself, 'It's O.K., somebody's moved it.' But when I came nearer I saw to my horror that only the roof was protruding from the crater in the road.

Bombed out South Londoners sit with their mugs of tea or coffee, as a nurse converses with a small child, in this oil painting *A Bermondsey Rest Centre*, created by Mavis Hutchinson (1941).

John Groser (1890–1966; left), the activist Anglo-Catholic priest who was instrumental in the Stepney Tenants' Defence League in the 1930s, went on to become an important figure in the organising of voluntary aid during the Blitz. He started rest centres, organised conscientious objectors to operate mobile canteens, and even helped to dig out the injured at incidents; he also administered to the wounded and dying.

The bomb had caused a 60-foot-deep crater, swallowing the bus and engulfing the Tube station platform, where 600 people had been sheltering. The water main, and sewer and gas pipes, were destroyed, with the result that tens of people were drowned as the water reached a depth of 3 feet, nearly a metre. The toll was 68 killed, including the stationmaster, the ticket office clerk and two porters. Nevertheless, Londoners kept on using the Underground shelters.

Thousands more Londoners also now got away from the metropolis entirely. The shock of the start of the Blitz saw many frightened East Enders rush to rural parts of Essex and Kent, including Epping Forest, for short-term safety, before they drifted back to make the best of it in the city. From September, another official evacuation scheme got underway, in which 20,000 departed in the first month. This second full-scale evacuation would eventually see as many as 1,340,000 people leave the capital, in some cases to be plunged into uncertainty. From Oxford, one lady described in a letter (to Henry Strong) '27,000 evacuees from the east side of London, and it is very pathetic to see them wandering about the streets here – in many cases absolutely unwanted and miserable'.

Those who remained faced not only the potential loss of life, but also the very real possibility they would lose their homes. By November 1940, tens of thousands of houses in London had been seriously damaged or destroyed. Badly hit districts included Stepney (for which the soon-to-be Deputy Prime Minister, Clement Attlee, was MP), where 40 per cent of houses were already destroyed, and Hackney (represented by the new Home Secretary and Minister of Home Security, Herbert Morrison). Those Londoners bombed out of their homes needed immediate relief, and those in poorer areas – like Stepney and Hackney – could not afford to pay for alternative accommodation. Despite all the pre-war predictions of the bomber always getting through, there was remarkably little government foresight about how to deal with those without roofs over their heads.

In the early days of the Blitz, much depended on voluntary action. In Stepney, Father John Groser (President of Stepney Tenants' Defence League) organised mobile canteens manned by conscientious objectors and personally helped dig out the injured at incidents, touring the area to pray with those wounded and dying. He worked with local MPs and petitioned the government to open the doors of the railway arches to make them habitable, with bunks, sanitation and food facilities (as well as play centres for the children, discussion groups, plays and dances). Impromptu rest centres also sprang up in schools – two-thirds of which had been requisitioned – or in church halls. However, suffering from haphazard organisation, they quickly became overcrowded, offering inadequate provision. Families in need required shelter, money, clothing and information about where they could possibly live if their home had become uninhabitable. Rest centres were meant to be temporary solutions, before people were allocated more permanent living spaces, but the reality was that many people lived in them for weeks at a time. In one school in Stepney, 300 homeless people had to depend on a mere

An open-air memorial service at a cleared bomb site in the Hendon area of North London (23 February 1941). Religion was seen as an important way of raising morale and encouraging unity during the war. The Ministry of Information created a Religions Division to help channel such feelings for propaganda purposes, but to mixed effect.

Wrecked and bomb-damaged shops in Bermondsey, South London (1 October 1940). While some premises were entirely destroyed in the bombing, a great number of partially damaged shops and businesses were quickly back in operation, their owners often employing considerable ingenuity and improvisation in the process.

10 pails and coal scuttles to serve as lavatories (which often overflowed) and basins without soap or towels. Worse, in a packed West Ham rest centre – also a former school and in an area suffering a dearth of public air raid shelters – local officials had promised coaches to evacuate the homeless to safer surroundings. But it was too late. The centre was hit on 10 September 1940, and hundreds lost their lives.

After the first six weeks of the Blitz, some 250,000 people had been made homeless, 10 per cent of whom were still in rest centres. Only 7,000 had been officially rehoused. The effects were palpable on the streets of London. As George Britton wrote to his daughter (on 26 September 1940), 'It is pitiable to see people walking about who have had to leave their homes because the houses are inhabitable.' One family he knew had been relatively fortunate: 'The Ramseys, after being sheltered in the Church Hall for several days, have now been sent to Baldock in Hertfordshire.' In West Hampstead, Gwladys Cox noticed on 25 September the 'numbers of strange-looking people with babies, children and odd parcels of clothes and bedding struggling up West End Lane. They turned out to be East Enders evacuated from bombed areas to empty houses all about here'. Many East Londoners were indeed sent to be rehoused in other parts of the capital, where a good few of them found it difficult to adapt.

In time, the infrastructure for temporary accommodation improved. The London County Council provided rest centres manned by volunteers from organisations such as the WVS, Salvation Army and the YMCA. By May 1941, there were 170 Londoner's Meal Service Centres, 27 community kitchens and 190 mobile canteens to try and feed the homeless. By the end of the Blitz the rest centres had become transformed with such facilities as bathrooms, comfy chairs and wireless sets.

As regards rehousing people, a Conservative MP, Henry Willink, was appointed Special Regional Commissioner for the Homeless, while welfare inspectors were appointed to deal with rehousing the difficult cases, and rehousing offices in each borough were centralised so that those affected by the bombing did not have to traipse all over the place to get the information and help they required. The repair of houses was prioritised, but there was a severe lack of builders and materials – although by April 1941 things were improving, when the Directorate of Emergency Works injected a workforce of 16,000 into London, in under a week, to boost the repairs to homes. These mobile squads included men specially released from the Army.

Nellie Carver left an evocative diary description of her own journey from familiar, domestic living in West Norwood to the uncertainties of homelessness, when her home, in Idmiston Road, was damaged by a landmine on 18 September 1940. She had been celebrating her birthday with her mother and elderly aunt:

> We were just finishing a glass [of port] apiece & about to go up to bed at 11.30pm when the whole house seemed to be torn apart by something we didn't hear fall. It was not so much a crash but like a shattering wind & thick dust rose up all round the room. We leapt from our seats & crouched together near the fireplace & waited, holding our breaths, for the roof to fall in. Nothing further happened in the kitchen but everywhere we could hear crashing glass both inside & out. I went to the front door which had burst open. The floor of the hall & the downstairs rooms were covered with glass & grit. I dared not show a light to explore further as guns were banging away overhead & I could hear a plane. A girl nearby shrieked out loudly & everybody from all the houses seemed to be in the street. We put on

> outdoor shoes, topcoats & hats & taking our gas-masks & case of 'valuables' went outside. Warden & Rescue parties had sprung from nowhere & were running along, banging on each door shouting 'Is everyone all right in there?'

The three women stayed with neighbours that night. When they returned home the next day, they found the front door hanging off, ceilings fallen in and all the ground-floor windows shattered. Had the women been in their beds, they would have been lucky to escape injury. The parachute mine had killed three people, and caused damage over a distance of about a mile. Neighbours waited for a lorry to take their furniture, piled up in the street, while 'A Mobile Canteen was serving out tea & food to them.' Such was the immediate sense of dislocation that, Nellie remarked, 'It seemed 2 years – quite – since we were all cheerfully drinking my health… last night.' Their own house was damaged beyond repair, so they temporarily stayed with friends in Leatherhead before moving back to a rented house in Tulsemere Road, West Norwood. But the sense of unease was pervasive. She wrote in mid-October:

> This would be a very nice house if one could take a real interest in it, but I can't get it out of my head we shall catch another packet before long & I can't settle down… I dread the long evenings & nights now, whereas at the beginning excitement & the 'newness' of it all kept us all going. The sirens are so much earlier now as well, as the darkness increases. What a horror that sound creates in one's mind, one never seems to get used to it even after all this time.

She was, in her own words, becoming increasingly 'apprehensive' during raids and hated feeling 'trapped and helpless', feelings which exacerbated her sleep deprivation.

On 1 October 1940, it was the turn of Gwladys Cox and her husband to find themselves without a home, as she recounted the following day:

> The bottom of our world has dropped out! Last night, most of our home, together with the whole top floor of Lymington Mansions, was destroyed by incendiary bombs.
>
> I am so dazed, so tired, so numb, I can hardly think, much less write, but I must try to put down what has happened in the past dreadful twenty-four hours, while I remember….

To go back to last night… there was a terrible crash quite close, to the east of us, making the building stagger. We sprang to our feet, dragged on overcoats, shut Bob in his basket & put out the lamps and stove. Almost immediately, the plunk, plunk, plunk of incendiary booms was heard above, on our own roof! The sound was different to anything in the nature of a bomb I had heard before, almost soft, in comparison to the loud bangs and crashes to which we had become accustomed….

Ralph immediately rushed out and up the area steps and found our A.R.P. Warden extinguishing a blazing incendiary in the street… he saw smoke curling up from the roof of the flat next door to ours, Mrs Price's. By this time, fire engines had come tearing down the pitch-dark street…

By now, the rest of us in the cellar, fearing we might be trapped or flooded out by the A.F.S. decided to leave at once. So, with my arms full of as much as I could carry, as well as Bob in the basket, I and the others stumbled along in the dark and utter confusion to the area steps. Looking up the shaft to the sky, we saw tongues of flame streaming out of the Prices' flat. Ralph then tried once more to get up to our flat, but was driven back by volumes of smoke pouring down the staircase. All was confusions now at the bottom of the area steps – Wardens and Fireman shouting at each other and giving contradictory orders. One Warden seemed annoyed we had left the cellar, and ordered us back, but we could not return as water was already pouring down from the fire-hoses above…

I pushed ahead grabbing at the iron rail-rings of the area steps, and halfway up, fell against Ralph.

'For God's sake, come quickly' he exclaimed 'the whole of the top story is on fire!'

He took Bob, dragged me up the rest of the steps and we faltered along the pavement. The Fire-Brigade, fed from the A.F.S. tank in Lymington Road, was working furiously

The road was becoming more crowded now as bewildered people ran out of the flats. An old lady clutched my arm 'Oh do let me come with you! I've lost my family and I am so frightened'. She clung to us, and, all together, we groped our way to the brick A.R.P. Street Shelter at the top of Sumatra Road. Here, in the dark and cold, we found other occupants of Lymington Mansions…

> Cigarettes were lit and we smoked and smoked, in silence at first....
>
> A.R.P. Wardens kept coming to the door of the shelter, taking a roll call, shouting out the names of missing people. Fireman looked in, occasionally, to report the progress of the blaze, with professional nonchalance....

The 'all clear' was called at 11.15 pm, but the Coxes were not allowed to return to their flat. Gwladys realised 'that we were literally homeless'. They stayed with acquaintances nearby. The next day revealed the full extent of the damage to their flat. 'My neat and orderly home was a scene of indescribable desolation. The dining-room was completely burnt out, neither roof no windows remained.' Ralph's library was gone, 'his hundreds of books, his chief hobby, collected during a life-time... congealed black masses of cinders'. Looters had already visited and taken a silver cigarette case, a gold watch and the contents of a trinket box.

The Coxes spent a month in another flat in Honeybourne Road, whose occupant had been anxious to leave London. Although, in Gwladys's eyes, it was 'ill furnished and shabby to a degree', it was a roof over their heads where they could at least 'dry our sodden effects'.

London experienced night-time raids for 57 consecutive nights between 7 September and 2 November, the worst-hit areas being the City and the docks, as well as Holborn and Stepney. However, if you couldn't see the damage for yourself, wartime censorship made getting precise news on the extent of it difficult, as George Britton described to his daughter on 11 October 1940:

> You remark in your letter how vague all the reports of localities at which damage has occurred are. I can assure you we get nothing more definite even in our local 'Guardian'. 'A school was hit', 'A public house was damaged' etc. It might give valuable information to the enemy if he knew the damage was in Marten Road and not in Cazenove Road. I know that the secretive system does encourage the circulation and belief in rumours which is so deprecated by the authorities.

Come Christmas 1940, Nellie Carver spent the time at her new home with her mother and aunt, having worked the previous day. She was at work on 30 December too, but her commute – by the No. 68 bus, as trains were not running – gave her a full view of the devastation caused by an enormous raid on the City area the night before. The conductor

The terraces of London's Silvertown district, Newham, with a yawning gap where once houses stood. The area derived its name from the Silver and Co. factory, manufacturing rubber and waterproof goods, where many local women worked. Its industrial works, dockside location and oil refineries meant this poor and densely populated area was targeted from the very start of the Blitz. Later, its battered streets were used to train troops in urban fighting.

told them that the whole City was still blazing away. She recorded later in her diary: 'I wasn't prepared for the horrible sights which met my eyes as I got out in Holborn, most of the station was gone and what was still in flames.' As she got to her workplace at the Central Telegraph Office, she admitted: 'We have often groused about our office… Most of us, in fact, at one time or another, but today many people were in tears – realising that we had seen the last of the old building & that one chapter in our daily lives was closed'. At lunchtime she followed some of the postmen up to the roof of the nearby King Edward Building, housing the Chief Post Office:

> The sight from up there was dreadful, more like the Great Fire of London. Greyfriar's Church was a just a shell, you could see downwards right into it as no roof was left – only the spire remained. Paternoster Row was in ruins, part of St. Paul's Churchyard, & most of Newgate Street also were gone… but it was very difficult to distinguish one place from another – the whole City looked to be either burnt out or still on fire.

On this night of 29–30 December, 136 Luftwaffe bombers dropped 127 tonnes of high explosive and 613 incendiaries mainly over the City and the East End, exacting a severe toll. The bombing ravaged the centre of London's book trade, as well as eight Wren churches – and this time St Paul's did not escape, having being struck by 29 bombs. The Guildhall was destroyed; Guy's and St Bart's hospitals had to be evacuated; and the Central Telegraph Office, the General Post Office telecommunications plant and three City telephone exchanges were all put out of action. Five railway stations and sixteen Underground stations had to be closed, too.

None of the St Paul's Watch had realised how much danger the cathedral was in, as they had been too busy manning stirrup pumps. It was the watch room at Cannon Street Fire Station that had called through to tell them that there were flames above the dome; luckily, the incendiary had not penetrated to the interior of the dome, and the Watch was able to take care of it. It was on this evening that *Daily Mail* photographer Herbert Mason, from the top of the newspaper's office building, captured his famous image of St Paul's dome emerging through the smoke. In his own words, 'After waiting a few hours the smoke parted like the curtain of a theatre and there before me was this wonderful vista, more like a dream, not frightening – there were very few high explosives. It was obvious that this was going to be the second Great Fire of London.' With this raid, and with this photograph, St Paul's became firmly established as London's principal icon of endurance, standing proud amid the turmoil of the Blitz.

Joseph Jackson, serving in the Royal Navy, was on his way back through London to HMS Collingwood in Fareham, after his Christmas leave, when he encountered the 'second Great Fire of London'. He left an extended description in a letter home. After getting off the train at Liverpool Street, he:

> ... went to the Tube to find it more crowded than usual. In my opinion it was hopeless to stay at the Y.M.C.A. with huge fires on all sides. It was 9.15p.m. and I decided to go across to Waterloo as I presumed [the] attack was local to Liverpool Street. The journey (at night time) involves two changes on the Tube, so I was on my way to Tottenham Court Road. A soldier came on the train with face blackened saying it was 'bad all over the place.' He had been on a train at London Bridge when an incendiary bomb had been thrown through the roof and on to the seat and set the carriage on fire in no time. He had to leave all his luggage behind – everything except his rifle.

Sir Muirhead Bone's chalk and ink drawing *St Bride's and the City After 29 December Raid* (1940), commissioned by the War Artists Advisory Committee. The roofless St Bride's dominates the foreground, while in the middle distance swirls of smoke linger over the firebombed streets of the City. In the distance, the dome of St Paul's survives, intact. For the Scottish artist and draughtsman, who was in his sixties by this time, the 1939–45 war represented his second outing as a war artist.

Having been told that Waterloo was also out of action, he exited Tottenham Court Road Station and walked along Oxford Street to Marble Arch. 'During the whole of that time it was a constant stream of fire engines and A.F.S. trailer pumps,' he observed, but he was also 'surprised at the small amount of damage in Oxford Street from the previous raids of high explosives.'

> Some buildings had been hit but were so strong that only the top 3 or 4 floors had been affected. As regards D.H. Evans and Selfridges, I could not see that they had suffered damage but I expect it was at the back. I saw one big shop which was really down and blown out completely, and that was the John Lewis block.
>
> In the Oxford Street Marble Arch area the number of incendiaries was not so great as in the City, and all were effectively dealt with. In the City and some other places they got beyond the control of the firemen. They had to deal with fires greater than any they have had to deal with in this war before.

He got back on an Underground train at Marble Arch, to return to Liverpool Street, only to discover that the YMCA had been evacuated just before his arrival:

> I went into streets surrounding [the] station to see the fires. There were 30 or 40 fires involving huge offices and shops as well as other buildings. I soon became surrounded by fires and the streets were simply jammed with fire engines and trailer pumps. Even though there were so many hundreds of fire engines, it was obvious they had not enough, nor enough hydrants to deal with such fires. Only those who saw them can imagine it.

Travelling by Tube to the Strand, he surfaced to cross the Thames on foot:

> From Waterloo Bridge one got a grandstand view of the terrific fires. It was a never to be forgotten spectacle – fires on both sides of the river, and I am sure that the Great Fire of London was not a more impressive sight, or so big; for although the Fire of London lasted many days, this was the night of hundreds of fires all burning on the same night in widely separated districts. Warehouses and buildings adjoining Waterloo Bridge were blazing furiously. I stood there for ten minutes.

> The only thing I can liken the scene to was a red sunset reflected by the river. Barges were moored in the middle, and the fire-lit sky was reflected all around them.
>
> The huge dome of St. Paul's and church steeples were surrounded by flames and it appeared to me that it was actually on fire – not the dome but the cathedral itself, but it is said in the papers that this was not so, although everything around it was burnt out. The flames rose many feet above the burning bridges and across miles of skyline. There must have been several square miles of fires. There was a big fire some miles down the river and many believed it to be at the docks.

At Waterloo Station he was prevented from going down to the Underground station, as it had been flooded by a burst water main. But he found refuge for the night in the Union Jack Club, just outside the station, although sleep was hard to come by:

> I was thinking about the great fires etc. I got up at 6.45 a.m. and went out again to Waterloo Bridge. I knew as soon as I stepped out the Club that the fires were as big as ever; the light was as bright as it was earlier in the night. On the Bridge, the scene was much the same. St. Paul's was still there, its dome a dark shape in the glow but the flames which earlier on had surrounded it, had been put out. But other fires seemed to be burning nearer the centre of London which I had not noticed a few hours before. The fires on the southern bank of the river seemed to have increased in intensity... Amongst other factories having been hit and set on fire was the Eldorado Ice Cream factory near Waterloo.

Joseph Jackson eventually made his way back to HMS Collingwood that day. Within a year, his own war – and life – would come to an end when, serving as a telegraphist on HMS *Dunedin*, the 25-year-old's ship was torpedoed in the South Atlantic.

When Nellie Carver toured the City a few days after the raid of 29–30 December, accompanied by her friend Edith, they both found an indomitable spirit amid the 'terrible clearance of so many our cherished landmarks':

> This would be very depressing if it were not for the cheerfulness & pluck of the City folk. In Cheapside, Bread St, Wood Street & Newgate Street, a string of cards has been hung out stating where the unfortunate owners have moved to (they appear to have already

A line of East Londoners snake through wreckage after a raid (20 March 1941), carrying water in buckets. Burst water pipes were not only common in Blitz-era London, necessitating recourse to temporary standpipes, but they could sometimes have catastrophic flooding effects.

found accommodation – if only half a room) & every now & then you come across girls & men loaded up with salvaged goods. Some alas have nothing to save – it's all gone into dust. There is not the slightest feeling of defeat in the air or on the faces of the clerks & shopkeepers – only a stern & grim determination to hold on to the end – Hitler's End.

Londoners' moods were even lifted from across the Atlantic, by one of President Roosevelt's broadcasts, his so-called 'fireside chats', in which he urged American industry to become 'the great arsenal of democracy'. The *Daily Express* translated it into the headline 'Hitler will not win, Roosevelt says'. The neutral United States was edging closer to being a war ally.

Not everyone regretted the damage caused by the raid. William Haslam, a property developer, rather callously told his nephew:

It is of course infuriating that Wren Churches and the Guildhall and City Livery Companies Halls should be destroyed or mauled about but we shall ultimately not regret the destruction of piles of antiquated buildings in the St. Pauls area. No legislation could have got rid of them without hideous sums of compensation and yet most of them were antiquated, many partially empty, and few of them susceptible to modernisation....

Such coolly rational views were, doubtless, a minority opinion. The stress was on damage limitation. In the aftermath of the December raid, 48 hours per month of fire-watching was made compulsory for all men between the ages of 16 and 60, although, to begin with, most undertook the task voluntarily. They included George Britton, who described his own routines to his daughter on 8 January 1941:

We have started a 'fire watching squad' in this road to ensure that if an incendiary drops it shall have immediate attention and not be allowed to develop into a fire. We watch in pairs and do two hours every other night. Mine for instance, with Mr Geary of No. 1, was 12 till 2 on Monday; tonight (Wednesday) 2 till 4; on Friday, 4 till 6am; on Sunday 10 till 12 midnight, and so on. If there is no raid warning we shall stay in our homes in the warm only being ready to sally forth in the event of trouble when it would be our duty to 'Turn out the Guard', that is to say call up the rest of the patrol.

In due course, from August 1941, the Fire Guard Organisation was created – it would become one of the biggest national civil defence organizations of the war, comprising nearly 6 million men and women of all ages, though few were very enthused about the somewhat low-status work.

From February 1941, a new type of domestic shelter became available to Londoners – the Morrison shelter, named after Herbert Morrison, the Home Secretary and Minister of Home Security. Measuring 6 feet 6 inches long, 4 feet wide and 2 feet in height (around 2 x 1.2 x 0.7 metres), it was a rectangular structure with a steel framework and wire mesh – effectively a steel cage – to be erected indoors on the ground floor. It could accommodate two adults and two small children or one older child, lying down; it was also dual use, supposed to serve as a table during the day. Families earning less than £350 annually received the Morrison shelter free of charge, as with the Anderson shelter, but the Morrison was especially useful for households with no garden or back yard of their own. The first recipient was not, though, an East Ender but instead – in a symbolic move – the prime minister. Between March and October 1941, more than 500,000 were distributed, and they were much in evidence for the later attacks on London. They also proved considerably more popular than the Anderson shelters, even though they could be less effective, having little protection from a lateral blast.

Just as the Morrison shelters began being rolled out, Londoners were experiencing something of a lull in the bombing over February and early March 1941. That relative peace was shattered on 8 March by 153 German bombers, 125 of which dropped 30,000 incendiaries on London. Fifty London boroughs were affected, and the buildings hit included the North Lodge of Buckingham Palace (a direct hit), three railway stations and (again) St Bart's Hospital. The most widely reported damage, though, was at one of London's most celebrated nightspots – the subterranean Café De Paris in Coventry Street, Leicester Square. To get to the restaurant one had to go down a long flight of stairs between the Rialto Cinema and the Lyons Corner House. The Café de Paris had been modelled on the sumptuous ballroom of the doomed liner *Titanic*, and, perhaps inauspiciously, the underground restaurant was advertised as the safest restaurant in town. But not on the night of 8 March, when, at around 10pm, it was struck by two 50kg bombs, one of which exploded just in front of the band. It killed 34 people, including the Guyanese-born Ken 'Snakehips' Johnson, leader of the dance band, and his saxophone player Dave 'Baba' Williams; they had been just about to perform the second chorus of 'Oh Johnny'. Leslie Hutchinson, the trumpeter in the band, remembered that Johnson had arrived at the restaurant in a hurry saying

'Man, it's terrible outside – just terrible'. Other casualties included Charles, the 'gracious' head waiter 'so much liked by all' (according to regular diner Miss Ballyn), and the manager, and a further 80 people were injured. One performer lucky to escape was the 'Bawdy but British' comic singer and songwriter Douglas Byng, who was the Café de Paris's entertainer for the week, but on that night was performing instead at a charity ball in Park Lane.

On the scene that evening was Lady Betty Baldwin, daughter of a former prime minister, Stanley Baldwin. She was working with an ambulance unit in Berkley Square. She remembered that nearly all the men there were in uniform, many of them Canadians, and there were Canadian nurses too – a young crowd, in a lively atmosphere. Also present was Ulric Huggins, an officer in the Royal Navy who was dining with his wife, along with a Belgian army doctor and his girlfriend, an Austrian nurse. They had just ordered champagne. After the explosion he remembered:

> The first impression I got was of darkness and dust, and I noticed the champagne bottle lying on the table horizontally. My first instinct at the moment was to pick up the champagne bottle and put it upright. It must have been a matter of some seconds afterwards that I remember I stood up, with the champagne bottle still in my hand, and poured out drinks for the other three people at the table. And a memory I have very clearly is that, as the champagne rose in the glasses, which incidentally were standing upright on the table unbroken, the foam on the top was grey with dust. And I remember quite clearly wiping the foam off with my finger before I drank. And then I turned round, and there at my feet was the waiter, who had been leaning over me pouring out the champagne – dead, of course.

He had a small hole in his back caused by a shard of glass. There were a few doctors, as well as the Canadian nurses, among the diners, who did as much as they could for the bomb victims before the first ambulances arrived from Charing Cross Hospital. Huggins and his Belgian friend Dr Limbosch cleared a central point where there was enough light to help those who were still alive. They used napkins to staunch wounds. Once Huggins and his wife had done as much as they could, they left what remained of the Café de Paris to be greeted by a small crowd asking questions – which they ignored – and caught the Tube home.

A Morrison shelter in the home (1941). Although a somewhat unusual centrepiece for a living room, the Morrison shelter proved its utility, and catered to the desire of many Londoners to have a safe space within the relative comfort of their own homes. Spacious enough for two sleeping adults (as here), it would have been rather more cramped when accommodating children too.

Huggins and his party had come to the aid of a young girl, Miss Hylton-Simpson, who had had her thumb blown off and was convinced she was going to die. He had also noticed two looters who, entering through the restaurant's back entrance, had picked up a lady's handbag and taken rings from the dazed diners: such criminals had spotters out in the West End, who would telephone through to the gang's headquarters if a bombing threw up a likely source for rich pickings. So quick were the looters, they would often arrive at a bombsite in advance of the ARP/Civil Defence personnel.

The Café de Paris was not alone among fashionable London venues to be hit by the Luftwaffe. Its sister nightclub, the Café Anglais, was wrecked in April 1941. Quaglino's and the Aperitif, Dunhill's, The Cavendish Hotel and Fortnum and Mason's were all victims of the bombing around Jermyn Street on 17 April 1941, just some of the destruction caused in the huge attack on the night of the 16th–17th. On that night, 685 enemy aircraft appeared over London to subject

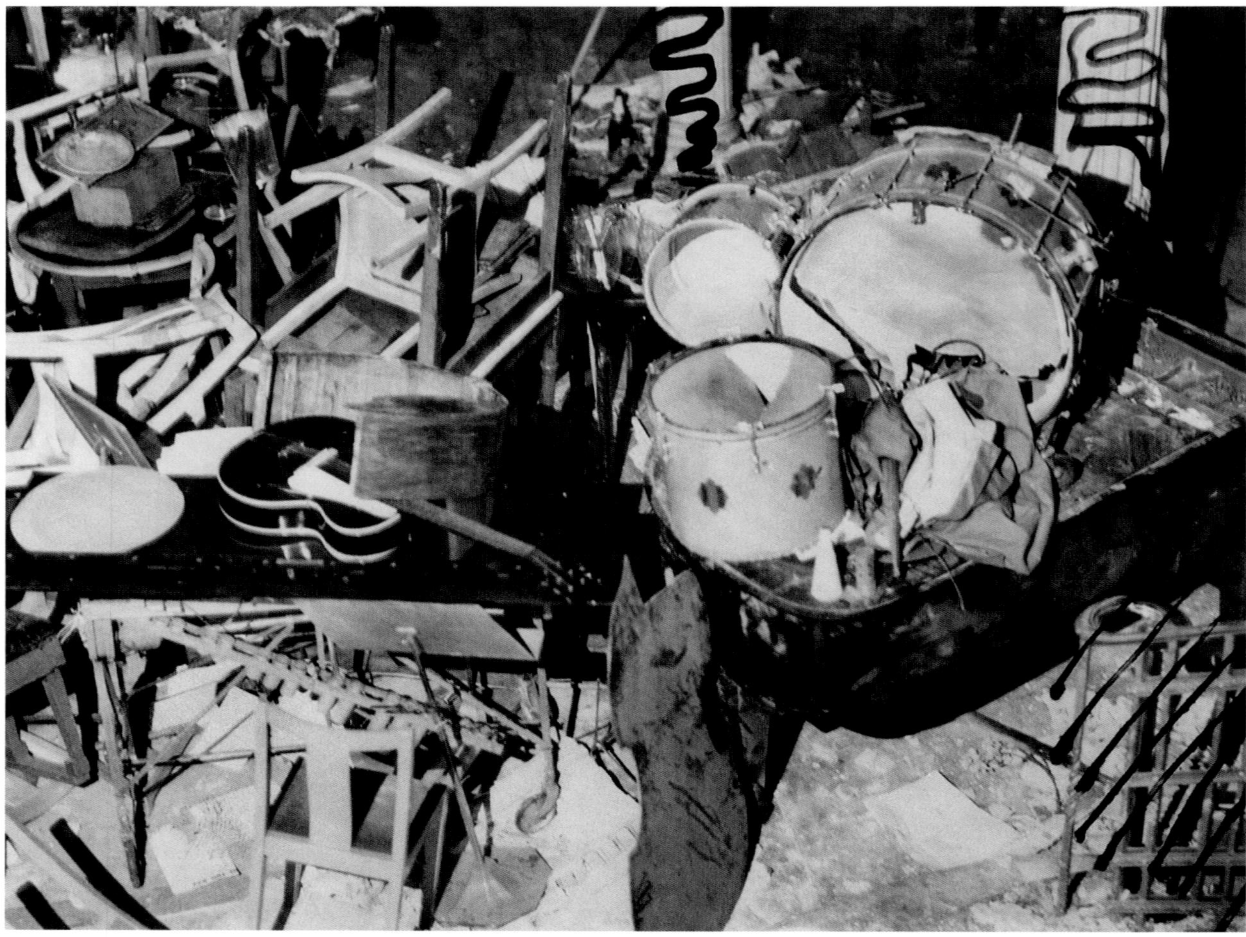

The wrecked bandstand of the Café de Paris, following the raid of 8 March 1941, which killed bandleader Ken 'Snakehips' Johnson and 33 others. The censor clearly thought the pillars and the staircase railings gave away the identity of this celebrated nightspot: they are marked for excision in this photograph.

the city to its heaviest attack so far of the year. Incendiaries, high-explosives and some landmines on parachutes, weighing up to 1,800kg, covered a broad swathe of the capital, from Chelsea to Pimlico and Westminster, and from Oxford Street to the City. Several hospitals were hit, as were a number of churches, including St Paul's, where a bomb penetrated its north transept. A few churches were entirely destroyed, including the Wren masterpieces of St Andrew's in Holborn and St Mildred's in Bread Street, in the City. Luckily for St Paul's, the worst was over. To the north, south and east of it, so much was – in the categorisation of the official Bomb Damage maps – 'damaged beyond repair', but after this night St Paul's would struggle on relatively unscathed.

Three days later, on the night of 19–20 April, another very large raid targeted the East End and the docks. In Bromley-by-Bow, 34 firemen died when their station was hit – the single highest toll suffered by the country's fire services, before or since. In just a few days, another 2,000 Londoners had died.

On the night of 10 May, the Luftwaffe mounted one more huge effort against London, comprising just over 500 bomber aircraft and leaving more than 3,000 Londoners dead or seriously injured. In its aftermath, about one in three of the capital's streets was judged unusable, the main train stations were out of action, bridges across the Thames lay damaged – and the House of Commons Chamber was wrecked. Ironically, MPs had just begun using the Houses of Parliament again, after months of conducting their debates elsewhere. At least Parliament's medieval masterpiece of Westminster Hall survived, as did the London Palladium near Regent Street, where a parachute bomb that had penetrated the roof failed to explode. Other landmarks were less lucky: the British Museum (housing the British Library) lost a quarter of a million books to fires, while the Tower of London, St James's Palace and Lambeth Palace were all hit.

Most Londoners mourned the loss of their city's historic landmarks, architectural gems, and famous shops and restaurants – and they were continually curious to view what had happened. Journalist Charles Graves called them 'blitz tourists' or 'gawkers', but one also gets a feeling that there was a sense of bereavement for the city. It was, though, the anxiety about the destruction of homes, neighbourhoods and workplaces that most affected people, at the heart of their everyday lives. The threat from the skies was out of anyone's control. But if you were an unfortunate victim, a strange kind of clarity could descend, as Teresa Wilkinson, an Air Raid Warden in West Ham, remembered:

> I was walking down a road where a whole row of houses were bombed and a man was sitting in the gutter. He laughed as we went by and said, 'I'm better off than you!' 'Why?' we asked. 'Because you're all worrying about your houses and your belongings. I haven't got anything to worry about. I haven't got anything left.

After 10–11 May 1941, London experienced a lull in the attacks. In fact, although Londoners could not know it, they were over the worst of it – and it would be February 1944 before Germany renewed its bombing of the British capital in such a concerted way again. Unbeknownst to them, Germany was on the verge of directing its energies elsewhere and opening a new front in the war, which

Opposite An aerial perspective of the City of London, taken from St Paul's Cathedral on 22 May 1941 and looking eastwards towards Tower Bridge. The scale of the destruction wrought over the eight months of the Blitz is plain to see.

materialised on 22 June in the shape of Operation 'Barbarossa' – the invasion of Germany's erstwhile 'Non-Aggression Pact' partner, the Soviet Union.

The Blitz of 1940–1 saw 354 aerial attacks against London, killing almost 20,000 civilians, which accounted for one in two British civilian deaths over the period. But morale had not been destroyed. By Christmas 1941, following the Japanese attack on Pearl Harbor, Hawaii, and the US declarations of war on both Japan and (reciprocally) Germany, there was a frisson of excitement in the air. Whatever the future held, Britain and its empire were no longer alone. 'What is London like on the first day of world-wide war?' Gwladys Cox asked herself. It was like this:

> Having to go to Wigmore Street for the umpteenth time about some bad war-workmanship on my glasses, we set out early – a fine, raw morning. After collecting my glasses, we walked to Mowbrays which was crowded, being Christmas time, and doing its best business of the year. After this, to Hamley's toy shop in Regent Street, to enquire about a Teddy bear for a Harward Court neighbour, who, with a small son, and no domestic help, cannot get out shopping. The smallest Teddy bear at Hamley's was 15/6. After lunch, we parted, I going to Selfridges on a further Bear Hunt. In the bus, I got chatting with an elderly dame, who told me of her great difficulty to get sweets for her grandchildren, 'but she had just succeeded at Swan and Edgars'. On parting, we amiably wished each other 'A Happy Christmas!'
> I noticed that strangers in the bus were chatting unreservedly; the atmosphere was exhilarating, not to say electric.

London and Londoners – though shattered by the Blitz – had learned how to adapt and endure.

W
W

IN FOCUS

LONDON'S DEFENDERS

When air raids occurred, London's first line of defence lay in trying to prevent the bombs falling in the first place – the role of Anti-Aircraft Command and the RAF. Thereafter, it was the job of the thousands of civil defence workers and volunteers to cope with whatever the Luftwaffe had been able to deliver.

Anti-Aircraft Command had been established in January 1939, but it was a poor relation among the military services, and by the opening of the war was deficient in both guns and personnel. In addition, before aerial bombing over Britain became a reality, there was a public dislike of the placing of unsightly and inconvenient gun positions in many civilian areas. Adding to these problems was a lack of equipment for proper targeting, which made the guns very inefficient. Over London, barrage balloons were in place to try and keep any attackers flying high, but this measure also made them harder to hit from the ground.

At the same time, the RAF's fighters could do little to intercept night-time raids. Despite advances in airborne radar, the problem was bringing those night-fighters that possessed the technology near enough to the objective, as they had to be within three miles of the other planes to register their presence. On the ground, there was as yet no radar equipment in place capable of detecting the course and height of the German bombers. (The technology was available but needed time to be deployed.)

On 7 September, as London was rocked by the first day of the Blitz, there was little in the way of counter-fire. A concerted effort then increased the number of London's anti-aircraft guns from 92 to 199, and during the raid of 10 September 1940, General Sir Frederick Pile, Commander-in-Chief of Anti-Aircraft Command, was determined to make an impression. He ordered all his guns to fire everything they had. The gunners used 'barrage fire' to try and saturate the skies and – with luck – bring down aircraft. In truth, none of the anti-aircraft measures were particularly effective during the Blitz period, especially at night, when most of the German raids took place.

However, what the sound and fury of the anti-aircraft guns succeeded in doing for the first time on 10 September was bolster morale and give Londoners a sense that they were fighting back. On 10 September 1941, diarist Vere Hodgson remembered it was 'exactly a year today that I returned [from Birmingham] to London to face the blitz. This was the night the anti-aircraft barrage took on a formidable tone, and gave Londoners some satisfaction. They had more to listen to than bombs falling one by one.' On 13 September 1940, Gwladys Cox offered her own impression of that same night:

Opposite Two ARP Wardens in a residential London road (1940). With their white steel helmets and gas masks, Wardens became familiar and essential figures on the streets of the capital. Their numbers varied over the course of the war, depending on the nature of the aerial threat.

Anti-Aircraft crewmen fire their 3.7 inch anti-aircraft guns at night, using targeting information provided by women of the Auxiliary Territorial Service (1942).

Women of the Auxiliary Territorial Service (ATS) operate the height and range finder on an anti-aircraft gun (1942). ATS contingents – 'ack-ack girls' – served with their male counterparts on both fixed and mobile gun batteries, although actually firing the gun remained the responsibility of the men of Anti-Aircraft Command.

The A.A. guns have a glorious sound, deep, full, commanding, challenging, like a lion roaring. The new gun barrage on Wednesday night seems to have been a great success. Messages from London to New York describe it as 'a curtain of fire', 'a screen of iron', 'a steel tent over London'. The barrage balloons were lowered while the intensive A.A. barrage was sent up with many more guns than have ever been used to repel a Nazi attack. The guns operated on a barrage system, the shells exploding in vast screens at different heights. This had the effect of sending the invaders up to an altitude from which they could not take proper aim, and of driving them hurriedly from one area to another.

General Pile was buoyed by the morale-boosting capacity of his organisation on this night. As he later wrote:

... it bucked up people tremendously. The midnight news said nice things about us, and when I put a call through to my wife the telephone operator said: 'By God this is the stuff. All the girls here are hugging each other.' Next day everyone said they had slept better, and for the first time A.A. Command hit the headlines. Apart from comforting the civilians, it stimulated the gunners, who had been feeling pretty frustrated during the long nights when they had been compelled to hear aircraft flying overhead and dropping their bombs without being engaged.

By the time of the later V1 attacks, London's anti-aircraft guns and the RAF's fighters were in a much better position to target the incoming bombs and missiles.

Once a bomber had dropped its load, coping with the results was a matter for the men and women of the civil defence bodies. From its creation in 1937, the organisation that served as the backbone of Britain's – and London's – civil defence effort was the Air Raid Precautions (ARP). At the outbreak of war, there were around 1.5 million voluntary ARP Wardens, spread across nine regions, one of which was London. These men and women initially spent much of their time

Meredith Frampton's painting of the London Regional Civil Defence Control Room (1943) contrasts precision of style with a certain informality in the grouping. Featured is the Senior Regional Commissioner for London, Sir Ernest Gowers, who stands in front of a map of Inner and Outer London, along with two colleagues. The Control Room lay in a specially constructed and highly protected building, sited half underground between the Geology and Natural History museums in South Kensington. Its function was to coordinate civil defence operations across London's local authorities, and to collect and evaluate information about the raids and their effects.

trying to get a reluctant population acclimatised to the inconveniences of the blackout. But, as the aerial bombardment evolved from the Battle of Britain into the Blitz, the ARP's roles diversified as they were augmented with first-aid, fire and rescue services and, in 1941, they were renamed Civil Defence. All of the ARP sub-groups were expected to work closely with the army and the regular police and fire organisations.

The capital's civil defence was quickly organised in May 1940 under a Senior Regional Commissioner, the MP Captain Euan Wallace, assisted by two Regional Commissioners, Admiral Sir Edward Evans and Sir Ernest Gowers; when Wallace resigned in January 1941, Gowers succeeded to the senior role. The London ARP region, encompassing 9 million people, had its headquarters at the Geological Museum (now part of the Natural History Museum)

A spotter on a London roof carries out his shift, looking out for signs of the approaching enemy (1941). Roof spotting rotas were organised from 1940, often drawing on volunteer staff of the offices and buildings, who could sound alarms when imminent danger threatened. In the words of Helen Jones (in *British Civilians in the Front Line*), roof spotting could be 'cold, lonely, boring, stressful and dangerous'.

Firemen douse flames, while other civil defence personnel attend to 'victims' of an attack in R. Vivian Pitchforth's watercolour *ARP Practice*. The artist was commissioned to cover the work of the Air Raid Precautions by the War Artists Advisory Committee.

Auxiliary Firemen Bernard Hailstone (with cigarette), Leonard Rosoman (at the back) and Richard Southern relax amid the rubble after an alert, somewhere in London (c.1940). Few roles on the home front were more hazardous than firefighting during the periods of aerial bombardment. Rosoman, a noted artist, captured the dangers inherent in such work.

in South Kensington. The next organisational level down was the borough, each containing a Report and Control Centre – usually the town hall – below which were the districts of up to 10,000 people. At street level, the most basic and visible manifestation of the ARP was the often sandbagged Warden's Post, manned by between three and six Wardens, and responsible for a neighbourhood of up to 500 people.

By the summer of 1940, when mass urban bombing had failed to materialise, many ARP personnel had left to join the Home Guard and other services. As a result, in London many of the Warden's Posts were understaffed. In response, the authorities 'froze' ARP, police, fire, rescue and stretcher-party personnel in their jobs – and in addition, men aged between 30 and 50 could opt for these roles instead of military service.

Under normal conditions, ARP personnel occupied themselves with issuing gas masks, patrolling to ensure the blackout was in place, and passing on any relevant information to their Control Centre. But during and after a raid, their tasks proliferated. For a start, Air Raid Wardens reported all incidents to their local sector and assessed what help was needed. Wardens would then often act as firefighters, rescue personnel or nurses, as necessary. And after a raid, Wardens would help with rescuing people from bombed-out buildings, dealing with unexploded bombs, and guiding newly homeless victims to rest centres. The efforts of ARP personnel were supplemented by the Women's Voluntary Service (WVS), founded in 1938, the fire service, the ambulances and the Heavy Rescue or Demolition squads administered by the London County Council.

However, Air Raid Wardens had no authority to make people take shelter. The consequences for individuals could sometimes be catastrophic, as Teresa Wilkinson, an Air Raid Warden in West Ham, observed:

One night, we were passing a block of flats and this man was standing outside. 'You should get into a shelter!' we said – and he told us what to do in no uncertain terms. So we left him standing there and walked on. When we came back, he was still outside the block of flats. His head was about four steps further along.

When a raid came, the principal responsibility for tackling fires lay at the feet of the regular London

The desolation of the City of London after the incendiary raid of 29–30 December 1940, which tested London's fire services to the limit. The view is from St Paul's. Beyond the gutted remains of the booksellers' quarter around Paternoster Row are the domed tower of the Central Criminal Court (Old Bailey) and the four-spired St Bartholomew's Church.

Fire Brigade, who were, at the beginning of the war, supplemented by the male volunteers of the new Auxiliary Fire Service (AFS). The numbers of AFS personnel swelled after June 1940, when such roles became alternatives to military service, and they included a number of conscientious objectors.

London's fire service bore the brunt of the government failures to put in effective fire-watching procedures. It was a dangerous, demanding and physically gruelling job. Just to get to a fire, firemen had to battle their way through diversion signs, craters and debris, past dangling telephone and trolley bus wires, over splintered glass and around people begging them to save their homes. Once at the fire they might have to climb a 100-foot water tower – only to find no water there as the pressure dwindled. Extremes of hot and cold, lack of regular nutrition and sleep, long hours (shifts of 48 hours on, 24 hours off, for AFS men), constant strain and a sense of never quite keeping up with the scale and frequency of conflagrations bedevilled their work. During the massive raid on London that occurred on the night of 29–30 December 1940, the City of London firemen battled the fires with 2,000 pumps from across the London region – and still it was not enough, for they needed another 300 from outside London. The pressures they faced contributed, just as the Blitz was ending, to the creation of a National Fire Service on 13 May 1941, amalgamating all the fire services under one unified command and control structure. The reorganisation was completed by the autumn. Fire personnel paid a price for their hazardous jobs: 793 firemen lost their lives during the war, as did 25 women working in the fire services, and 7,000 other fire personnel were injured.

Inspired by Ellen Wilkinson, Parliamentary Secretary at the Home Office and Ministry of Home Security, women took part in all aspects of ARP/ Civil Defence, acting as Air Raid Wardens, fire-watchers, messengers, drivers, as well as being employed in clerical work and as telephone operators. In March 1942, the number of women serving full-time in Britain's Civil Defence reached its peak, at 19,400, while a further 127,200 were employed part-time – and that figure would rise to nearly 180,000 by June 1944, when London was under attack yet again from Germany's new flying bombs, the V1s. They gave their lives too: 618 ARP/Civil Defence women were killed across the country as a result of enemy action during the war.

At the beginning of the Blitz, the small proportion of full-time ARP workers (and Auxiliary Fire Service men) were paid £3 5s a week and women £2 3s for a 72-hour week, though their actual working hours were usually much longer than that throughout the Blitz. But the vast majority of ARP workers were part-timers, and many of these were women. The thousands who flocked to join them reflected the enormous voluntary response to the outbreak of war, including also such organisations as the WVS and casualty and fire services. Over 1.5 million people were serving in some sort of voluntary capacity by December 1940; by December 1943, nearly 2 million civilians were serving in Civil Defence and the fire, ambulance and police services, most as part-time volunteers.

After the Blitz, there was considerably less work for Wardens to do. As Teresa Wilkinson remarked, 'After May 10, 1941, we didn't get a bad raid again. The worst of the blitz was over and air raid wardens went back to £3 a week for doing nothing and I got bored.' By 1942, the government expected Civil Defence workers to double up and work in war industries or some other useful capacity. The Heavy Rescue men and stretcher-bearer units amalgamated. At the height of the Blitz there were 127,000 people in London's Civil Defence, but this number had fallen to 70,000 by 1943. Similarly, by 1943 200 London fire stations, no longer overwhelmed by having to fight the flames, were engaged instead in various types of war work and toiling on allotments, instead of battling the ravages of aerial bombing.

Two members of the Women's Voluntary Service (Patience 'Boo' Brand and Rachel Bingham) distribute tea and buns in one of the trench shelters constructed in London parks (1941). In such ways, the WVS provided temporary sustenance to thousands of those made homeless or seeking refuge during the Blitz and later attacks. The occupants of this shelter have made it rather more homely by installing their own chairs, tables and lamps.

Customers enjoy eating out at a packed Lyon's Corner House on London's Coventry Street, between Piccadilly Circus and Leicester Square (1942). The well-established Lyon's tea rooms and Corner Houses, with their smartly dressed waitresses, were a popular London institution.

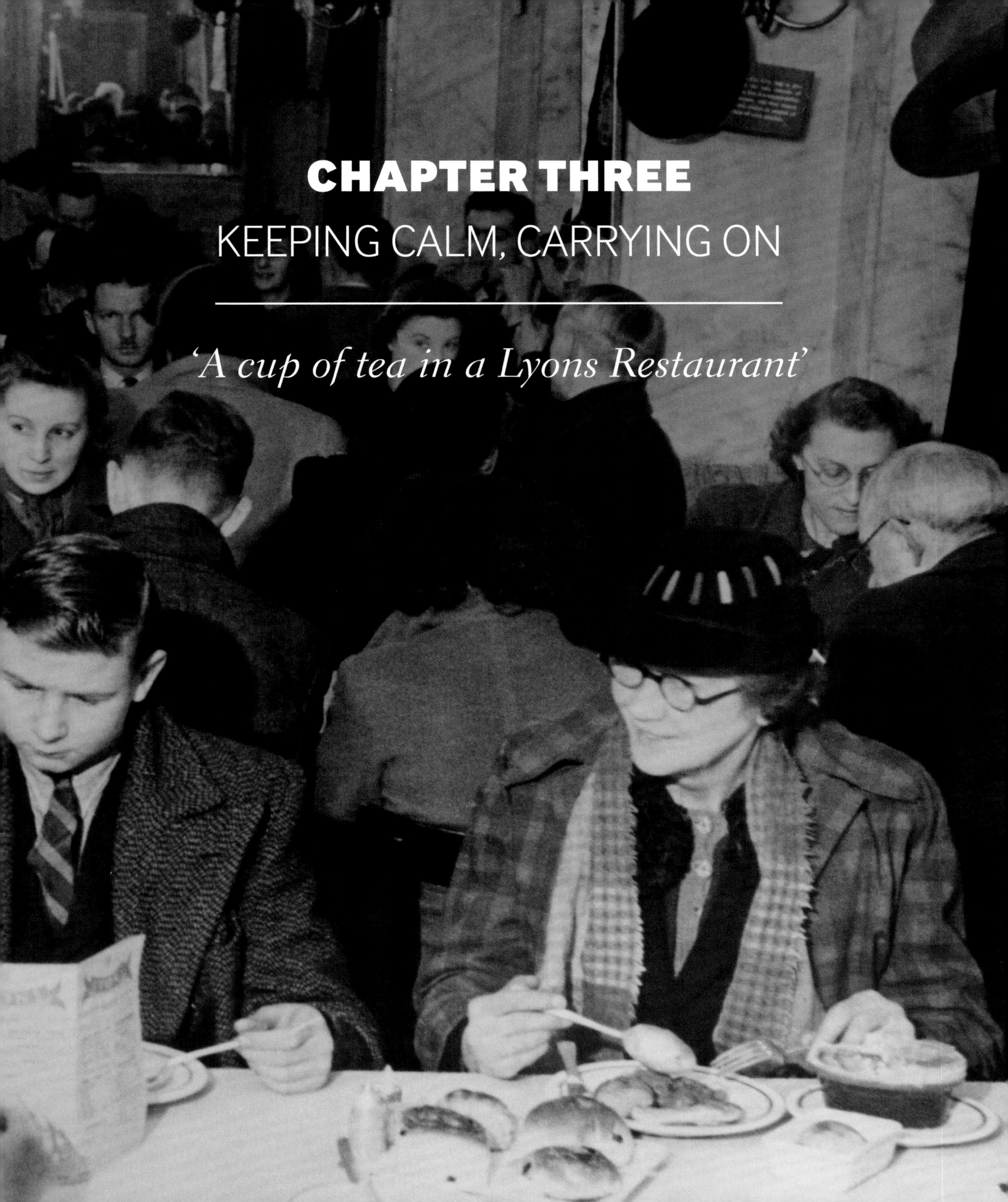

CHAPTER THREE

KEEPING CALM, CARRYING ON

'A cup of tea in a Lyons Restaurant'

The qualities of adaptation, endurance and a sense of being 'in it together' that enabled London's people to get through the Blitz came to be summed up in the cliché of the 'Blitz spirit'. Of course, it was more complicated than that. There was indeed a sense of shared identity that often brought communities together, but it was not all-encompassing across London; it ebbed and flowed. Nevertheless, those qualities of endurance, of sticking it out, became apparent in many of the published and unpublished diaries of the time. In the words of one Londoner remembering the dangers faced by fighting men in the First World War, 'if they can do it, I can, and so can anyone else. They were just ordinary people, and so am I.'

It was much harder, of course, when the bombs first started to fall in such shocking numbers. At first, there was resentment among some that it seemed to be the urban working classes who were bearing the brunt of it. As Mrs Hilda Neal of Kennington noted in her diary, 'An aggressive Labour bus driver told me the East End people were saying that their houses were destroyed, or allowed to be destroyed and no one cared; but when the West End was touched the government started a barrage!' And as the raids wore on, guilty terror could easily still swallow individuals. As late as May 1941, Miss Vera Reid, a London WVS worker could still admit to her 'Fear, Paralysing physical fear. It grips you and you feel contaminated, unclean.' Yet for the most part, Londoners learned to adapt remarkably quickly. As Paddington bus driver Henry Penny wrote in his diary on 12 September 1940, 'Although the past week has been very Trying with Bombs and Sleepless nights we are still not "Downhearted" for as it has been said, We are all in the "Front Line" and we realise it.' Vivienne Hall echoed those feelings four days later, describing how the 'pavements and roads are thronged with people trying to get to work and there's absolutely no panic or grumbling anywhere. We picked up odd people on the way and two to four hours to get to work seems quite the usual time, but still we go to work, Mr. Hitler!' The early evacuations had contributed to a sense of neighbourliness among those Londoners who remained, even before the hardships of the Blitz were felt, but the bombing itself intensified that sense of connectedness for many people. It was true for Gwladys Cox, who recorded that 'People we have known for years by sight and have passed without recognition, have suddenly become very friendly – it seems to require a war to break down "English reserve".'

Such adaption to the 'new normal' was reiterated a few months later in an official memorandum by Home Secretary Herbert Morrison, describing the bombing between September and November:

Anthony Gross's pen and wash drawing *A Gas Main on Fire in Chelsea* (1940), commissioned by the War Artists Advisory Committee. The area depicted is Paulton Square. As the Home Secretary and Minister of Home Security Herbert Morrison well knew, the rupture of gas pipes was just one of the many pressing threats to London's infrastructure.

The effects of the raids can be considered as the transient and the durable. The transient effects were those on morale and general disorganization. London people lost much sleep and suffered anxiety and discomfort, but there was no breakdown, no panic and no mass evacuation, except in small heavily bombed areas. The effect was largely one of surprise. After a few days the first horror of the raids wore off and people became adjusted to the new conditions of shelter life.

Disorganization was more serious. The complicated network of railways was cut at many places at once. In three weeks, 104 railway bridges were put out of action for periods ranging from a day to a month. Roads were blocked by craters and debris. Thousands of water and gas mains were broken, interrupting supplies over large areas. Telephone exchanges were put out of action and postal deliveries hampered.

His assessment of morale was generally reflected in people's personal correspondence as well as the regional morale reports from London and around the country.

Daily morale reports were the job of regional officers working for the new Ministry of Information's Department of Home Intelligence, set up in December 1939 under Mary Adams. They drew on a range of evidence, including the wartime social survey, and reports from the social scientists of the Mass Observation project. In London, MOI staff also had large networks of friends and connections from all walks of life, who in turn suggested other individuals whom they contacted by phone or visited, with the result that the morale reports were generally more detailed than for other regions. Although there was much adverse press coverage for 'Cooper's snoopers' (named after Duff Cooper, the Minister of Information at the time), the reports generally tended to confirm the resilience of Londoners during the Blitz.

The reports were not, though, uniform. One early London report, for 9 September, painted a picture of contrasts:

> No signs of defeatism except among small section of elderly women in 'front line' such as East Ham who cannot stand constant bombing. Districts sustaining only one or two shocks soon rally, but in Dockside areas the population is showing visible signs of nerve cracking from constant ordeals. Old women and mothers are undermining morale of young women and men by their extreme nervousness and lack of resilience. Men state they cannot sleep because they must keep up the morale of their families and express strong desire to get families away from danger areas. Families clinging together, however, and any suggestions of sending children away without mothers and elderly relations considered without enthusiasm... Lack of sleep already showing signs of undermining morale and working capacity of the population.

A day later, the report noted the kind of divisions evoked by Hilda Neal's bus driver:

> Class feeling growing because of worse destruction in working class areas; anti-Semitism growing in districts where large proportion of Jews reside owing to their taking places in public shelters early in the day... Districts less regularly bombed, such as Lewisham and Chelsea, report great neighbourly feeling.

A child at play among what were once South London homes (14 September 1940). Although another evacuation scheme began when the Blitz started, many children had returned to the capital in the months before. For those who stayed, the bombing created a landscape of new, sometimes dangerous, but fascinating playgrounds.

In later September however, spurred on by the reassuring noise of anti-aircraft barrages, Londoners' morale was lifting, according to the reports, with feelings in the East End of 'We'll give them hell now', while residents of Croydon were 'determined to see it through'. The authorities, though, did not get off the hook for their ill-preparedness to cope with consequences of aerial bombing. The reports noted in late September 1940 'a lot of bitter feeling about the Government's slowness in coping with the emergency'.

Along with the evolving stoicism of those on the receiving end of the war's punishment, there was admiration and sympathy for the victims, who were increasingly visible as the bombed-out East End refugees spread across London. One correspondent, writing on 17 September 1940 to Henry Strong, was 'terribly sad to think of the appalling havoc that has been wrought in London':

> We could see the docks blazing from here or rather the terrific red glow in the sky. We have a refugee family from Wapping in an empty house in our road, they arrived about 7 o'clock last Friday night with bedding but practically nothing else. No black-out or anything done for them, all the neighbours rallied round and lent different things. But the woman was amazingly brave, she really staggered me, but she certainly proved that what the papers say about the morale of the East Enders is quite true.

But feelings and responses to the Blitz were by no means simple or unqualified. With the acceptance of death, destruction and homelessness as everyday affairs, it was also necessarily true that the thresholds for sympathy rose. Eugenie Chaudoir, writing to her sister, deplored this development in herself:

> I think the most horrid thing about this war at the moment is the utter lack of feeling we are cultivating towards people we don't know. You are told that 6 died on Argyle Street etc. and it just means nothing to you. Less feeling than when Chelsea won a match. I can stare without blinking at the ruins of someone's home. It is far more a marvel that a bomb could do so much damage than the whole of some poor devil's life has been removed, and so we go on staring and the belief becomes stronger that it couldn't happen to me. The horrid thought is that if it misses me it may hit the next.

Even after the Blitz, a sense of the war's everyday tragedy loomed over people's lives – unwelcome news could intrude at any moment. Gwladys Cox remembered how 'One of our neighbours on the top floor, hearing that her only son was missing, threw herself out of a back window. Most mercifully, I was not in the garden at the time.'

For many children still in the capital – and so long as they were not themselves victims – the Blitz could be a source of thrills, an utter and captivating contrast to the tedium of the usual routines. John Simonson, then a boy in Southgate, North London, remembered:

> ... it was strangely exciting going to school to see what might have happened overnight, and of course quite a few gaps in the houses started to appear. A popular activity with us school boys at this time was to collect shrapnel, as there was always quite a lot to be found after extensive anti-aircraft fire. Even the milkman would leave bits on our doorstep!

For some primary school children, classes in the capital continued where it was still safe enough, as here in the Greek Road School's basement, South-East London (1941). Inevitably, the interruptions of war, especially in hard-hit areas such as the East End, took their toll on levels of educational attainment.

Normal school life was, anyway, disrupted. Many schools had been turned into rest centres, and many other schools had been damaged, especially in the East End. In West Ham, out of 60 local council schools only 16 remained functioning because of bomb damage; although this number had climbed back up to 39 by the end of 1941, there was still a deficit in children's education. In one primary school, not a single child aged seven could read.

What anchored the majority of grown-ups, by contrast, was the simple necessity of trying to impose order on extraordinary times. From government ministers and faceless bureaucrats to London's ordinary workers and housewives trying to feed their families, there was a huge task of organising and managing daily life, and of coping with the raids.

Simply getting around became difficult. For a start, the movement of freight and troops took priority over the needs of the ordinary traveller. Civilian train services were reduced, so they became overcrowded, and restaurant cars almost disappeared. The country became geographically mysterious, as station signposts were removed in 1940 for security reasons. During the Blitz, train services out of London were blocked, sometimes for months. With so many of the traditional London buses out of action, buses from across the country were brought into the city to compensate: in one week alone, 472 buses, of 10 different makes from 15 different owners, arrived, 82 of the vehicles being single-deckers. And the buses carried on, throughout the Blitz and the rest of the war, as did the London Underground – which of course served its dual role as protection. Private road transport, though, became problematic. Travelling was not only more difficult because of the blackout and exposure to the possible danger of air raids, but was officially discouraged. Petrol was rationed from September 1939, and in 1942 the petrol allowance for private motorists was stopped completely. In war conditions, to travel unnecessarily was regarded as anti-social. However, rather than ration the number of journeys the public could make, the government relied upon persuasion with slogans such as 'Is Your Journey Really Necessary?'

Every bomb that struck home required an effort of toil to respond to the damage and to help the victims. First Aid Posts were established to treat minor injuries, while the more seriously injured were sent to hospitals, where doctors and nurses worked extremely long hours. Many of the hospitals were themselves hit by bombs. (The non-physical traumas of war, by contrast, got less attention: in the early days of the Blitz, there was little help available to orphaned children or to those suffering mental breakdowns.) Mortuaries found themselves busy. Sometimes, the dead were only discovered under rubble in demolition work, months after the attack that killed them, whereupon the remains would be sent to the mortuary – and pieced back together, if identifiable.

London's infrastructure – as Herbert Morrison's memo suggests – took a battering. Every time a bomb hit a road, it damaged the mass of pipes and cables that ran beneath it. In the first three months of the Blitz, 4,124 water mains were broken. But repair work went on even as the bombs fell, not least because the bomb damage could create new hazards. When a gas main was shattered, the end of it had to be plugged, or the supply cut off – which involved going through the flames to get to the necessary area. Even burst water pipes could be fatal, as the Balham Underground Station bombing testified, and as Air Raid Warden Teresa Wilkinson could confirm with regard to her friend 'who had just got engaged and she went to spend the weekend with her fiancé's family. They had a shelter in their cellar and when she was there, a water main burst and the cellar filled with water and

Right In North London, the WVS-run East Barnet Pig Collection Unit goes into action, as Winifred Jordan (left) and Kathleen Kent, head of the Unit, empty kitchen scraps into a designated trailer (1943). The recipient would have been the nearest pig farmer. The Women's Voluntary Service grew from 165,000 in 1939 to over a million by 1942. It broadened its base away from purely civil defence work, playing a leading role in evacuation, collecting salvage, running canteens, distributing ration books, staffing Incident Inquiry points (to provide information after air raids), as well as comforting the bereaved.

Below A South Kensington resident, Mrs Day, separates her cardboard and tin for re-use (1941). Long before environmental worries about landfill and dwindling natural resources, the war effort was inculcating its own habits of recycling.

Mrs Bertha Martin (left, foreground) does her bit at Perrings furniture showroom, Kingston, on the outskirts of West London. The company was making small parts for RAF aircraft, and the cricket-themed scoreboard for 'Perrings v. Hitler' shows the daily totals of good armature coils produced. In London, as elsewhere, the conscription of women brought thousands of workers into factories supplying the armed services.

they all drowned.' Massively labour-intensive was the job of repairing the damaged telephone cables: when one was severed, up to 2,800 individual wires might be broken, and each would need reconnection.

In dealing with such aftermath, the men of the Heavy Rescue teams played a vital role, many of them being builders, bricklayers, plumbers and carpenters – men who knew how buildings were made. Less clear was who was in charge on any incident site, where senior ARP Wardens and police frequently came into competition. Usually the police took over, but it took two years before the problem between these services was ironed out.

To respond to these conditions, and to enable 'ordinary' life to go on at the same time that the fighting war and armaments production were sucking in people and resources, the government exercised new levels of control. In 1941, it assumed powers to direct and allocate labour; and, for the first time in British history, it introduced conscription for women, in December 1941, offering women a choice of working in industry or joining one of the services. Extremely arduous, low-paying and monotonous though factory work often was, many women endured it. Working in a factory – while not as rosy as the 1943 fictional film *Millions Like Us* depicted it – could create a sense of camaraderie, even if social divisions remained. At the Ford Factory in East London, the workforce showed its dedication by continuing to work their 15-hour shifts, with very little absenteeism, throughout the Blitz.

National membership of the WVS, under Stella, the Dowager Marchioness of Reading, also grew, from 165,000 in 1939 to over 1 million by 1942. The vast majority of members were middle class and they could afford to give their time entirely unpaid. Local councils helped, by providing free premises and furniture. The WVS had helped with the evacuation of London's children, and during the Blitz its members provided a range of support services beyond the core civil defence functions to help the victims of air raids: collecting salvage, distributing ration books and clothing, and running mobile canteens, for which pre-war training in emergency cooking in dustbins and home-made ovens came in very useful. Later, WVS volunteers also staffed Incident Inquiry Points after air raids to provide information and to comfort the bereaved. One of the earlier ones was in Putney's public library, South London, after the Dance Hall nearby was bombed in 1943. In Willesden, North-West London, the WVS staff of a nearby rest centre even stepped in to provide the choir for a local wedding. In wartime, weddings often had to be improvised affairs, done in a hurry when leave was cancelled or relocated when churches were bombed out – as depicted in the 1942 film *Salute John Citizen* (1942), about the fictional Bunting family.

The outspoken Labour Party MP Dr Edith Summerskill made her own contribution to London's female volunteer organisations by establishing the unofficial Women's Home Defence. It was her reaction to discovering that women were not permitted to join the Home Guard or undergo weapons training. 'In this war, it has been found that women are capable of doing most things,' she proclaimed, and earned the nickname 'Flossie Bang Bang' for her pugnacious efforts. Eventually her organisation was disbanded, in 1944, when women were finally allowed to become Home Guard Auxiliaries.

By June 1944, across Britain unemployment had virtually disappeared, as some 10 million men and 6.5 million women engaged in civilian war work. London in 1940 saw the reappearance of female bus conductors – as in the First World War – except that this time they were greeted without any raising of eyebrows. By March 1943, there were 32,200 women serving full-time with the National Fire Service (NFS), and an additional 54,600 women served in a part-time capacity. While female members of the NFS did not tackle major fires, they provided important back-up to their male colleagues. Many acted as drivers taking up supplies to firefighters, and they also served as despatch riders. Others performed the role of mobilising officers at fire stations, covering fires in their division or district. After 1941, thousands of other women became members of the Fire Guard Organisation, trying to combat the danger from incendiary bombs. To help women work in all their new capacities there was an effort to improve the provision of nurseries for those who could not rely on family help to take care of their young children.

For men and women alike, daily life in London gradually improved as the war went on. Along with full employment, wages gradually rose. However, although the average weekly wage rose by 38 per cent between 1938 and 1943, prices had risen by 42 per cent in the same period, and people were working more hours for their money – an extra four hours per week, on average, for a man. The city's population had reduced from its pre-war level – the East End, battered by the bombs, had witnessed the flight of half of its people, while London as a whole was, in mid-1943, a quarter down. Yet, perhaps surprisingly, shops sales remained relatively buoyant – at just 7 per cent lower than pre-1939 levels.

Almost all household expenditure went on price-controlled goods, for which people queued: life in wartime London meant queuing for everything – for shops, for buses, for restaurants. And in the Sunday newspaper of 1 June 1941, Gwladys Cox – now relocated with her husband and cat to Honeybourne Road, West Hampstead – discovered the disappearance of yet another piece of pre-war normality: 'Clothing is to be rationed. For a year, each person is allowed 66 coupons – so many for a dress, so many for underwear, shoes etc.' In the new system, coupons would allow each person to buy a basic variety of clothes of his or her choice. But more than that, the new controls of the Utility scheme, from 1942, meant that garments had to be cut as economically as possible. Men's suits lost their turn-ups, women's skirts became slimmer, and even the number of buttons was restricted. Otherwise it was a matter, as the government and newspapers encouraged, of 'make do and mend'. Many an adult's overcoat was turned into a girl's skirt, while unrationed fabric such as curtain net or blackout material could be transformed into novel, fashionable outfits.

For Gwladys at least, clothes rationing was not going to be a great privation: 'I scarcely think these restrictions will worry me at all for I had no idea of buying anything, except warm stockings.' Perhaps she would have regretted more the rationing of soap in February 1942. For many people though, the everyday escapism of such little luxuries of shopping or eating out remained important ways to counteract the oppression of the Blitz. In the West End, hotels, restaurants, cafés and shops were often open again just a few hours after

Shoppers waiting to buy products from the baker Williamson's spill out of the store and along Wood Green High Street, North London. This photograph was taken in 1945 – by which time Londoners were thoroughly used to the routines and tedium of five years of rationing and queuing.

a raid. The story of the Hungaria restaurant, on London's Lower Regent Street, is an example of the typical insouciance, tenacity and adaptability witnessed all over the city.

By the time of the Blitz, the Hungaria was still in the hands of one of its original 1928 founders, an Italian-turned-British-citizen Joseph Vecci. On 3 September 1940, a regular diner, Robert Herrmann, was celebrating his eleventh wedding anniversary with his wife when, as he wrote in his diary:

> ... the band leader made the following announcement through the microphone 'For your information (not that you're interested, of course) there is an air-raid warning on', after which everything went on as before. When we left an hour later the commissionaire told us that the all clear had sounded some time ago.

BERKERTEX
Utility Frocks
60/-
UTILITY

Opposite A shop window displays a variety of 'Utility' clothes for women. In wartime, it would not do to waste precious resources and materials on frills and ostentation. The rail nearer the front contains a row of the unglamorously named 'Berkertex Utility frocks', but, despite the plainness of all the garments seen here, they boasted a glamorous designer: Norman Hartnell

Within weeks, as the Blitz got fully under way, the restaurant had moved downstairs to the subterranean grillroom, which offered diners refuge in the restaurant's cellar, on couches behind screens, during raids. Should a raid go on all night, breakfast would be served in the morning. A month after his anniversary celebration, Herrmann was back again. Unlike the recently bombed Royal Automobile Club in Pall Mall, which now had (in Herrmann's view) a 'forbidding' atmosphere, the Hungaria was 'one of the few pleasant spots in these dreary days':

> Dinner was served in the Grill Room; itself an underground shelter, and while I was fortunately unable to test the management's assertion that it is bombproof and blastproof it certainly was soundproof. I heard nothing of the warning and the only sounds were the pleasant strains of the orchestra which made quite a change. The dinner was excellent and there were a few cheery people about.

The grillroom was indeed something of a fortress – it had been fitted with steel doors to make it bomb- and splinter-proof, and other London restaurants and hotels were quick to follow. The Hungaria went on to become even more popular in the later war years, during the V1 attacks, playing host to such celebrity diners as Flanagan and Allen, Will Hay and Jack Hylton. In this respect, it had rather taken over the earlier wartime role of the Savoy Grill.

The Savoy was a haven for many American newsmen such as Ed Murrow and Quentin Reynolds in the early years of the war. Its basement had been a banqueting hall, but was turned into an underground shelter for hotel guests, with a restaurant and a dance floor that was converted into a dormitory providing permanent sleeping quarters, with different sections for men, women, married couples – and even for heavy snorers. To add to the comfort, raids could not be heard in the restaurant. But when, in December 1944, the Savoy's windows were smashed for a seventh time (this time by a V2 rocket), it lost its status as a favoured hotel for visiting journalists and celebrities. It was, as journalist Charles Graves put it, rather too near the 'vulnerable side of the Thames'.

Other smart London hotels made the necessary adaptations to continue their business. The Dorchester had underground shelters, which induced many guests to stay on during the war on a semi-permanent basis. Duff Cooper, Minister of Information from May

MARTINEZ RESTAURANT

SWALLOW STREET PICCADILLY LONDON WI

'Phone REGent 5066

PLATOS DEL DIA

(TO-DAY'S SPECIAL)

Thursday 23rd April 1942.

Smoked Salmon 5/- Fresh Caviar 6/6

Hors D'Oeuvres Variés 1/9 Paté de Foiegras 2/6

Scallops Mornay 2/-

Sopas — Soups

Crema de Legumbres 1/3 Consomé Brunes 1/-

Potage de Alubias 1/3

Pescados — Fish

Calamares con Arroz (Ink-Fish & Rice) 3/6

Fresh Scotch Salmon (Boiled or Grill) 6/6

Merluza Catalana 3/6 Cold Lobster Bayonaisse 7/6

Entradas — Entrees

Pelaff Casera 3/- Minced Chicken & Rice 3/-

Pierna de Cordero 3/- Roast Leg of Lamb & Veg's

Chile con Carne 3/- Meat & beans 3/-

Pollo Riosera 5/- Casserole Chicken 5/-

Legumbres — Vegetables

Patatas 6d — Col flor 1/-

Espinacas 1/- Guisantes Frescos 1/3

Dulces — Sweets

Gateau Martinez 1/- Vanilla Ices 1/-

Welsh Rarebit 1/3.

SPECIAL SPANISH DISHES

still available.

Served daily-to order.

Lenguado Alfonso XIII.
Sole garnished with tomatoes, pineapple, etc.
15 mins.

Zarzuela a la Andaluza.
Turbot, lobster and mussels, stewed with tomatoes, etc., flavoured with aniseed.
15 mins.

Pollo a la Martinez.
Chicken cooked with red peppers, orange, olives, mushrooms and sherry wine.
15 mins.

Arroz a la Valenciana.
Chicken and rice with red peppers, saffron, mussels, various vegetables, etc.
25 mins.

Suprema de Pollo Hortelana.
Wing of Chicken done in bread crumbs, served with various vegetables and a rich sherry sauce.
15 mins.

□□□

The Restaurant is open daily, Sundays included, until 10.15.

USUAL PRICES. NO MUSIC.

□□□

DINNER AND DANCE
In our vaults, official A.R.P. Shelter, every night except Sundays 7.15 to 11.45.

Minimum charge for food 8/6 per person.

CHEQUES AND SIGNED BILLS NOT ACCEPTED.

A 1942 menu from Piccadilly's Martinez Restaurant shows that wartime London did not always mean the ration regime – if you could afford to upscale. Customers here could choose chicken, salmon, lobster, lamb and much else. Indeed, after dining at the Dorchester in November 1941, Henry 'Chips' Channon was moved to write: 'London lives well: I've never seen more lavishness, more money spent, or more food consumed than tonight, and the dance was packed. There must have been a thousand people.'

1940 to July 1941, and the Foreign Secretary Lord Halifax inhabited the old gymnasium (where a sign read 'Reserved for Lord Halifax'), which contained eight beds behind screens. After her home, at No. 7 Grosvenor Square, was bombed, the society hostess Lady (Emerald) Cunard was somewhat bolder, adopting a three-room suite on the Dorchester's seventh floor as her London abode and the centre of her social gatherings.

Early in the Blitz, the Savoy was also the location of one of the rare occurrences of popular political unrest witnessed in London during the war. The hotel's magnificence was about as far as one could get from the wretchedness of parts of the East End and the pounding it was taking from the Luftwaffe, and on 15 September 1940 left-wing activists sought to make a point about the lack of shelter provision for ordinary people. About a hundred members of the Communist Stepney Tenants' Defence League, led by Phil Piratin and Tubby Rosen, congregated in the nearby Embankment Gardens. In 1938, Piratin had written a paper on deep air raid shelters and put it before the Civil Defence Committee, but it had been rejected. By the beginning of the Blitz, he was leading a campaign to open up the Underground to provide shelters. When the air raid sirens went off on 15 September, this group marched into the Savoy demanding to be let into the hotel's basement. After consultation, the manager acquiesced. Piratin left a vivid recollection of what followed:

> After we came in, the other Stepney groups came in at ten-second intervals. In all, 78 people turned up. Among them there were a number of children and a couple of dogs. That – as you will agree – is typically English. Nothing is good enough for the English dog.
>
> People came forward to protest but I told one of the waiters to get me a wooden chair and I stood up and made a speech. I explained what we were doing it and why we were doing it. The senior Savoy man – an Italian type who spoke in broken English – tried to intervene and I said, 'I'm taking no interest in you! I will only discuss this matter with English people!' Now that might be wrong – but on the other hand, we were feeling very bitter.
>
> Then a police inspector came in with about 12 or 15 police. He asked if I was in charge. Then he said, 'You're not worried about shelters, are you, Mr Piratin?' 'No', I said, 'I'm not worried about shelters. I'm only waiting for my call-up. But what would you do if your wife were put in the position of that woman over there. Her husband's in the army. She's got four children. What would you do?' The inspector said to me, 'You're right, guv, you're right. Well, what do you intend to do here?' I said, 'We don't really want this place. We want the Tubes opened!' He said, 'Oh, quite right!' But his duty was to take names and addresses because we were now occupying a place where we had no right to be. Meanwhile, a number of the English waiters got together. One of them came over and said, 'Can we do

> anything for you?' I said, 'Yes, everyone's tired. They want tea. And the little ones want milk. What's your price?' The waiters laughed. I said, 'We'll pay you the price of a cup of tea in a Lyons restaurant. We'll pay you tuppence,' and they agreed. So they came in with silverware trays, serving teas and providing milk for ladies with babies. The inspector said, 'When do you intend to leave?' 'When the all-clear sounds, we'll go,' I said. So when it did, that was that. Everyone left, elated and there was publicity in the Sunday papers.

The 'all clear' came soon, after 15 minutes, and for the next siren most of the Stepney insurgents were escorted to a public shelter – although a small number remembered staying the night in the Savoy, with breakfast in the morning, all at the hotel's expense. Despite the Savoy's favour among American journalists, the incident received relatively little newspaper coverage, except for the *Daily Mail*. It was, however, reported widely in the German press, which was presumably optimistic about this possible sign of a collapse in London's social cohesion.

Elegant hotels, smart restaurants and upmarket clubs remained beyond the reach of most Londoners, whose daily lives were circumscribed by the austerities and uniformities of rationing. During the First World War, nationwide rationing had come late, only in July 1918 – a few months earlier in London for meat, butter and margarine. By the time of the Second World War, contingency plans were better advanced, after the Food (Defence Plans) Department of the Board of Trade had been established in 1936. Thus, in September 1939 a fully-fledged Ministry of Food came into being. It was headed up by William 'Shakes' Morrison – so called for his love of quoting Shakespeare – who, on 1 November 1939, announced that rationing would be introduced at some point, garnering a storm of protest. This was, asserted the *Picture Post*, 'the most unpopular Government decision since war began', while *Daily Mail* readers were warned:

> Your butter is going to be rationed next month. It would be scarcely possible – even if Dr Goebbels were asked to help – to devise a more harmful piece of propaganda for Great Britain. Our enemy's butter ration has just been increased from 3ozs to just under 4ozs. Perhaps because of Goering's phrase 'guns or butter' has given butter a symbolical significance. But mighty Britain, Mistress of the Seas, heart of a great Empire, proud of her wealth and resources? Her citizens are shortly to get 4ozs of butter a week. There is no good reason to excuse Mr Morrison, the Minister of Food, for this stupid decision.

However, the British people and ordinary Londoners were less hostile, because they were already experiencing problems such as continually rising food prices in a time of war. In October 1939, Elizabeth 'Lylie' Eldergill, who lived in Bethnal Green, and who worked full time as a machinist as well as caring for her blind husband, wrote to an American friend:

> It is one rush for me from morning till night. The shops shut at 6 o'clock, so I have to go out in my dinner time to get errands. It is a fight to get a bus in the morning and another to get home at night. The prices of food are going up. I don't know how some people manage. I'm glad I haven't any children. It is hard enough to manage on the money.

According to the researchers of the Mass Observation project, 'On one point grocer and customer are at accord. A hundred times a day the sentiment is expressed on both sides of the counter, "I'll be glad when they start rationing". It'll put an end to all this.' Polls bore out this sentiment. The truth was that people wanted a reliable system for food supplies that would remove the anxiety about what they might be able to obtain, and which would stabilise prices.

The moment came in January 1940. The introduction of food rationing was intended to ensure fair shares for all in a country now deprived of so many of the imports that normally made up 70 per cent of the nation's food, for both people and livestock. It represented an unprecedented regulation and reduction in consumption, and transformed the country from an essentially free-market economy to one based on centralised control and planning. Londoners, and everyone else, were issued with their ration books, allowing them to buy limited weekly quantities of basic foodstuffs from specific shops at which they had to register. The butter ration, which had so alarmed the *Daily Mail*, was set initially at four ounces, though it would later vary. In Carshalton Beeches, Viola Bawtree and her family were just some of the millions of Londoners who made the best of it:

> Its amusing the way we each eke out our 2oz of butter. Sylvia has margarine all week, & then a treat of much butter. Elaine has both, but mostly margarine. I don't care to eat margarine, so have dry bread, dry or fried for breakfast, & dry with cheese at tea, & one piece of bread & butter with jam. This just ekes it out with none to be lavish with.

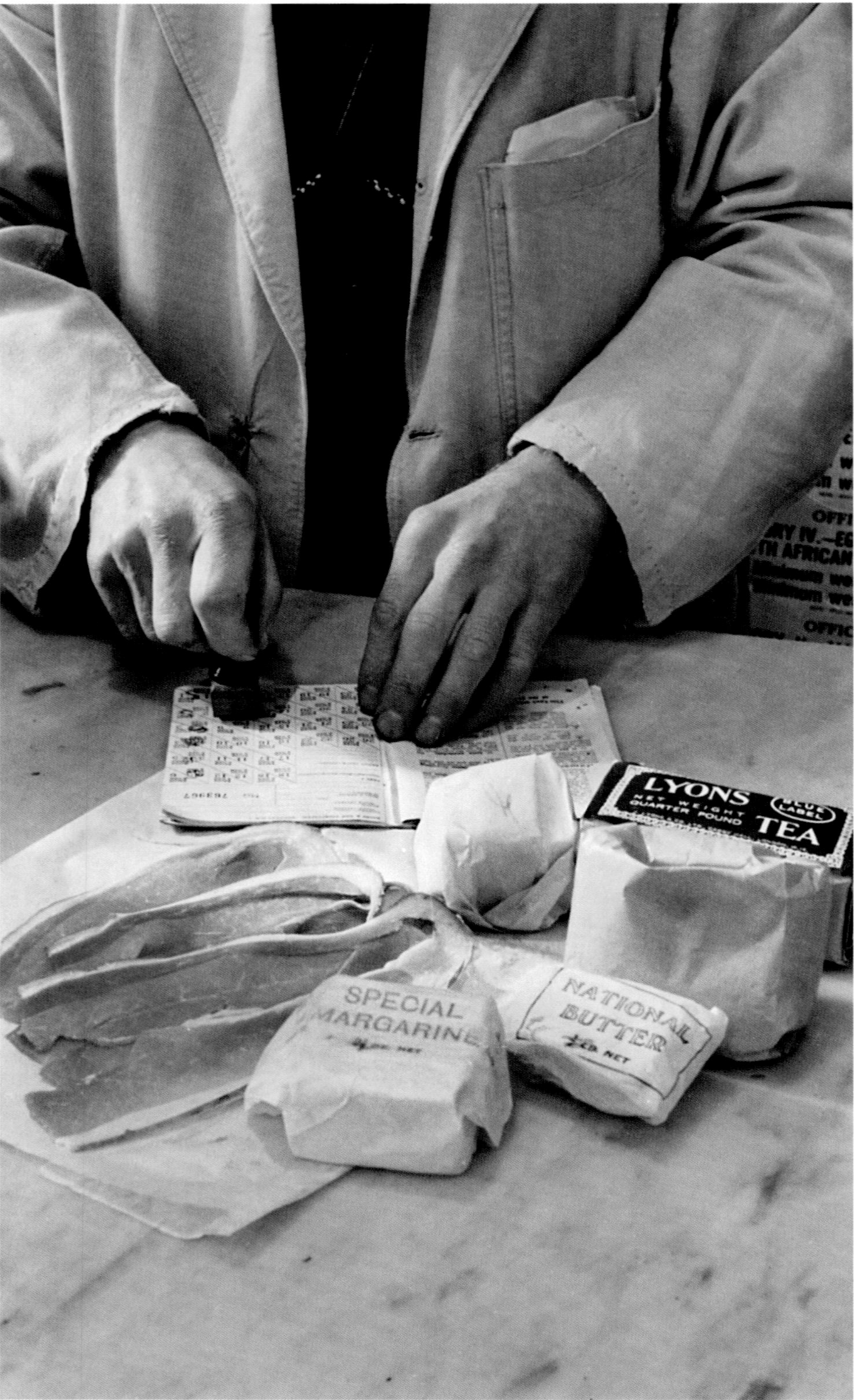

A shopkeeper stamps Mrs Olive Day's ration book, during her shopping trip along the King's Road, Chelsea (1941). In the foreground are her purchases: a weekly allowance of tea, sugar, 'national butter' and 'special margarine', cooking fats and bacon. Failure to properly stamp books or handle coupons could land retailers in trouble if the authorities found out.

In March, meat was limited to a per-head expenditure of one shilling and sixpence a week, and it remained relatively plentiful during the Blitz, owing to a glut of slaughtering; but it was reduced to one shilling and tuppence in mid-1941, where it remained for the rest of the war. Offal was excluded from the restrictions, and fish was unrationed but became increasingly difficult to get hold of. In July 1940, tea was rationed to two ounces a week. From Walthamstow, George and Helena Britton explained to their daughter across the Atlantic how they were managing, in a letter of August 1940:

> There is no shortage of anything except eggs. We have lost our main sources of supply in Holland and Denmark. The producers are selling a large proportion of the home production to the large catering establishments at the maximum retail price of 2–3/4d. so that if the retailer wants any in his shop he must be content to deal in them with no profit. The Co-op produces some of its own so that occasionally we are lucky enough to obtain some. Last week we got half-a-dozen from the milkman. There is plenty of bacon but the maximum price is so high that many people can't afford to take their ration of half-a-pound so it stays in the shops. We find that the allowance of half-a-pound of sugar is just about sufficient for our needs as we neither have a very sweet tooth and anyhow we have a little in hand for emergencies. In the case of tea were are restricted to two ounces a week and we have been obliged to draw on our reserves for the last two or three weeks but we are told that the ration is to be increased very shortly. Butter and margarine is now six ounces a week and the proportion of each is optional so that three-quarters of a pound of butter just about keeps us going.

The Brittons had one advantage, in that their own rations were continually augmented by parcels sent over by their daughter, particularly of tea, for which they were very grateful because, as George Britton put it, 'our consumption regularly exceeds our ration'. The United States helped in a much larger way, too. When President Roosevelt's Lend-Lease Bill was passed in March 1941, shipments of dried eggs, evaporated milk, tinned meat and cheese started arriving in the summer and were to prove essential in the maintenance of the nation's diet. A curious result was that many people hoped that America would stay out of the war, so as to ensure the continual arrival of food aid.

In 1941, jam, marmalade and syrup were rationed, then mincemeat, lemon curd and honey, followed by cheese in May. The next year, sweets

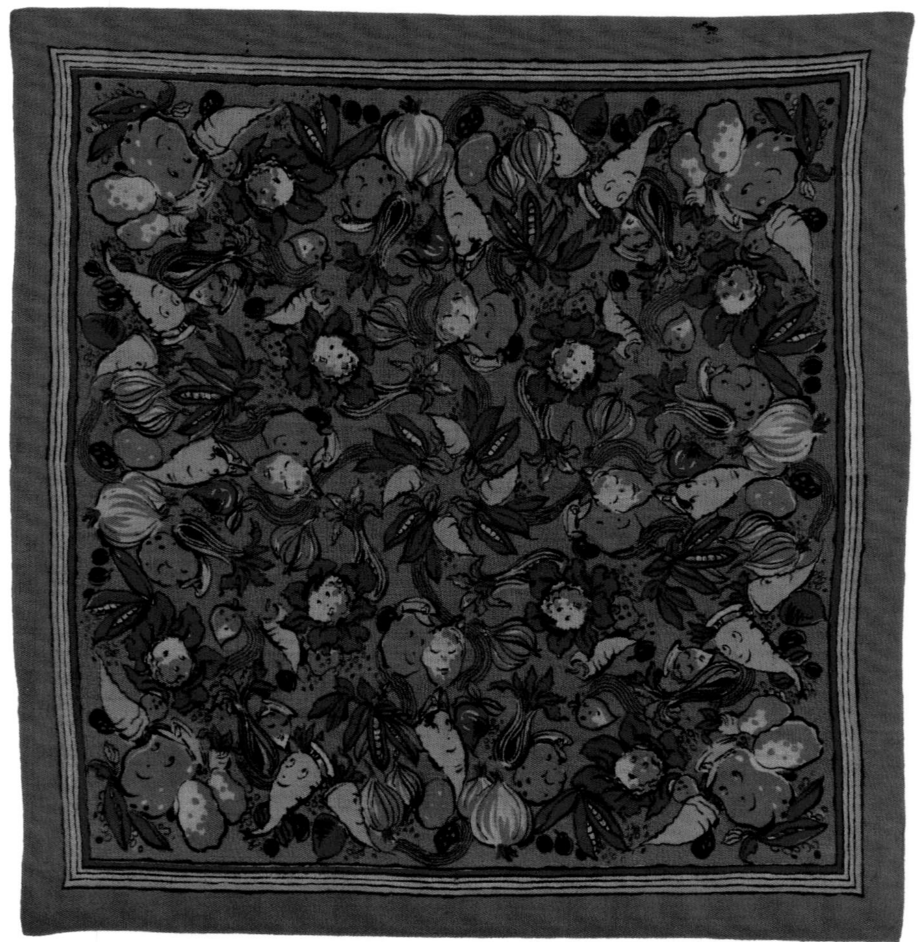

Left A scarf featuring 'Potato Pete' and 'Dr Carrot', and (*opposite*) a poster boasting of Potato Pete's suitability for soups. These anthropomorphised vegetables were part of the Ministry of Food's campaign to encourage everyone to eat more of what was both available and nutritious. Potato Pete's Fair, held on London's Oxford Street in December 1942, drew 100,000 visitors, some of whom went home with the free potatoes handed out by Father Christmas. By 1944, the BBC was broadcasting a Potato Pete song four times daily. Such initiatives helped increase potato consumption by 50 per cent.

were rationed to 12 ounces a month. From 1 December 1941, 'points' rationing – where items could be bought from any shop that stocked them – was introduced for tinned goods, dried fruit, cereals, pulses, syrup, treacle and biscuits. George Britton tried to explain it all to his daughter in July 1942:

> We are to be allowed 4 ozs more cheese a head per week making 8 ozs. but so that we shall not be overdosed with protein foods they have reduced the monthly points from 24 to 20. I am not quite sure that you know what I mean by points. This, shortly, is how it works. A great number of articles, although not rationed, are given a 'points' value. For instance 1-lb. tins of best salmon is 32 points. Sultanas and prunes are six points per pound. Pilchards in tins, sardines, rice, tapioca, tinned meats, figs, dates and other things have a points value and are also price controlled.

While not explicitly rationed, milk, eggs and oranges were controlled to ensure availability for those deemed to need them most, such as babies, expectant mothers and invalids. For the rest of the population – unless you had access to hens – eggs became very scarce, as George Britton could testify. Whereas, prior to the war, the average person ate three eggs a week, this dropped to one per fortnight – when available – with most people seeing no more than thirty eggs in a year. Ration books instead offered packets of dried egg. Bananas and other exotic fruits disappeared almost totally from wartime London. In July 1943, the actor Derrick de Marney auctioned off a single banana for £5, while an onion – another rarity – went for £4 in the London offices of *The Times*. Some meats, and some types of cheese, escaped rationing, such as the 'Gruyere-type' and 'Roquefort-type' cheeses imported from South America; but they were accordingly expensive, sold at four times the price of Cheddar.

'Dig for Victory' was the slogan for the concerted campaign encouraging people to grow food and vegetables – in gardens, allotments, any portion of land that could be turned to the purpose. In London these included royal parks and even the Tower of London's moat. The message was encapsulated in this and other posters, and there were similar campaigns throughout the Empire and Commonwealth.

A Dig for Victory poster adorns the front of the Swan & Edgar department store, Piccadilly. Even when shopping at the more upmarket places, Londoners were reminded that growing your own was a priority.

Whatever Londoners needed, they had to queue for it, and food was never simple, as Gwladys Cox noted in her diary (26 April 1941):

> Food is beginning to be a problem these days. We do get enough to eat; the trouble is to collect it. Fish is very dear, but think of the risk of catching it! Sausages have rather more in them lately, but goodness knows what. Milk has been reduced, so that cheese can be made. On Monday and Wednesday we get only one pint instead of two. We get our weekly tea, sugar, butter, margarine, bacon, cheese and meat rations regularly, but are sure of nothing else. Tinned fruit is getting very scarce; jam is rationed; only 2 eggs this week.

The largely meatless sausage epitomised a decline in food standards in the early war years. As Helena Britton told her daughter, 'Now, the water content of sausages is so great that they are only held together by the skins otherwise they would be nearly liquid so quite unsuitable for selling as sausage meat.' People quickly adapted, however. They looked for the best buys. They also found ways to eke out their food, as evidenced in all the inventive recipes that appeared for stretching a joint of meat to two, even three, meals, encompassing concoctions such as 'Mutton Charlotte' or 'Scotch Rissoles', as described By Beatrice Dawson in a 1943 issue of *Vogue*. For Mollie Panter-Downes in her *New Yorker* 'Letter from London' (10 August 1941), 'The classic English topic of conversation, the weather, has vanished for the duration... Everyone talks about Food. An astonishing amount of people's time is occupied by discussing ways and means of making rations go further....' Food was becoming a national obsession.

Part of that obsession manifested itself in a revolution in agriculture. In a nation now committed to self-sufficiency, every acre of land was vital, and not only in the countryside and on the farms. Patriotic citizens in towns and cities were encouraged to 'Dig for Victory'. In London, the parks and open spaces were turned into allotments, and flowerbeds and lawns were dug up to grow carrots and potatoes instead. The nation's number of allotments almost doubled, from 815,000 in 1939 to 1,400,000 in 1943. One of them belonged to George Britton, and, as he told his daughter on 19 November 1940, it did indeed bring some self-sufficiency: 'The allotment is keeping us going with all the vegetables we need. We are just using the last of the beetroot. Another year I must sow for a succession. Our brussel sprouts are very good.' More and more people also reared animals for the dinner table: rabbits and chickens were popular, but, more ambitiously, so too were pigs – and the war saw the emergence of pig clubs. In these ways, the Londoner with the right resources and access to some land could go a long way to ameliorating the limitations of ration-book life.

Eating away from home, for many ordinary Londoners, meant school dinners, factory canteens – and the British Restaurants, born during the London Blitz. These had emerged from the Londoners' Meal Service organised for the London County Council by Valentine Bell, the retired head of Battersea Polytechnic. By Christmas 1940, he had established 104 centres (also known as Citizens' Kitchens) serving 10,000 meals to those affected by the Blitz. In addition, there were about 200 mobile canteens, a food convoy and water trailer, 2 lorries with cooking facilities as well as 3 mobile canteens that could be despatched anywhere in London, accompanied by 4 despatch riders. Among their offerings were 'Blitz meals' such as vegetable soup and a cup of tea (for adults) or milk (for children). The Ministry of Food funded much of this provision.

The British Restaurants that evolved, both in London and across the country, were non-profit ventures organised by local authorities, and they were very much opposed by commercial restaurants. The Ministry of Food paid part of the expenses and provided advice on equipment, layout, nutrition and catering, including exhibitions mounted as part of the official War Artists scheme. In practice, the restaurants were somewhat makeshift affairs offering basic food that was popular rather than particularly healthy; but they came into their own during the Blitz for their combination of comfort food and a friendly, informal atmosphere, adopting the self-service system also being introduced elsewhere. By 1941, London had 203 British Restaurants, a figure that rose to 250 by 1943. Tom Harrisson, one of the originators of the Mass Observation project, noted that their most popular offerings were stews, boiled beef and carrots, and toad in the hole, with milk pudding, fruit pies, plum duff and spotted dick for pudding. For fourpence, you could (in 1942) get roast beef, two veg and treacle pudding, along with bread and butter and a cup of coffee.

Gwladys Cox, sampling her local British Restaurant on the Finchley Road in October 1942, was somewhat underwhelmed: 'The fare was passable, but, of course the clientele a mixed bag & service somewhat rough and ready.' Others were much less impressed. William Regan, an ARP Warden bombed out of his home on the Isle of Dogs and living in South-East London, paid ninepence for a 'rotten dinner' at a British restaurant in January 1942:

> 1 potato, 1 piece of carrot, and 2'x 3' rectangle of boiled beef, followed by a small piece of boiled pudding, spoilt with an evil tasting sauce. It is supposed to be run on a Non profit making basis, it is not.

By 1942–3, about one in five of the population were using British Restaurants across the country. But particularly in London, eating out was becoming more common.

Presiding over the mammoth task of control, administration and distribution of food was the Minister of Food, businessman-turned-politician Frederick Marquis, Lord Woolton. He was appointed in April 1940 to turn around a ministry that was failing, and he and his wife largely remained in London during the war even after the ministry was evacuated to Denbigh. The ministry ran a very active public relations and public education effort, in collaboration with the BBC and co-opting popular entertainers to deliver the right messages;

Diners tuck in for lunch at a British Restaurant in Woolmore Street, Poplar , in London's East End (1942). British Restaurants served up no-nonsense food. The somewhat elderly clientele here, whose names are recorded, include at the front table (clockwise) a carpenter, two men working on iron recovery, and a 77-year-old retired merchant seaman.

Woolton himself became a popular broadcaster, coached by the BBC commentator Howard Marshall (who became the Ministry's first Director of Public Relations). The minister also appeared on film, and at public meetings and weekly press conferences. To ensure a good press, he had regular meals with newspaper proprietors, but also found time to deal personally with a vast volume of daily correspondence, up to 200 letters a day by the time he left the ministry in November 1943. To the public he soon became 'Uncle Fred'. He took them into his confidence, warning them of impending shortages, and frankly admitting and correcting the occasional errors of judgement and maladministration by his ministry. One of these misfires was the recipe for the eponymous Woolton Pie, devised by the Savoy chef Francois Latry. Comprising stewed swede, turnip and cauliflower underneath shortcrust pastry or mashed potato, it was served in British Restaurants and hotel restaurants. Unfortunately, and

The ornate interior of Fishmonger's Hall, near London Bridge, doubles as a self-service canteen run by the Londoners' Meals Service (1942). Here, City workers and others could get a two-course lunch for a shilling (with a third course for an extra threepence), and a three-course supper for a shilling and sixpence. Coffee, at tuppence, was marginally more expensive than tea, at one and halfpence.

despite its Savoy credentials, it was universally disliked. Even Lord Woolton could not manage a convincing performance of eating it.

A poor recipe could not, though, dent Woolton's popularity. 'Lord Woolton is the only Minister about whom one rarely hears a grumble; some conscientious Britons feel that he does his job as purveyor to the national stomach perhaps a shade too well,' wrote Mollie Panter-Downes in her 'Letter from London' (19 July 1942). Ordinary Londoners vouched for him too – people like Nellie Carver, who wrote: 'One thing we are thankful for – our food rations – those have kept mostly the same. Thanks to our thrice blessed Lord Woolton we are adequately fed.'

While the authorities could keep Londoners eating during the Blitz and beyond, a more intractable problem was putting a roof over the heads of those who had lost their homes. In contrast with the government's pre-war plans to feed the population in wartime, they were caught on the hop by the explosion in homelessness. The numbers were staggering. About 1,400,000 Londoners – one in six – were made homeless by the Blitz. In Central London, only one house in ten escaped some kind of damage. The East End was badly affected not only because of the volume of bombs that fell there, but on account of its poorer standard of housing.

The better-off often escaped London in the early years of the war, as Gwladys Cox noticed on a walk into Hampstead:

> Very pleasant & quiet up there, but also, rather depressing. Nearly every other house in the district is either to let, or for sale, the gardens are running wild, and the houses – houses of the rich – are shabby and forlorn in the extreme, already looking like the Sleeping Beauty's Palace after 100 years' sleep.

The more wealthy returned to their large houses later in the war, but already a social change was under way. The number of servants available to run these properties declined dramatically during the war years, and it would never recover – a certain upper-middle-class way of life was about to disappear.

At the other end of society, the government's lack of foresight meant that the voluntary services had to step in. Initially, these homeless had to rely on the poor law for feeding stations and shelters; but the large number of homeless overwhelmed the system and it was

The popular Lord Woolton, Minister of Food from April 1940 to November 1943, accepts a cup of tea from a mobile canteen operated by volunteers working for the Young Men's Christian Association (YMCA). Other YMCA 'tea cars', providing refreshment for those in need, are visible behind. Woolton made himself the public face of his ministry, and helped to earn people's trust for its messages, earning the nickname 'Uncle Fred'.

abandoned by the Ministry of Health. The London County Council was given a free hand to improve the rest centres manned by the WVS, Salvation Army and the YMCA. The LCC and local boroughs had requisitioned empty houses, but there were still not enough billets to go round once the Blitz began. Attempts to place East Enders in West End mansions created unhappy experiences, as people found it hard to adjust. The concerted surge in manpower, including from the army, to repair London's housing stock in 1941 did make a difference: by August 1941, more than 1,100, 000 homes had been made wind- and waterproof – and therefore just about habitable – with another 50,000 still to be repaired. Overall, many of the local councils were unable to cope with the demand for their services, so the LCC took over control.

While homeless Londoners had enough to do taking care of themselves, those in a better position were encouraged to dip into their pockets and

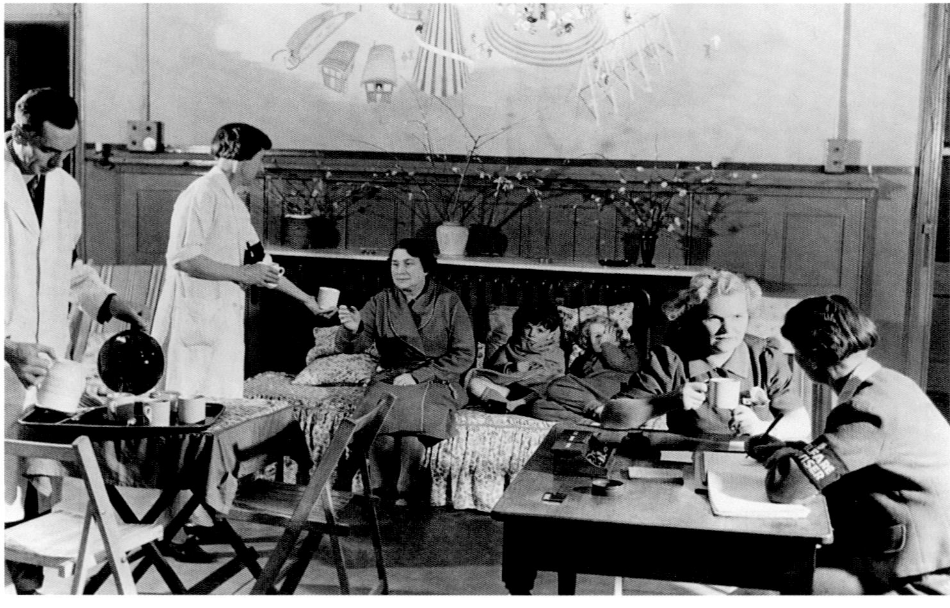

Left Just one of the many men and women drawn from across the Empire, who came over to Britain and its capital to help on the home front. India made a large contribution to the war effort, including this engineer.

Below A somewhat idealised impression, from the Ministry of Information, of an efficient looking rest centre (1942). To the right, the mother of the children on the sofa speaks to a Welfare Adviser. It was true, though, that after a poor start rest centres greatly improved once the London County Council, under government direction, coordinated arrangements with the voluntary and local organisations.

help the war effort. The government was tackling the massive costs of waging war through, for example, the introduction of a purchase tax, but also by encouraging people to invest in War Bonds and National Savings. These voluntary savings not only made extra funds available but also, by cutting individuals' spending power, helped to prevent high inflation. By June 1940 nearly a quarter of the population belonged to one form of savings group or another. Patriotic Britons contributed enthusiastically to campaigns such as 'Salute the Soldier Week' and 'Spitfire Funds'. London War Weapons Week in May 1941 raised, according to Gwladys Cox, at least £120 million, representing an average of £20 per head of London's population. London's Warship Week in March 1942 had a target of £125 million, while the city's Wings for Victory Week the following year aimed to hit £150 million (and saw almost £57 million raised on the first day alone).

At the same time as generosity in the cause of patriotic revenue-earning was encouraged, so austerity was preached in all other areas of life. The 15th of June 1942 was, Gwladys Cox noted, 'austerity day in the West End. Five shillings became the legal maximum price for lunch.' Any tendency towards personal overspending was frowned on by the 'Squander Bug', whose evil swastika-covered body appeared in posters and advertisements. And if saving money was important, so was the saving or salvaging of every raw material: Scouts, Guides, the WVS and public-spirited citizens were involved in collecting paper, bones and metal for recycling.

One notable feature of the war generation would be long remembered by their children: a horror of wasting *anything*.

THIS MAN IS NOT YOUR MATE
HE IS HITLER'S
TREAT HIM AS SUCH

IN FOCUS

LAWBREAKING IN LONDON

If the Blitz brought out the best in thousands of Londoners, for a minority of people wartime, the blackout and the Blitz presented opportunities to continue, or even begin, a life of crime. For many more people, the advent of so many new rules and regulations governing everyday life made it so much more tempting to cheat the system, and claw back some sense of pre-war normality.

Before the war, the main types of crime in London were theft, prostitution, murder and protection rackets, and these continued in wartime. Although London was the centre of illicit drug use, the problem was relatively small – in 1938, there were only 519 registered drug addicts. Gang violence, though, was more serious. Before the war, South London gangs had smashed up milk bars and cafés, and now such violent incidents increased, aided by a smaller police presence and the darkness of the blackout. A notorious site was the coffee stall and King's Head pub near the Elephant & Castle Underground Station. On Saturday 21 March 1942, James Bolitho Harvey and his brother came out of the station's exit on their way home from a West End show. They were at the coffee stall, intending to board a tram to Brixton, when they were set upon by a gang and robbed. Harvey died from the beating, and only three of the seven-man gang were caught and sentenced, for manslaughter.

Just two months into the war, diarist Gwladys Cox found out how useful the blackout was to those with malevolent intent. She was walking along the Embankment on 27 November 1939 when:

... a man among the passers-by put his hand stealthily on my handbag and tried to snatch it. I was holding it firmly with the leather handle wrapped around my waist, so I wrenched it away and said 'No, you don't!' He actually turned to look at me, blinked, the moon lighting up his face, and then disappeared among the other dim figures.

The blackout was also rather useful for gang leader Billy Hill, who had been released from Chelmsford Gaol in 1939. He and his gang were suspected of a number of West End smash-and-grab raids in the first year of the war, both by day and in the blackout. The victims included jewellers Ernest Lowe in Mayfair, attacked in daylight on 4 December 1939, and Longman & Strongitharm in the West End, cleared out four days later, at night. Hill was finally arrested for a raid on Carrington's in Regent Street on 20 March 1940, after its window was smashed and gold rings worth £6,000 stolen. But still his luck held, for he failed to be picked out in the ensuing identity parade.

Hill was responsible for a new method of smash-and-grab, in which a gang-member stood on the passenger seat of an open-topped car, smashed the glass of a store front, and made off quickly with the stolen goods. It was the method his gang employed on 21 May 1940, for a raid on a jewellers in Wardour

Opposite In one of the finger-wagging posters that equated pilfering with helping the enemy, a warehouse worker figures that if he gives one loaf of bread to his mate, it's all okay. The reality was that many ordinary people, in London and elsewhere, were trying to make the strictures of the ration book more elastic by bending a rule or two – or looking away when a rule was bent in front of them.

A recruiting poster for the Corps of Military Police is quite specific in its requirements: only 'smart' men need apply. The influx of servicemen into London during the war, and their intermingling with the civilian populace, meant that the maintenance of law and order in the capital inevitably meant collaboration with military police, including those of Allied nations.

Street, and in another attack, on Phillips' jewellers in upmarket New Bond Street later that month. Arrested again, Hill once more escaped justice when failing to be identified in a line-up. But his good fortune was running out. Hill's last raid, carried out with a bookmaker, Harry Bryan, was on Hemmings & Co. in Conduit Street, on 26 June 1940. However, the car driven by Bryan got stuck as Hill was about to smash the window with a sledgehammer. They both ran for the second car, driven by Georgie Hall, but it stalled as a policeman hurled his truncheon through the windscreen. The gang had to hot-foot it, running down Bruton Street, with two policemen in pursuit. The thieves were caught in one of the buildings, having clambered along the roofs. Both Bryan and Hall pleaded guilty to stealing the cars and receiving stolen goods, and they were gaoled for three years, while Hill got two years after pleading guilty to conspiracy.

With so many people in uniform because of the war, the nature of domestic policing changed. The Metropolitan Police often found itself working with military police in combating London's crime. The murder in December 1940 of Morris Scholman, manager of the Coach and Horses pub in Covent Garden, was one such case – it was eventually cleared up by the Canadian Provost Corps and the Metropolitan Police together. A soldier had been seen running away from the scene of the crime, so all the soldiers in the area were quickly rounded up before moving back to their units. A Canadian Provost sergeant noticed that a Canadian serviceman was missing from his hostel in Tavistock Square; he also heard a rumour that this soldier had a girlfriend in Craven Street. They were both found there, and the girlfriend admitted she had persuaded the soldier to rob the pub. A struggle had broken out, a gun had gone off, and the bullet had pierced the soldier's wrist before entering Scholman's head. The Canadian soldier was condemned to death, but the sentence was commuted to life imprisonment.

Another case involving a foreign serviceman and his British girlfriend was the Bonnie and Clyde-style adventure of US deserter Private Karl Gustav Hulten, of the 101st Airborne Division, and Elizabeth Marina Jones. He styled himself 'Lieutenant Ricky Allen', while she had taken the stage name 'Georgina Grayson' for her striptease-dance routines, which she had performed at the Blue Lagoon club (near Regent Street) and the Panama Club (South Kensington). Hulten, born in Stockholm but raised in Massachusetts, had a wife and child back in the United States by the time he deserted in August 1944. Jones, born in Neath, Wales, had had a troubled upbringing, running away from home at age 13 and then spending time in an approved school until, aged 16, she had married an army corporal ten years her senior: she left him on their wedding night, after he had hit her. Jones moved to London, where she began working as a dancer, supported by an army marriage allowance; but then she joined the 'Piccadilly Commandos' – the burgeoning number of prostitutes who gathered around Shaftesbury Avenue's 'Rainbow Corner', the

The American Red Cross club at Rainbow Corner, near Piccadilly Circus, London. This thriving social centre for US servicemen on leave also provided a source for hard-to-find goods that made their way into London's black economy. It was a magnet, too, for wartime prostitutes, the 'Piccadilly Commandos', who scandalised some members of polite society.

US servicemen's main recreation centre in London. However, it was near Hampstead Underground Station, at the Black and White Café, that Hulten and Jones first met on 3 October 1944, introduced by a mutual friend.

Just two days later, Hulten picked up Jones from her flat in King Street, Hammersmith. They decided they would rob a taxi, so, having followed one to Cricklewood and thinking it empty of passengers, Hulten used his army truck to block the vehicle, before pulling a gun on the driver; but inside the cab was a US officer, who drew his own gun in response. Hulten ran back to his truck – and on this occasion, the couple escaped. The next night, they tried a different plan. They hired a taxi from Hammersmith and drove out of London, at which point Hulten shot the driver, George Heath. Hulten then drove the taxi while Jones went through Heath's pockets, discarding whatever was of little value. The law caught up with them on 9 October, when Hulten, still in possession of the stolen car, was arrested in Fulham. The US military authorities allowed Hulten to be dealt with by the British judicial system. Both Hulten and Jones were convicted and sentenced to death, although Jones was reprieved and sentenced to life imprisonment instead. According to the *News of the World*, she wrote from her cell in Holloway: 'I would rather die than serve a prison sentence. God – what a jury! How I hate the London people.'

War created new crimes and new punishments. After an initial warning period in September 1939, war profiteering was punishable by a fine of £500; later on, hoarding became an offence too. But the most controversial crime during London's Blitz and the later air raids was looting.

Looting during the Blitz, as occurred during the Café de Paris bombing, was a major problem. By the end of November 1940, 390 cases had been reported. In response, Scotland Yard's Criminal Investigation Department established an anti-looting squad of 300 officers. Mrs Mary May, who lived in Sandgate Street, Camberwell, was just one of the unfortunate victims of looters. After having to evacuate her bombed-out home in 1940, she stayed with friends; but on returning to her house she found it had been robbed by her *neighbour*, who had gone off with her piano, armchairs and sewing machine, among other items.

Occasionally 'looting' could border on the farcical. After one man was given permission to take some soap from a bomb-damaged Croydon factory in August 1940, the press pilloried him as 'The Air Raid Looter'. In October 1940, three sappers and a lance corporal, who had worked in the bomb disposal squad at St Paul's, were imprisoned for taking shaving brushes from a shop nearby.

That same month, after bombs had struck Gwladys and Ralph Cox's home, they returned the next morning to find her 'silver cigarette lighter had disappeared from its drawer':

Under my bed, my trinket box was lying open, its contents scattered over the wet carpet. It had been taken out of my dressing table drawers which had been forced and everything of the least value taken. Ralph's room had been ransacked and most of his underclothing, as well as a gold watch, taken. All the work of looters.

By the end of 1940, more than 4,500 cases of looting had occurred in London. The press urged no mercy, with headlines such as 'Hang a Looter and Stop This Filthy Crime' in the *Daily Mirror* (November 1940), while the *Observer* called looters 'the dregs of Society'. The following year, the numbers did begin to drop: by 22 February 1941, only three cases had come before the Old Bailey.

Pervasive, in a time of shortages and rations, was the black market – if you knew who to ask and could afford the prices charged. Shopkeepers sometimes kept special supplies 'behind the counter', and 'spivs' – petty criminals – traded in goods often obtained by dubious methods. Indeed, on his release from prison, Billy Hill turned to black market racketeering, dealing in anything from army bedding to whisky: it was a less dangerous occupation than smash-and-grab raids, and it proved rather more profitable. Minor offences generally went unheeded. But for more serious offences, 2,300 people were prosecuted and severely penalised for fraud and dishonesty in the period up to March 1941.

Most of London's black market was centred on Soho, where servicemen on leave – and deserters – congregated. The soldiers, and particularly the US troops when they arrived, had plenty to sell, including cigarettes, surplus rations and nylon stockings. The deserters had services in kind to offer, such as selling on these desirable goods. The biggest trade was in selling and buying coupons for petrol or clothing, but pretty much anything was available on the black market for a price, from fur coats to underwear. Nylons and other undergarments were highly prized, and therefore a temptation to the light-fingered. As Vere Hodgson wrote in her diary (for 18 June 1944), 'The Last thing I must record in my diary is very *serious*. I have lost my best satin nightdress, my best silk underskirts and a dress. They are just the things people steal nowadays.'

In other ways, enterprising crooks took advantage of the capital's Blitz conditions. When London Underground stations introduced ticketing in October 1940, the purpose was not only to prevent queuing, but also to stop the black market operated by 'droppers'. They would entice or threaten a Tube worker to let them in ahead of the queue and then take up the best spaces, subsequently charging shelterers sums of up to two shillings and sixpence. By January 1941, organised gangs were scouring the Tube stations, pretending to sleep next to their victims and then making off with their valuables. Similarly, a spate of thefts occurred at empty homes while their owners were in the shelters.

The many customers of black marketeers effectively aided and abetted the rule-breaking. Vere Hodgson, whom Leonard Mosley described as 'a brisk good-looking women in her middle thirties of an English type no one (except official registrars) would ever call a spinster', later published her own diary under the title

An 'entrepreneur' sets up shop in London from a couple of suitcases (1941). His goods might have been legitimately obtained, but customers became used to not asking questions when offered something desirable at the right price.

Few Eggs and No Oranges. She relished her own 'under the counter' experience on 22 February 1941:

Managed to get a few eating apples yesterday to my great joy. I treated myself – they are one shilling and one penny per pound. I carried them home as if they were the Crown Jewels. Also had some luck over cheese. Went for my bacon ration and while he was cutting it had a word with the man about the Cubic Inch of Cheese. He got rid of the other customers and then whispered, 'Wait a mo'. I found half a pound of cheese being thrust into my bag with great secrecy and speed!

Sometimes, the gamekeepers turned poachers. In March 1942, five people were sent to prison for selling sugar at three times the regulated price: one of them was a member of the Willesden Food Control Committee, while another was a War Reserve policeman. Eight months later, Ministry of Food officials were caught taking bribes from a Brixton butcher, though one of them was defended by his superior as an otherwise excellent officer who had brought in more than £3,000 in fines since 1940.

In the normal course of things, it was Ministry of Food officials and their informers who were doing the snooping on restaurants and retailers, to make sure the war strictures were being adhered to. In November 1942, a woman lunching at the café of the Astoria Cinema, Streatham, noticed that meat and fish were being served in the same sitting – an offence. She contacted the local Ministry of Food office, which sent out an official to 'test' the accusation. As a result, the cinema manageress and even the two waitresses were fined. In another incident, a woman asked a shop assistant in the Hendon branch of Woolworths for an extra ration of tea, because she had forgotten her ration from the previous week; when the assistant did not take the correct coupons from the ration book, the customer returned with the Ministry of Food inspector. In late 1940, the local inspector had a small army of women who made such 'test visits' at up to 30 shops a day. As a result, 59 shopkeepers in the Hendon area were prosecuted.

These practices were later forbidden by both Lord Woolton, Minister of Food, and Hugh Dalton, President of the Board of Trade. Ministry officials were told they should not prey on a shopkeeper's sympathy to lure him or her into breaching the rules; also, that they should avoid buying from young and more inexperienced shop assistants. All the regulation that had built up in wartime society was beginning to breed discontent – conveyed later by novelist of London life Patrick Hamilton in his *The Slaves of Solitude* (1947), in which his character Miss Roach is worn down by the nanny state propaganda with its constant reminders not to waste food or fuel, its injunctions to curtail travel, and the pressure not spend her own money unless it was on government savings.

Such was the proliferation of restrictions, and such was the demand for products over and above wartime allowances, that all kinds of organisations found themselves in the dock. The Savoy Hotel and the East India Club were both in court for rationing offences. The grocers J. Sainsbury sold meat without coupons; the department store Swan & Edgar, among others, was prosecuted for taking loose coupons rather than ones cut from ration books; and Woolworths broke price regulations in its Bond Street shop. Two Cities Films, which made the wartime classics *In Which We Serve* and Laurence Olivier's *Henry V*, fell foul of the law for using £2 of petrol in an emergency while filming for the Ministry of Information in January 1941.

Neither were the great and the good immune from the law. Among those caught in the net were Noël Coward, the writer of *In Which We Serve*, who was then at the height of his fame, with his play *Blithe Spirit* running in the West End. His somewhat rarefied offence was of not offering dollars that he had brought back from the United States for sale to the Treasury. Before the war, Coward had also kept quiet about his American investments. In his defence, Coward admitted his incompetence in financial affairs, declaring that his papers were in disarray as his London office had been damaged during the Blitz. He pleaded guilty to 'moral' innocence and was fined £1,600 instead of the larger penalty of £22,000. (In his memoir, Coward suggested that someone high up – Lord Beaverbrook no less – was out to get him.)

Coward's fellow actor and composer, Ivor Novello, was imprisoned for a month for misusing petrol while he was starring in his musical *The Dancing Years*. He had been refused a licence for petrol to return home on the weekends to recuperate – he had only recently recovered from pneumonia. One of his devoted fans, 'Grace Walton', suggested that his Rolls-Royce be transferred to the commercial firm she worked for, because a large amount of travel was integral to the business. The firm had a branch at Reading where the Rolls-Royce could be kept during the week. However, the company was initially unaware of the arrangement by 'Walton' – in reality one of their clerks named Dora Grace Constable, who had become obsessed with Novello. Once this was discovered, Novello's solicitor informed the Petrol Board. Novello was prosecuted under the Motor Vehicles (Restriction of Use) Order 1942 and summoned to appear before Bow Street magistrates in April 1944. Both Novello and Miss Constable pleaded not guilty. She received a fine of £50 and had to pay £25 costs, while Novello was sentenced to eight weeks' imprisonment, and had to stump up for £25 costs and £20 bail. The next month, despite the appearance of the great artistic patron Sir Edward Marsh, and the husband and wife actors Lewis Casson and Sybil Thorndike as character witnesses, Novello's appeal was dismissed – though at least his imprisonment was reduced to four weeks. His experience in Wormwood Scrubs prison clearly affected him. He not only sent a large cheque to the prisoners' welfare fund and gave pianos to both Wormwood Scrubs and Holloway prison, but also sent complimentary tickets for *The Dancing Years* to the warders and organised a monthly concert party for his fellow prisoners. On his return to the show on 20 June, he was greeted with thunderous applause and at the conclusion he received a standing ovation to the tune of 'For He's a Jolly Good Fellow'.

While he was in prison, Novello gave up smoking, but some weeks after his release he was back on 60 'Abdullahs' a day. A huge percentage of civilians smoked during the war, while for those in uniform army life seemed 'to be fags, fags, fun and food' – as one recruit wrote from Edinburgh's Redford Barracks. But when, in 1942, soldiers were unofficially rationed by the military supply organisation NAAFI (Navy, Army and Air Force

Noël Coward entertains sailors on board HMS *Victorious*, accompanied by Norman Hackworth on the piano (1944). Although the playwright, actor and singer became a stalwart in Britain's morale-boosting efforts for civilians and services alike, he was not immune to the long reach of the law regarding his financial affairs.

The musical star and actor Ivor Novello is flanked by actresses Diana Wynyard (left) and Margaret Rutherford (right) on board a troopship, while working with ENSA (1945). But after circumventing government restrictions on private petrol allowances, he briefly had to swap the musical stage for a prison cell.

Institutes) to five cigarettes a day, cigarettes became ideal black market material. In May 1944, the director of the Piccadilly Billiards Club was found guilty of having 3,000 NAAFI cigarette packets in his possession. By the end of the war, cigarettes were becoming scarce on the home front too, and 'shop crawlers' would roam around London's tobacconist shops and kiosks to buy up stocks for resale in the West End for three shillings rather than the standard two shillings and fourpence. Cigarettes became the unofficial currency of liberated Europe and the main target for military and civilian thieves: it was this illicit trade that, in the later 1940s, really cemented in people's minds the image of 'spiv'.

Overall, the crime statistics for the war period paint a sobering picture. Between 1940 and 1945, the numbers of those found guilty of criminal offences increased from 150 to 223 per 1,000 of the population. Property crimes rose, and male juvenile delinquency increased by as much as 70 per cent, while for young women it more than doubled (a 120-per-cent rise) in the six years up to 1944. In January 1945, the *Montreal Gazette* relayed warnings from John Gibson Jarvie, a leading London banker, about how a British culture of oppressive 'wartime controls' was creating an explosion in organised crime: 'There is not a market which has not its racketeers, no department which is not riddled with deceit and evasion.' As early as September 1939, one lady was telling diarist Gwladys Cox of her 'sore trials with profiteers over sugar and matches'; by January 1945, Jarvie feared 'the same conditions that existed in America during prohibition. Gangsterdom will become the major industry and the best paid.'

The spirit of camaraderie and mutual support associated with the Blitz undeniably had its darker side.

King George VI and Queen Elizabeth pose atop a pile of rubble after one of the raids that hit Buckingham Palace, while the somewhat grim-looking workmen pause their clearance work (1940). The presence of the head of state in London contributed to a sense that all of society, high to low, took a share of the dangers.

CHAPTER FOUR

LONDON FACES, OLD AND NEW

'There's no place I'd rather be'

Then as now, London was different to the rest of Britain, and the circumstances of war exaggerated some of those differences. In wartime, the capital remained the seat of the Establishment: the centre of the national and imperial government, and the natural habitat of the great and the good, and of the leaders to whom people now looked for steadfastness, encouragement and determination. London's survival during the Blitz, especially in international eyes, stood for Britain's defiance and for the anti-Nazi cause as a whole. But in addition, London also became the centre for an array of governments-in-exile from Occupied Europe. And while a sizeable proportion of Londoners left their homes and neighbourhoods, London's more transient population was swelled by an influx of foreign troops, not least US personnel after 1941, making a diverse population even more cosmopolitan.

At the apex of Britain's Establishment were, of course, the King and Queen. The stature and popularity of royalty had taken a dip following the short-lived reign and abdication of Edward VIII in 1936, but the war would cement the Royal Family's popular appeal. Gwladys Cox, listening to Queen Elizabeth on the wireless in November 1939, was impressed: 'Her Majesty has a very pleasant, fresh young voice and her delivery and enunciation was perfect; I never heard better. At the mention of separation from her children, evacuated as they are indeed to Scotland, her voice wavered ever so slightly.' Luckily for both British morale and the Royal Family's war reputation, the King and Queen – rejecting advice from Churchill and others – did not stay in Scotland, nor did they always keep themselves safe from danger. It would be the royal couple's presence in London that came to define the wartime bonds between people and monarch. As Gwladys Cox wrote in her diary for 12 September 1940, 'Papers today show pictures of the bomb damage to Buckingham Palace. With much thankfulness we read that the King and Queen escaped injury.' It was another attack the next day, shattering windows of the room in which the King and Queen were sitting, that allowed Queen Elizabeth to feel, in her famous words, she could 'look the East End in the face'. The fact that the palace was damaged by several raids during the war, and that the royal couple had – it was generally judged – shared the dangers experienced by ordinary Londoners increased their popularity. The Queen later told poet Stephen Spender that the war years had been the happiest of their lives, during which the bombing of Buckingham Palace and their tours of London and the East End had helped them empathise with the suffering across London and throughout the home front.

Brendan Bracken (1901–58; left), later 1st Viscount Bracken, with one of the many politicians-in-exile, the Greek Prime Minister Emmanouil Tsouderos. As the most successful of the wartime Ministers of Information (from 1941 to 1945), Bracken was a key member of Churchill's government.

His Majesty's Government, in the shape of the various ministries of state, initially moved out of London early in the war. But they too, for the most part, returned to the capital as the war progressed. One new ministry, the Ministry of Information (MOI), was based in the University of London's imposing new Senate House, which had been opened in 1936. Designed by Charles Holden, an architect notable for his many London Underground stations, the distinctive and towering Portland-stone-clad building would become the inspiration for George Orwell, who cast it as his Ministry of Truth in *Nineteen Eighty-Four.*

Unfortunately, the ministry had an unhappy bedding-in period, witnessing no less than four ministers in less than two years. As a result, a ministry intended to uphold confidence in the government and maintain morale suffered from low morale within its own ranks and became the object of general ridicule, exemplified by another novelist, Evelyn Waugh, in *Put Out More Flags*. Even the second,

Opposite One of the more well known photographs of Prime Minister Winston Churchill, inspecting a Tommy gun (31 July 1940). He exudes what, by 1940, seemed to most of the British people an appropriate air of aggression.

short-lived Minister of Information, Sir John Reith (the former director of the BBC), saw 'incredible incompetence' at the ministry. It was a widespread view. According to Gwladys Cox, the newspapers were full of the 'mismanagement' of the Ministry of Information. After Brendan Bracken, a close friend of Prime Minister Winston Churchill, became the new minister in July 1941, perceptions of the ministry improved, and its work became more successful.

If the King and Queen represented reassuring continuity at the highest levels, and the ministries of Food and Information were manifestations of how much the country had changed in wartime, at the centre of power was the dominating figure of Churchill – a figure both familiar and newly energised. When Winston Spencer Churchill had finally succeeded Neville Chamberlain as prime minister on 10 May 1940, he was sixty-five. It was the summit of an almost continuous Parliamentary career, since 1900, during which time he had held most of the major offices of state. However, it was the failure of appeasement (which Churchill had vehemently opposed) and the outbreak of war in 1939 that had rescued him from his so-called 'wilderness years' over the previous decade and brought him back into government as First Lord of the Admiralty. Although many of Churchill's Conservative Party colleagues had very mixed feelings about Churchill's suitability for high office, some regarding him as a dangerous and egotistical adventurer, Gwladys Cox did not share their views. Rather, she welcomed a politician who spoke his mind, writing on 12 November 1939:

> This evening, we were heartened by a robust broadcast from the First Lord of the Admiralty Mr Winston Churchill. 'Ten Weeks of War'. It is really very jolly listening to Mr Churchill because he is not afraid to speak up and make no bones about his contempt for the gangsters now ruling Germany. Unfortunately, all do not agree as to the suitability of his language and call it 'undignified' and 'war-mongering'. There have been several letters to the Press from these white-livered gentry, who object to the Germans being called 'Huns'. If however, they behave like Huns, I cannot see the objection.

When Chamberlain stood down, Churchill had assumed the office not only of prime minister, but also of Minister of Defence. As such, he was responsible for both the conduct of military operations and the supervision, through the Lord President's Committee, of the war on the domestic front. In September 1940, and in the face of animosity from Conservatives, he added the leadership of the Conservative Party to his roles. But more than these heavy official and Party responsibilities, Churchill took it upon himself to harness all his considerable powers of persuasion and eloquence to inspire courage and build morale in the civilian population through his speeches, broadcast to the nation via the BBC Home Service. In the opinion of poet Stephen Spender:

> England was in a way held together by a kind of patriotic poetry and by language, really, and above all by Churchill. Churchill was a kind of throwback, in a way, of a kind that at that moment in our history we needed very much and I think his speeches were magnificent. They expressed what people realised, the moment it had been expressed, was what they most deeply felt.

More specifically, Churchill, who seemed to be unbothered by threats to his personal safety, continued to govern from London, which meant that he was able to embody the city's spirit of defiance during the Blitz. Gwladys Cox and her husband Ralph listened to one of his broadcasts at the beginning of the Blitz, on 11 September 1940, which she thought worth recording in detail:

> At 6pm, we listened to another grave but inspiring broadcast by Mr Churchill. 'These cruel, wanton, indiscriminate bombings of London' he said 'are, of course, a part of Hitler's invasion plan. He hopes by killing large numbers of civilians, including women and children, that he will terrorize and cow the people of the mighty Imperial city and make them a burden and an anxiety to the Government, and thus distract our attention unduly from the ferocious onslaught he is now preparing. Little does he know the spirit of the British nation, or the tough fibre of the Londoners... This wicked man, the repository and embodiment of many forms of soul-destroying hatred, has now resolved to try and break our famous island spirit by a process of indiscriminate slaughter and destruction. What he has done is to kindle a fire in British hearts here, and all over the world, which will glow long after all traces of the conflagrations he has caused in London have been removed....

Churchill's chief staff officer General Hastings 'Pug' Ismay provided in his memoirs a testament to Churchill's popular appeal during a visit to the London Docks, after the first Blitz raids on 7 September 1940:

> The destruction was much more devastating than I had imagined it would be. Fires were still raging all over the place; some of the larger buildings were mere skeletons, and many of the smaller houses had been reduced to piles of rubble. The sight of tiny paper Union Jacks which had already been planted on two or three of these pathetic heaps brought a lump to one's throat.
>
> Our first stop was at an air-raid shelter in which about forty persons had been killed and many more wounded by a direct hit, and we found a big crowd, male and female, young and old, but all seemingly very poor. One might have expected them to be resentful against the authorities responsible for their protection; but, as Churchill got out of his car, they literally mobbed him. 'Good old Winnie,' they cried. 'We thought you'd come and see us. We can take it. Give it 'em back.' Churchill broke down, and as I was struggling to get him through the crowd, I heard an old woman say, 'You see, he really cares; he's crying.' Having pulled himself together, he proceeded to march through dockland at breakneck speed.

In some ways, Churchill's ability to strike the perfect popular note went against his entire background and habits of life. After all, this was a man with aristocratic lineage, born in Blenheim Palace, and a consumer of expensive cigars and copious amounts of Pol Roger champagne. At the Savoy Hotel, the barman Joe Gilmore not only kept Churchill's private bottle of Black & White whisky for whenever he dined there, but invented three new cocktails in Churchill's honour – the Blenheim, the Fourscore and the Churchill. The prime minister had never ridden on a bus, and had travelled on the London Underground just once in his life. He knew little of the lives of ordinary people, and yet he seemed to be in step with them, fostering and epitomising national identity.

In return, vast numbers of the British people were mesmerised by Churchill, including Vere Hodgson: 'The one thing that kept us going was Mr Churchill's indomitable courage.' She compared him with such national heroes as Horatio Nelson and Alfred the Great; she listened to all his speeches (as did the majority of the country), read biographies of him, and often wrote about him in her wartime diary. Of President Roosevelt in March 1941, she accounted him 'a great man, but not so great as Churchill… His speeches are wonderfully heartening to us – but they lack the touch of magic Mr Churchill gives.'

Left Churchill strolls in the garden of No. 10 Downing Street with a Soviet delegation, including Foreign Minister Molotov (centre) and (left of Molotov) the long-serving Soviet ambassador, Ivan Maisky. Behind Molotov is Anthony Eden, the British Foreign Secretary who succeeded Lord Halifax. They had just signed the Anglo-Soviet Alliance (26 May 1942).

Below US Ambassador John Winant (front row, third from right) along with Roosevelt's close confidant Harry Hopkins (left of Churchill), US Admiral Ernest King (right of Churchill) and other representatives of the US government and navy pose with Winston Churchill for the camera. Hopkins and Churchill liked one another, while Winant had done much to sweeten the diplomatic tone after his predecessor, Joseph Kennedy. They were all being entertained by the Board of Admiralty, at Greenwich (25 July 1942).

While Churchill continued to run his government from London, the city also became home to governments-in-exile that found their way to, or were reconstituted, in the British capital following the German conquests of 1939–40. Here were the 'official' governments of Belgium, Czechoslovakia, Luxembourg, the Netherlands, Norway, Poland and Yugoslavia. Also present was the charismatic if prickly military officer Charles de Gaulle, whose broadcasts from London in June 1940 had launched the Free French movement, to keep the flame of French freedom alight.

One foreigner in London was making himself distinctly unpopular early in the war. Joseph Kennedy, who was father of future president John F. Kennedy, had been made Roosevelt's Ambassador to Britain, or, more technically, Ambassador to the Court of St James's, in 1938. Displaying limited love for Britain, a feeling perhaps reinforced by his Irish Catholic lineage, and possessing little confidence in Britain's ability to hold out, he had been an advocate of appeasement and an intimate of Neville Chamberlain, and he firmly believed that the United States should stay out of the war. Now that the bombs were falling he could envisage only inevitable and speedy defeat for Britain. As Churchill developed his own relationship with Roosevelt, Kennedy's position became more fragile – and in October 1940 he returned home. In London, he was replaced as ambassador by John Winant, who set a very different tone as soon as he landed: 'I'm very glad to be here. There is no place I'd rather be at this time than in England.'

Winant was instrumental in improving US–British diplomatic relations. At the same time, Ivan Maisky, the durable Soviet Ambassador to Britain (since 1932), at a time when so many ambassadorial careers were cut short by Stalin, was proving similarly influential in improving Soviet–British diplomatic contacts. He entertained regularly at the Soviet Embassy in London, his visitors ranging from politicians such as Churchill and Anthony Eden to writers like H.G. Wells and George Bernard Shaw. Whatever Churchill's loathing of Communism, and despite the unfortunate period of the Nazi-Soviet Pact, the prime minister was keen to cultivate Maisky for the larger goal of supporting and emboldening Russia against Germany.

Perhaps what Joseph Kennedy had failed to appreciate fully was that, even in 1940, Britain was never alone – however much a post-war myth developed about Britain's isolation. From the beginning, the war effort was sustained by the men, materials and resources of the British Empire and Commonwealth, and London was the control centre and magnet of that empire. Gwladys Cox appreciated this global dimension,

Left One of the many Polish soldiers that could be seen in an ever more multilingual and multicultural London, photographed towards the end of the Blitz (10 May 1941). He reads a copy of *Polska Walcząca* ('Fighting Poland'), a weekly for the Polish Armed Forces in Britain.

Opposite Soldiers of the Royal Indian Army Service Corps enjoy a feast following the Eid ul Fitr ceremony marking the end of Ramadan, at the East London Mosque (1941). The war increased the ethnic and religious diversity of London, too.

no doubt partly because she herself had been born in Jamaica. A month into the war, on 6 October 1939, she wrote in her diary:

> On the wireless this evening, we listened with deep appreciation to the Empire Broadcast of 'How the British Commonwealth went to war with Germany'. We heard speakers in Africa, India, Burma, Malaya, Hong Kong, Australia, New Zealand, the South Sea Islands – special reference being made to the Queen of the Tongo's loyal offer, the Falklands, the West Indies, Trinidad being singled out, Jamaica omitted to my sorrow, also Barbados and Canada, describe how the news of the war was received in their respective countries. Recordings were given of speeches by Dominion and Colonial Prime Ministers. We were very touched by the deep patriotism shown by all these diverse units of the Empire.

Even in the 'finest hour' of the Battle of Britain, when Britain's fate seemed to rest in the hands of so few young fighter pilots, there were Polish, Czech and French squadrons, as well as volunteer American

pilots fighting the RAF's cause. And even before the United States entered the war, London's international mix was swelled by large numbers of Allied and Commonwealth service personnel, along with European troops such as the Poles, Czechs, Dutch, Norwegians and Free French. Forces from the self-governing Dominions were based in Britain in large numbers – mainly Canadians, but also New Zealanders and Australians. The Canadian Army provided the first ever imperial troops to guard the Royal Palaces, while, in 1940, the French-speaking Royal 22nd Regiment, as well as the Toronto Scottish, who had the King and Queen as their colonel-in-chiefs respectively, provided the King's Guard.

Gwladys Cox seemed to relish the 'lively' cosmopolitan atmosphere, enjoying, for example, on 11 June 1941, 'the varied scene' that was 'enhanced by a detachment of Indian soldiers in Whitehall, evidently on their way to India House, which was being visited today by the Duchess of Kent'. One of her West Indian friends, however, on her first arrival in Britain 'was shocked to notice how indifferent to Empire the average person was, seeming to know little, and care less, about the British Commonwealth'. Perhaps the experience of London during the First World War, which had seen an earlier presence of Empire servicemen on leave and many Belgian refugees, had inured Londoners somewhat to new faces in times of war.

Undeniably novel and fascinating, though, from April 1942 onwards were the large numbers of US troops who started arriving in the UK, many of them gravitating towards a London now free of the incessant bombing of the Blitz to spend their leave, to socialise and to fraternise. Coming from what seemed to ration-regulated Londoners a land of plenty, they brought with them highly desirable consumer goods such as razor blades, Lucky Strike cigarettes, Hershey chocolate bars and – most importantly – nylon stockings. London's children loved the excitement of their presence. Others were less sure – and thus the GIs, with their plentiful supplies of luxuries, earned from their envious but impoverished British rivals the reputation of being 'over paid, over sexed and over here'.

The American Red Cross set up clubs for US serviceman across Britain – and the WVS responded by establishing 200 British Welcome Clubs. A favoured London destination for US serviceman on leave was the American Red Cross Centre, which opened on Shaftesbury Avenue, near Piccadilly, in November 1942. Better known as 'Rainbow Corner', it became the main recreation centre for American troops. It was a taste of home, offering entertainment, diversion, and American food and drink, 24 hours a day. The facilities included accommodation, a dance hall and a library.

A rayon headscarf from the Mayfair company Jacqmar of London celebrates 'The American Forces in London'. US airmen, soldiers and navy personnel mingle with Londoners around landmarks including the US Embassy, St Paul's Cathedral and what are described as 'bits of Blitz'.

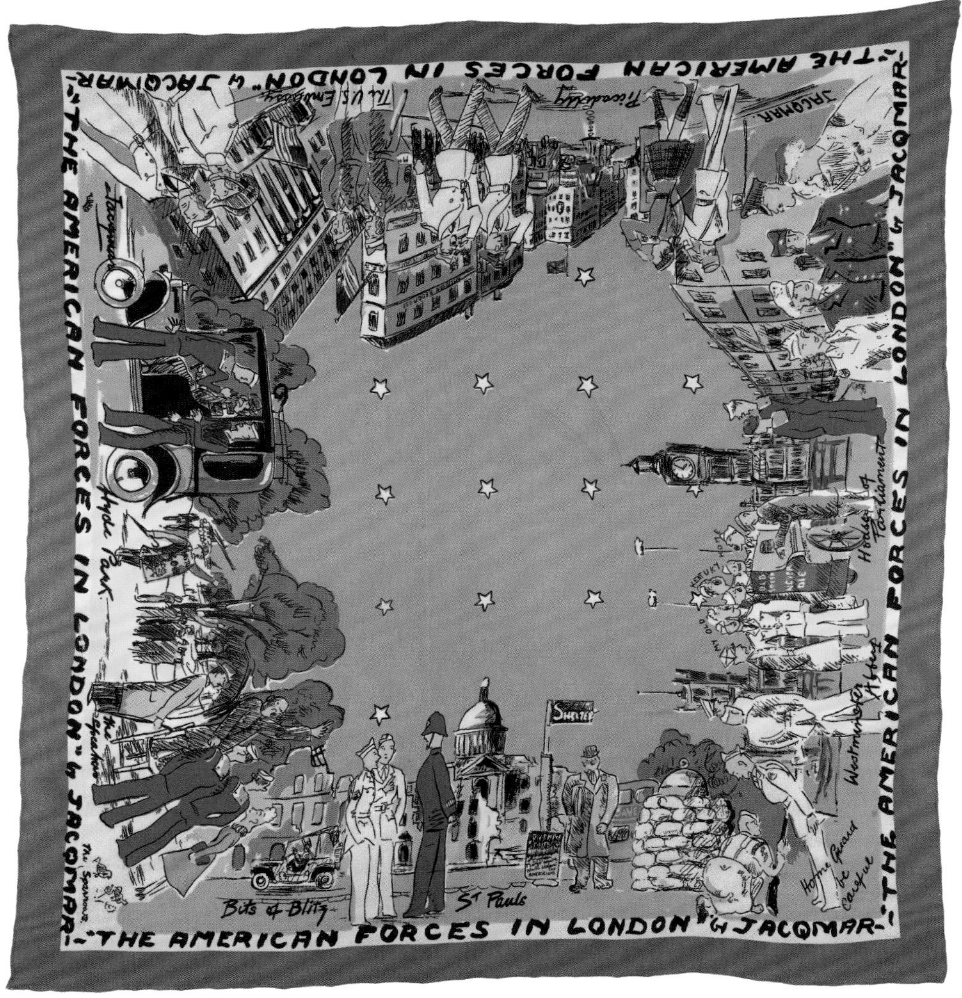

Rainbow Corner proved to be a huge draw for the locals too. For a start, British youths tried their best to gain access to this wondrous palace of New World life. Then there were the young women of the 'Piccadilly Commandos', who offered GIs other sorts of pleasures, for a price. The arrival of American forces created a surge in the number of prostitutes working in London. Many were young girls who had gravitated to the capital from the Midlands and Wales, or who were trying to avoid the call up into the services or factories; but there were also deserters from the Auxiliary Territorial Service (ATS) and Women's Auxiliary Air Force (WAAF). Vivienne Hall, for one, deplored the whole display:

> The country is stiff with Americans and many are the stories one hears of their behaviour – we British are so prone to expect the whole world to think and act as we and it doesn't – well the people who are different

to us are, of course, wrong – damned impudence we've got really! I feel the Americans must think just the same of us as unfortunately the only ones who show the general mass any friendliness are our most crude specimens of girl and womenhood, who flock around the Americans, doing anything they want them to do and fleecing them in payment – its disgusting to see our young girls cheapening themselves and screaming about the West End and suburbs; it's they and not the Americans who are bad. Here speaks the crusty old maid I suppose, but I hate to have the British judged by these little bitches who are showing only our bad side to the Americans.

She was referring, more broadly, to the giddiness that seemed to overcome so many young British women when confronted with the attractions of these smartly uniformed, extrovert and generous newcomers. US servicemen had a mixed reputation for the way in which they behaved with their unattached (or even attached) escorts. Some treated their 'girls' like movie stars, and struck up enduring relationships. For many others, things were much more casual. With only two days off per month, GIs saw a trip to London as a chance to let off steam. Pub crawls in London (a favoured activity) could end up in a stranger's bed, and sometimes feelings of remorse the next day. By December 1942, cases of venereal disease among US troops in Britain had risen by 70 per cent since April. Not for nothing was one of Rainbow Corner's less publicised facilities a prophylactic centre.

By the end of the war, the more durable relationships – some of which had already spawned children – were reflected in a flood of Anglo-American marriages. Some 70,000 British women became 'GI Brides'. Anticipating a transatlantic life, they could attend a 'School for Brides' at Rainbow Corner, where lessons, held on the first Sunday of the month, introduced them to the American systems of government and education, as well as providing information about shopping, American customs and other matters. By October 1945, 60,000 of the war brides were still waiting to be transported to the United States. These ignored 'wallflower' wives demonstrated outside the US Embassy in London's Grosvenor Square, but, unsurprisingly, the return of servicemen took priority.

London was not just the magnet for GIs on leave; it was also the centre for the US Army High Command in Britain. London had to accommodate 33 officers' billets, 300 buildings for accommodation for other ranks, and a further 2.5 million square feet covering 'PXs' (Post Exchanges – American shops), messes, clinics, dispensaries and other services for the US armed forces. The US officers' mess in Grosvenor

House, Park Lane, nicknamed 'Willow Run', served up to 7,000 meals a day. Despite the social and behavioural freedoms that GIs seemed to bring with them, in one respect there was a stark divide that sat uneasily with London's cosmopolitan nature: the racial segregation policies enacted among the US armed forces, which confined African Americans to separate military units and facilities. And yet discrimination was not entirely an American affair. In 1943, West Indian Test cricketer Learie Constantine was banned from staying at the Imperial Hotel in London's Russell Square. He blamed the decision on 'American pressure', successfully sued the hotel for breach of contract, and went on to pen a book entitled *Colour Bar*.

Despite the social excitements and tensions created by the influx of US servicemen, some Londoners paused to remember why the Americans were present in the first place. One friend of George Britton wrote to the latter's daughter in the United States on 10 February 1943: 'When I go to London town I see many American soldiers, they look so different from our own, but seem to have settled down and it is quite a common sight to see them fraternising with our Soldiers, Sailors and Airmen and of course people generally'. He continued: 'We feel now we are surrounded with help, and we know just what America is doing for us and are thankful believe me.'

BBC
BBC

IN FOCUS

CHURCHILL'S LONDON

From London's centre of government, Winston Churchill seemed to radiate unremitting energy and drive, fuelled by his overarching faith in his own abilities as a war leader.

On becoming prime minister, Churchill maintained Chamberlain's War Cabinet structure, with the sole aim of winning the war, but now on a coalition basis. He kept on Chamberlain and the Foreign Secretary, Lord Halifax, in order to maintain Conservative Party support; but they were joined by the leader and deputy leader of the Labour Party, Clement Attlee and Arthur Greenwood. By the end of 1940 the War Cabinet had increased to eight members with the additions of: press baron Lord Beaverbrook (Minister for Aircraft Production), who had in the previous war served as Minister of Information in the 1918 Cabinet; the Labour Party luminary and leading trades unionist Ernest Bevin, who became Minister of Labour; and Sir Kingsley Wood, Chancellor of the Exchequer. Chamberlain fell ill and died in November 1940, to be replaced by Sir John Anderson as Lord President of the Council, while in December 1940 the Conservative MP Anthony Eden took over from Lord Halifax as Foreign Secretary – and Halifax was despatched across the Atlantic to be Ambassador in Washington, DC. The Labour politician Herbert Morrison became Home Secretary and replaced Anderson as Minister for Home Security.

Of these men, it was Morrison who connected experience of London life and politics at the local level with the concerns of national government. Of a vastly humbler background than Churchill, Morrison was born and brought up in Brixton, the son of a one-time maidservant and a policeman. He had been a conscientious objector during the First World War, before rising through Hackney Borough Council, as a Labour councillor, to lead Labour to victory in the London County Council elections of 1934 (becoming LCC leader) and 1937. His pursuit of progressive reforms in education, health and housing in London helped propel him to national attention, as did his book *Socialisation and Transport* (1933), which outlined a blueprint for nationalisation that was later adopted by the Labour Party. Morrison's first portfolio in the wartime government was as Minister of Supply in Churchill's coalition, until his promotion to the War Cabinet. Together with his Parliamentary Secretary 'Red' Ellen Wilkinson, another pacifist, with whom he was having an affair, he visited many bombed-out sites in London during the raids of 1940–1 and later the V-weapon attacks. He was not lionised in the way that Churchill was, but Morrison was much admired by many Londoners – and the advent of the Morrison shelter made sure he was, literally, a household name.

In anticipation of the need to protect Morrison and the other core members and functions of

Opposite Churchill makes a radio address from his desk at No. 10 Downing Street, wearing one of his distinctive 'siren' suits, his own quirky variation on a boiler suit. He was happy to greet world leaders and generals in what he called these 'romper suits' (and occasionally even in his underwear), perhaps demonstrating an aristocratic disregard for middle-class notions of etiquette.

Prime Minister Winston Churchill sits at the centre of power in this formal group portrait of his Coalition Cabinet in 1940. Standing at the extreme right is the politician who knew London municipal life intimately, Herbert Morrison. The others are, left to right (*back row*) Sir Stafford Cripps, Ernest Bevin and Lord Beaverbrook, and (*front row*) Sir John Anderson, Clement Attlee and Anthony Eden.

government, the underground Central War Rooms were established in Whitehall on 27 August 1939. In December of that year their name was changed to the Cabinet War Rooms. However, at the beginning of his administration, Churchill spent most of his working day in the more usual environment of No. 10 Downing Street, and thereafter he was generally reluctant to go underground even during the Blitz. But, sometimes he would do so in the evenings, or use London Underground's offices in the former Down Street Underground station in Mayfair: lying between Dover Street (now Green Park Station) and Hyde Park Corner, the station had been closed to the public in 1932. One advantage that would have appealed to Churchill was its excellent dining facilities.

At 10 Downing Street itself, a shelter was built in the basement, including dining and sitting rooms. However, in December 1940 Churchill moved to a ground-floor flat in the No. 10 Annexe, above the Cabinet War Rooms, which was fitted with heavy steel shutters that could be closed during air raids. Not long afterwards, he proudly showed General Alan Brooke, then commanding Britain's Home Forces, around the flat, where they visited the 'study, sitting room, kitchen, scullery etc.' Churchill was, in Brooke's view, 'just like a small boy showing his new toy and all it could do! He had certainly been very comfortably fitted out.' This was where Churchill slept, and he would use the flat for the remainder of the war. Brooke would often find himself being summoned there, to Churchill's

The subterranean office-bedroom designated for the prime minister, in the Cabinet War Rooms. In the end, Churchill did not use it much, preferring his private flat in the No. 10 Annexe, which, though above ground, was shielded against bomb blasts.

bedroom, where he would find the great man lying in his dressing gown smoking a cigar. On one occasion, Churchill had just finished his bath:

However he received me as soon as he came out looking like a Roman Centurion with nothing on except a large bath towel draped around him! He shook me warmly by the hand in this get up and told me to sit down while he dressed. A most interesting procedure, first he stepped into a white silk vest, then white silk drawers, and walked up and down the room in this kit, looking rather like 'Humpty Dumpty', with a large body and small thin legs!

The Cabinet War Rooms themselves were used most intensively in the evenings, during the Blitz period itself, and then during the subsequent bombing phases of the 'Little Blitz' and V-weapons attacks, with lesser use in the relatively bomb-free period of 1942–3. There was an early near miss for the government, when the House of Commons was badly damaged in the final Blitz raid of 10 May 1940.

Although Churchill accepted these wartime exigencies, lurking in a bunker under London's streets was antithetical to everything he stood for. He relished any opportunity to be on the move, attending the wartime conferences, travelling to see Roosevelt, or visiting battlefield successes. As Vivienne Hall wrote in her diary, 'that man will always be where there's any excitement; he's like a schoolboy with power to indulge his every wish for

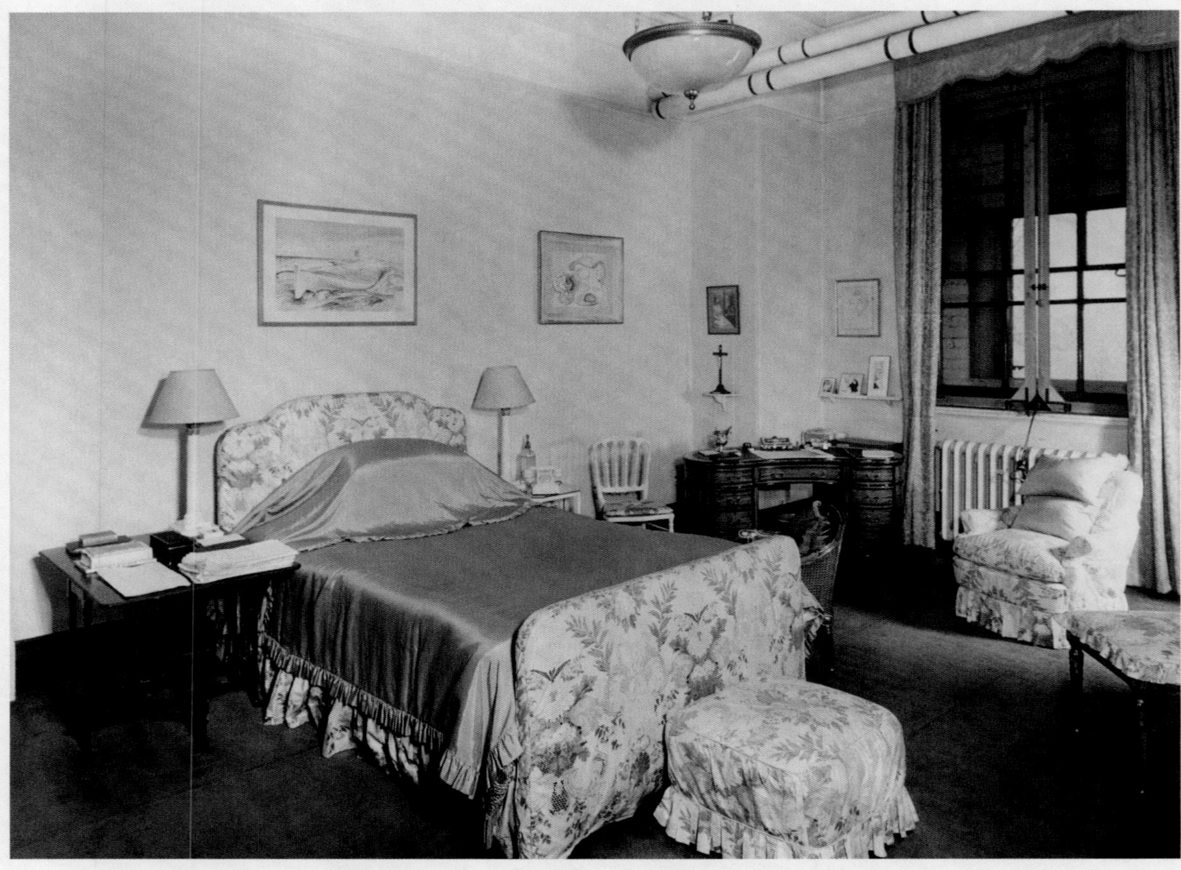

Clementine Churchill's bedroom in the No. 10 Annexe, above the Cabinet War Rooms. The protective steel shutters visible at the window are a stark contrast with the floral upholstery and bedlinen. Clementine's presence by Churchill's side provided a bedrock of support throughout the war.

being part of mighty adventures!' He drove himself hard, and he drove those who worked for him hard, consulting at all hours of the day and night. In London, he convened War Cabinet meetings on bank holidays and generally did not believe in taking time off, his hectic schedule ably supported by his wife Clementine and other members of his family. Perhaps surprisingly, the majority of people who worked for Churchill were glad of the opportunity to do so. General Alan Brooke collaborated closely with his prime minister from 1941 until the end of the war – though in his case, the experience left him exhausted.

On the whole, Churchill ran the military elements of the war, but he did allow his colleagues to get on with their jobs with little interference. Those colleagues included, beyond the War Cabinet itself, his unofficial 'cabinet', who were all allocated rooms in the Cabinet War Rooms and the No. 10 Annexe – men like Frederick Lindeman, Churchill's scientific adviser, or Brendan Bracken, his Parliamentary Private Secretary (until persuaded to head up the Ministry of Information in 1941), and Major Desmond Morton, who advised on intelligence matters.

The permanent inhabitants of the Cabinet War Rooms included the staff working in the map room, the Joint Planners and Joint Intelligence Staff with their support staff of telephonists, typists, stenographers and Royal Marine orderlies and guards. Olive Christopher was one of the secretaries working there; she later became personal assistant to General Sir Leslie Hollis, Secretary to the Chiefs of Staff, and she left a description of a 'typical' day in the underground labyrinth:

Official time of arrival – 9 a.m. The hours of the week were dictated, of course, by the demands of the wartime regime. Any personnel on night duty, such as the Map Room officers, for instance, would have to respond to urgent signals and emergencies of any kind which would have repercussions occurring through 24 hours, or even longer. So, one might arrive on duty at 9 a.m. only to find that 'all hell was breaking loose'! The Committee Rooms would be occupied by the Joint Planning Staff and the Joint Intelligence Committee, the Cabinet Room by the Chiefs of Staff and, also, sometimes the Prime Minister. Officers would be rushing up and down corridors and in and out of the typing pool with urgent draft papers for copying, etc. Operation TORCH (invasion of North Africa) comes to mind! Interspersed with all this activity were breaks for tea, lunch, dinner, etc., in the Staff Canteen. If we were very busy, the Royal Marine Guards would take pity on us and bring us the odd 'cuppa' from their kitchen. If all was peaceful we were sometimes allowed out for fresh air or dinner, which was usually taken at Lyons Corner House at Charing Cross in their Salad Bowl Restaurant – cost 5/-! One has to remember that our working hours were officially three days on duty (sleeping in the C.W.R. dormitory) and two days off.

Although relatively safe underground, those working in the Cabinet War Rooms shared the above-ground dangers with other Londoners when getting to and from their place of work. Fortunately for Olive Christopher, her job may have saved her life: one night at the War Rooms, she received a telephone call to say that her home in Croydon had been destroyed by a bomb. Indeed, luck seemed to attend her, for she also missed being in the Café de Paris, because of a cancelled date, when it took its direct hit on 8 March 1941.

The novelist Anthony Powell worked for a brief period as a military assistant secretary in the War Rooms. In his evocative novel *Military Philosophers*, Book 9 of his magnificent 'Dance to the Music of Time' sequence, he vividly encapsulated the concentrated intensity that characterised the inner sanctum of Churchill's London powerbase during the war:

In this brightly lit dungeon lurked a sense that no one could spare a word, not a syllable, far less gesture, not of direct value in implementing the matter in hand. The power principle could almost be felt here, humming and vibrating like the drummings of the teleprinter. The sensation that resulted was oppressive, even a shade alarming.

Men and women, soldiers and civilians, sway to the music of a violin in London's West End (1941). Those not dancing enjoy the music from the comfort of their tables. Despite the dangers, Londoners congregated for dancing of every kind, from polite tea dances like this to the more energetic American imports of the jive, jitterbug or swing.

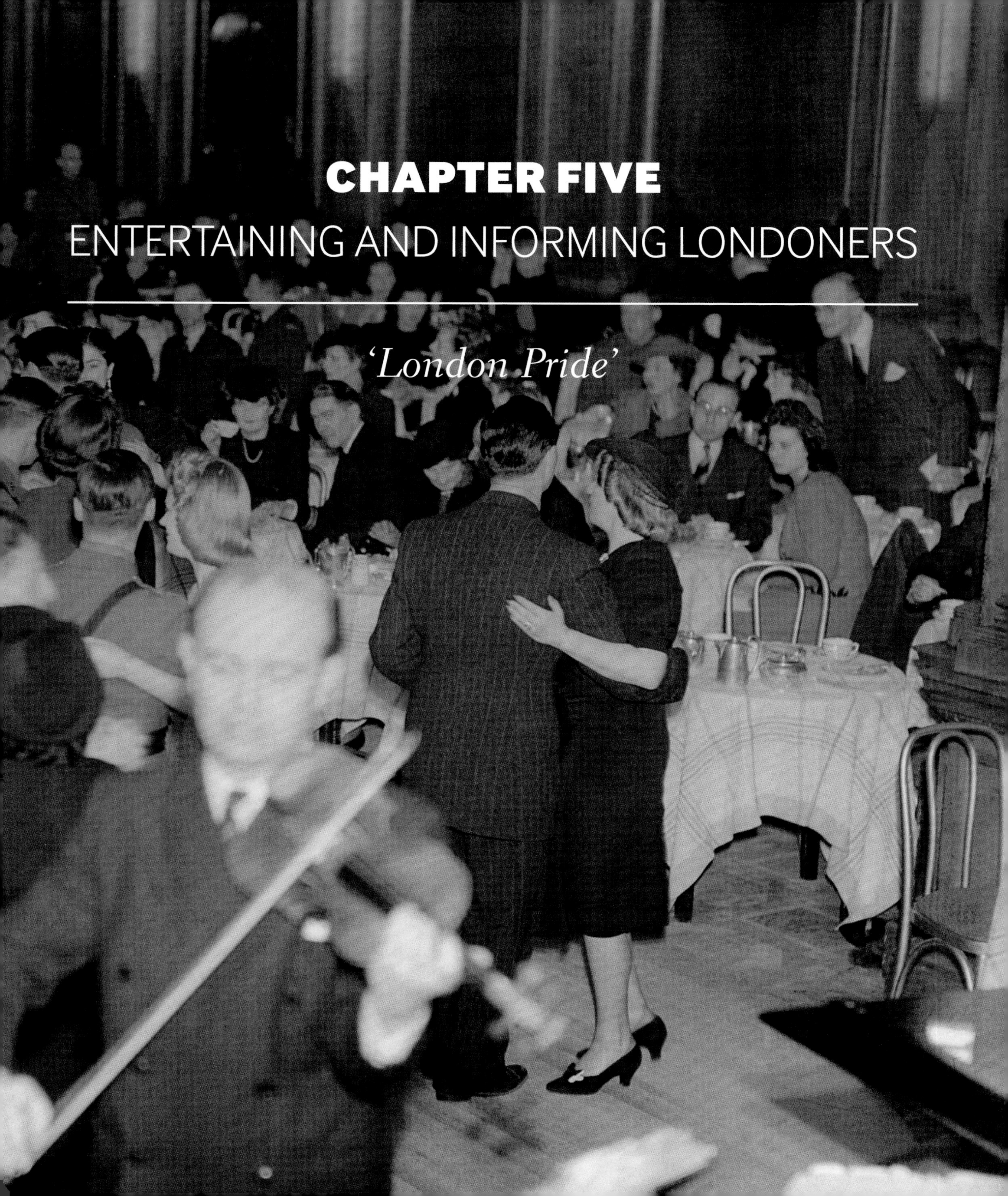

CHAPTER FIVE

ENTERTAINING AND INFORMING LONDONERS

'London Pride'

The outbreak of war in 1939 had caused disruption across so many facets of life, and not least British cultural and recreational life. And in this respect there was a disproportionate effect on London, the nation's cultural as well as political capital. As elsewhere, the immediate impact was the mandatory closure of many theatres, sports grounds, dance halls and cinemas – at least until it became apparent that the country was not going to be obliterated just yet, and until it was realised that war, if anything, would increase the demand for culture, for diversion, for information and entertainment. Indeed, although most people's free time was limited, over the war years their spending on sources of entertainment rose by 120 per cent, as they looked for ways to fill those few spare precious hours between work and sleep.

After the initial scare, a kind of normality returned quite soon. The cinemas were re-opened after a fortnight. Within weeks, many of London's theatres and sports grounds were also open again. Some things were already different, though. Football grounds and other sports venues reduced their maximum capacity by 50 per cent, to ensure that spectators could get to shelter quickly enough if the sirens sounded; and many of the best sportsmen would go on to serve overseas. Pubs, on the other hand, were fuller than ever, and live music and performance were thriving. In one of his broadcasts to America, on 16 November 1939, journalist Ed Murrow reckoned there were more dance bands playing in the West End than prior to the war; places like the Embassy Club, Quaglino's, the Paradise and Café de Paris were full every night. On New Year's Eve 1939, there were no less than three cabarets at the Savoy, topped off by the trumpeters of the Life Guards seeing in the New Year. Similar entertainments, if on a lower scale, were enjoyed in the Regent and Strand Palace hotels, and in Lyons Corner Houses; and in South London, at the Streatham Locarno, the dance floor could be packed with 800 dancers (and hundreds more in the balcony). Other theatrical offerings in the 1939 festive season were the dancing girls at the Prince of Wales's Theatre (popular with servicemen on leave), the husband-and-wife revue performers Jack Hulbert and Cicely Courtneidge at the Palace, and pantomime at the Coliseum. At Soho's Windmill Theatre, the Windmill Girls performed their famous routines, including risqué *tableaux vivants*, throughout the war under the theatre's proud motto 'We never closed' – wittily reinterpreted by others as 'We never clothed'. In the West End, the generation's leading actors were still performing: John Gielgud, Edith Evans and Peggy Ashcroft starring in Oscar Wilde's *The Importance of Being Ernest*, Sybil Thorndike and Emlyn Williams in the latter's autobiographically inspired *The Corn is Green* (1938),

The two respectably clad women wandering past Soho's Windmill Theatre give little clue as to the somewhat racy fare on offer in its 'Revudeville' entertainments, which had been running since 1932. Statuesque nudes, decorously posed, contributed to the theatre's draw, and the Windmill was famously the one London theatre that always remained open during the Blitz.

and Godfrey Teale in Shakespeare's *Julius Caesar*. And the actor and music hall artist Lupino Lane was starring in the hit musical *Me and My Girl*, whose standout song, 'Lambeth Walk', had been reconfigured for the new times by Al Bollington, an RAF pilot and BBC organist:

> Down the inky avenue
> Inky, pinky, parlez vous
> You'll find your way
> Doing the 'Blackout Walk', Oi!

War was creating odd new juxtapositions in people's lives, as they juggled their evenings out with taking the necessary precautions. On 18 November 1939, Vivienne Hall went to see *Goodbye Mr Chips*, after which she:

Opposite The bomb-damaged Old Vic Theatre in Waterloo, London (September 1941). The theatre renowned for staging Shakespeare and the classics got off to a glorious start during the war, with John Gielgud in *King Lear*, before the Blitz brought about its closure. Disaster struck during the last big raid, on 10 May 1941, when it took a direct hit; it did not reopen until 1950. This watercolour (with crayon and pencil) was done by Gwendoline May, who painted several scenes of the damaged theatre.

... wept and wept at the film and coming out of the cinema hoped to avoid seeing anyone as my face was in such a mess with crying. I bumped into three sets of people before I got home who all asked me what happened to me!! To the cellar again with tiny pink eyes and a headache – but I enjoyed the film immensely!

London's cultural life inevitably suffered a shock when the Blitz began in earnest. On its first day, 7 September 1940, there were twenty-four plays and musicals running in the West End; one week later, just two theatres were open. But theatre managers, performers and audiences again adapted to the new circumstances. When venues reopened, theatre shows and concert programmes started earlier than they used to, to try and avoid the night-time bombing raids.

On the West End stage, the war witnessed great highs as well as moments of disaster. At the Vaudeville Theatre, there was a Shakespeare revival, including *Henry IV, Part One* and *All's Well That Ends Well*. The larger-than-life actor Donald Wolfit gave lunchtime Shakespeare readings at the Strand Theatre. John Gielgud played King Lear at the Old Vic, before the Blitz closed the theatre, and then toured in *Macbeth* before returning with the play for its London run at the Piccadilly Theatre. Among contemporary plays in London, two of the biggest successes were Noël Coward's *Blithe Spirit*, whose run began in 1941 and would last for nearly 2,000 performances, and Terence Rattigan's *While the Sun Shines* (1943), set in wartime London and containing topical references to Spam, the Beveridge Report and the shortage of razor blades. Esther McCracken's *No Medals*, about a wartime housewife, was equally successful when it opened in October 1944: it ran until after the war and in 1948 spawned a film version, *The Weaker Sex*. As for the theatres themselves, the Old Vic was bombed on 10 May 1941, and it was not the only one to suffer. The Holborn Empire was destroyed, and the historic Theatre Royal, Drury Lane was badly damaged during the Blitz.

War seemed to create an appetite for Shakespeare, to which Britain's theatrical aristocracy responded. Laurence Olivier and Ralph Richardson re-established the Old Vic Company in 1944, its productions put on at the New Theatre (today the Noël Coward Theatre). They included *Richard III*, in which Olivier starred. Stage met cinema in the patriotic and morale-boosting feature film of *Henry V*, starring Olivier and produced by Two Cities Films with government subsidy. John Gielgud established a rival theatre company at the Haymarket, where he played in *Hamlet*, William Congreve's Restoration comedy *Love for Love* and Somerset Maugham's 1921 drama *The Circle*.

That the arts flourished was partly down to a desire to escape the drabness and uniformity of ration-book life, but also, more practically, because of government backing through the Council for the Encouragement of Music and the Arts (CEMA), the forerunner of the Arts Council. Set up in January 1940, and chaired from 1941 by the economist and Bloomsbury Group luminary John Maynard Keynes, CEMA enjoyed an annual subsidy from the Treasury, enabling it to mount concerts, operas, ballets and dramas, and even to sponsor touring art shows. With CEMA backing, London companies such as the Sadler's Wells Ballet (also called the Vic-Wells Ballet) and the opera company normally based at the same theatre took their work to the 'provinces'.

As with other arts during the war, interest in ballet grew steadily. And in a way, the war did the art form a favour. At a time when Britain was starved of international touring companies from the more well developed ballet traditions of, for example, Russia and France, the importance of a home-grown ballet company like the Sadler's Wells only increased, and an 'English style' of dancing developed. When the Sadler's Wells Ballet returned to London, after touring both nationally and internationally (where it had to beat a hasty retreat from the advancing Germans during a tour of the Netherlands in May 1940), its usual base was no longer available: it was being used as temporary accommodation for homeless Londoners. The company was based initially at the New Theatre, where nightly queues stood through air raid sirens and braved bombing raids. In 1944, the company relocated to the Princes Theatre. For the company, Ninette de Valois – once a young Irish dancer named Edris Stannus, but who would go on to become the grande dame of British ballet – choreographed *The Prospect Before Us, Orpheus and Eurydice* and *Promenade* during this period, to scores by Constance Lambert.

The public flocked to see the ballet stars, at the apex of which was prima ballerina Margot Fonteyn, who had formed a celebrated dance partnership with the company's leading male dancer, the versatile Australian Robert Helpmann. His career embraced film and theatre acting too (he had a role in Olivier's *Henry V*), and in 1942 he added choreography to his range by devising three pieces – *Comus*, *Hamlet* and *The Birds* – for Sadler's Wells. (By this time, the Sadler's Wells' regular choreographer, Frederick Ashton, was serving with the RAF, and would not return to the company until after the war.) The

Right Actor Lewis Casson drives an ex-furniture van containing the Old Vic's scenery for the company's wartime tour of South Wales (1941). They were performing Bernard Shaw's *Candida*, starring Casson and Sybil Thorndike, and directed by Tyrone Guthrie. London's loss was the regions' gain, as war prompted many arts companies to take to the road, with the financial backing of the Council for the Encouragement of Music and the Arts (CEMA).

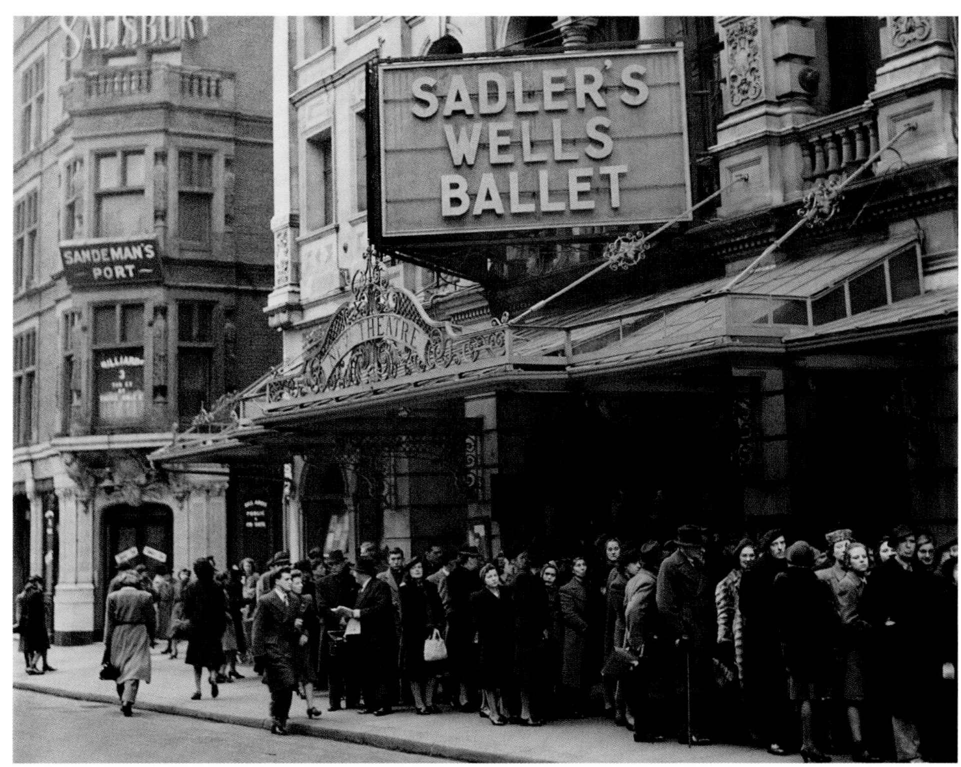

Below Wartime crowds queue for tickets to see the Sadler's Wells Ballet at London's New Theatre in 1944 (later the theatre was renamed the Albery Theatre, after one of its managers). In unanticipated ways, the war years laid the foundations for the future development of English ballet companies and their performance styles. And clearly, there was a hunger during the war for what ballet offered.

Sadler's Wells Ballet would go on to become the Royal Ballet. Another company that would endure was led by Marie Rambert, whose Ballet Club gave as many as four performances a day to packed houses at London's Arts Theatre during the Blitz, before touring the country under the auspices of CEMA.

Opera in London fared less well: the showpiece venue, the Royal Opera House in Covent Garden, was turned into a dance hall, and the Sadler's Wells Opera company toured the country in 1940–1, with Mozart's *The Marriage of Figaro* and Verdi's *La Traviata*, in a reduced company of twenty-six, including an orchestra of just four. It was not until June 1945 that the company was back at the Sadler's Wells Theatre, to perform Benjamin Britten's new opera *Peter Grimes*.

The circumstances of war meant that the government was keen to co-opt artists, writers, entertainers and broadcasters in the larger cause, and to make best use of the media at its disposal – for public information, for propaganda, and for the maintenance of morale. One manifestation was the large number of information booklets, pamphlets postcards and posters produced under the auspices of the Ministry of Information and published by His Majesty's Stationery Office (HMSO). Indeed, the ministry became a popular refuge for writers such as John Betjeman, Graham Greene, Laurie Lee and A L Lloyd. The output included the book *Frontline 1940–1941*, which was published in 1942 and told the story of the civil defence effort across Britain, but particularly in London. It was heavily illustrated with telling images – of St Paul's, the East End and destruction across London – that became central to the story of the Blitz. The book pictured the lives of civil defence workers, firemen in action, and it suggested continuity too – the milk and the post still being delivered. George Britton sent a copy to his daughter in the United States, and she, it seemed, appreciated it:

> So you like 'Front Line'. Then I am glad I sent it. It is very real, and I thought it might help Americans to understand a little of what London had during the period of blitz krieg. I can assure you that in whatever direction you go from the centre of London results of the bombing are manifest for five or six miles. Yet most of us are still alive and on the whole quite recovered and very cheerful.

The Ministry of Information worked closely with the BBC, which had put into action its own wartime plans two days before the official declaration of war. Its national and regional services were combined into the Home Service, and every transmitter across the country operated on the same medium wavelength, so that if any were damaged, the BBC could continue to broadcast. Although the government did not take direct control of the BBC, it had the right to broadcast whenever, and whatever, it wanted. Weather forecasts disappeared from broadcasts – in case they aided the enemy. In fact, the BBC also undertook its own self-censorship, taking care not to compromise security.

The BBC's fledgling television service was closed down on 1 September 1939 – a decision that affected mainly London, where the majority of the nation's 20,000 television owners lived. At this period, broadcasting really meant radio: there were some 9 million licensed wireless sets across the UK. In West Hampstead, Gwladys Cox was not much impressed with the initial wartime programmes, commenting on 28 September 1939:

> The wireless, during the first three weeks of the war, has been pretty poor; but with, with the performers carrying on under all sorts of makeshift conditions, this is scarcely surprising. For the first week, we got nothing but records and Tommy Handley and Leonard Henry. But we are spoilt now – during the last war, there was no such thing as broadcasting for the public.

The Home Service kept the public informed about such things as evacuation plans and rationing. In wartime, news was of paramount importance. Half the nation tuned in to the Nine o'Clock News each evening, delivered from Broadcasting House in London, and the announcers became household names. Three times Broadcasting House itself was bombed – on one occasion, as listeners heard, during a live news bulletin.

Beyond the news, the BBC broadcast many programmes to boost morale and to try to keep the population cheerful and informed. They were not always from London – the Variety Department evacuated to Bangor in Wales. Programmes with a local London flavour included *In Town Tonight*, featuring interviews with London characters and visitors to the capital, while many people rushed home of an evening to catch Frances Durbridge's popular *Paul Temple* mystery series, set in the pre-war world of cocktails, beautiful women, expensive cars, London flats and murderous villains. (The character was later parodied as 'Peter Tremble' in another popular BBC series, the comedy show *ITMA – It's That Man Again*, starring Tommy Handley.) In London's *Evening*

Time for curtain up at the New Theatre in St Martin's Lane, as Peter Gellhorn prepares to conduct the overture to Verdi's *La Traviata* for the Sadler's Wells Opera Company (1943). It was one of the relatively rare outings for opera in wartime London, and compromises were necessary: the theatre's orchestra pit was too small to accommodate either the percussion player or the harpist, both of whom occupied boxes at the sides of the stage.

Standard newspaper, every Friday, readers could also follow a Paul Temple short story. Throughout the war, the Overseas and European Services grew: from Bush House, Aldwych, the BBC was broadcasting in 40 different languages, and the sound of 'This is London calling…' and the signature march 'Lilliburlero' became familiar worldwide. The service also published a monthly magazine called *London Calling*. The BBC's staffing numbers alone, almost tripling to 11,417, suggest how important 'Auntie BBC' became during the war. By 1945, it had also tripled its output to 150 hours worth of material across its services.

People got their news from newspapers too, of course, which were avidly digested. Initially, the Ministry of Information was very unpopular with the press, but under Rear Admiral George Thomson, the chief press censor, good relations were re-established. But newspaper coverage was always limited by the general constraints on the dissemination of information deemed sensitive. During the Blitz, the Air Ministry allowed the names and locations of damaged sites to be

Londoners young and old learn about army life and the progress of the war at the 1943 Army Exhibition, staged on the spacious site of the bombed-out John Lewis department store in Oxford Street. This exhibition, created for the War Office, was the largest to be mounted by the Ministry of Information. It was then recreated in Birmingham and Cardiff.

revealed only 28 days after the event. With information murky, rumour abounded. Factories were not allowed to be mentioned, and while lists of casualties could be posted locally, they could not be published. The tragic disaster at Bethnal Green Underground Station in 1943 – when, after a siren sounded, the blacked-out staircase became a deathtrap for 173 people trying to get down it – was reported, but without reference to the place or the panic.

As had happened in the First World War, the government sought to put the visual arts at the service of the war effort. Accordingly, the Ministry of Information established in 1939 the War Artists Advisory Committee (WAAC), which held monthly meetings at the National Gallery, chaired by the Gallery's director Kenneth Clark. The WAAC commissioned both established and lesser-known artists to paint bomb-shattered ruins, factory workers and other home front scenes as well as sending them overseas to record the fighting in every theatre of war. Under this patronage, conditions in the London shelters were chronicled not just

The Ministry of Information at work (November 1941), in this case civil servants at the MOI's Photograph Division. Initially, the Division collated photographs taken by official and agency photographers and made sure they were implementing their self-censorship correctly. The images were then distributed to various bodies, including the MOI's publicity and news sections.

by photographs but also in drawings by Henry Moore and Leonard Rosoman. Moore had initially refused Clark's request to work as a war artist, preferring to concentrate on his own projects. However, when returning to Belsize Park with his wife one evening in September, his curiosity was aroused:

> As a rule I went into town by car and hadn't been by Tube for ages. For the first time that evening I saw people lying on the platforms at all the stations we stopped at. When we got to Belsize Park we weren't allowed out of the station for an hour because of the bombing. I spent the time looking at the rows of people sleeping on the platforms. I had never seen so many reclining figures, and even the train tunnels seemed to be like the holes in my sculpture. Amid the grim tension, I noticed groups of strangers formed together into intimate groups and children asleep within feet of the passing trains.

On the following nights he made a number of sketches, and when Clark contacted him again, Moore felt he could no longer refuse the invitation to work as an official war artist.

Moore's roving commission took him all over the London Underground stations, resulting in his memorable shelter sketches.

He visited other public refuges too, including the notorious and large Tilbury shelter. 'But,' he wrote, 'the shelter which interested me most of all was the Liverpool Street Underground Extension. A new tunnel had been bored and the reinforcement of the walls completed, but there were no rails, and at night it was occupied along its entire length by a double row of sleeping figures.'

Leonard Rosoman, by contrast, served as an Auxiliary Fireman. His painting *A House Collapsing on Two Firemen, Shoe Lane, London, EC4* was purchased by the WAAC in August 1941. It depicted a real incident – two of his colleagues in the shadow of a falling wall, the moment before they were crushed, a fate which Rosoman himself barely escaped. In later life, he regarded this work as 'sentimental and superficial', and as the war went on he preferred to paint the machinery of warfare for the WAAC.

Other artists, such as R Vivian Pitchforth, Graham Sutherland and Sir Muirhead Bone, were commissioned specifically to convey the damage being done to London. Sutherland was employed by the Ministry of Information for six months from January 1941, and he spent his time in the City of London and the East End, areas of London that for him represented very different qualities: 'In the City one didn't think of the destruction of life. All the destroyed buildings were office buildings and people weren't in them at night. But in the East End one did think of the hurt to people.' He was aware of the sensitivities surrounding the act of turning distress and destruction into art, and wanted to take photographs initially because 'it is difficult to draw in some places without rousing a sense of resentment in the people'.

Art became increasingly democratised, as exhibitions sprang up everywhere – in Underground stations, in bombed-out department stores, and in British Restaurants. CEMA also bought new works of art for travelling exhibitions, after many museums had re-opened by mid-1942. In September 1943, it was estimated that half a million people had been to the thirty 'Art for the People' exhibitions organised by CEMA in the previous eighteen months. Sometimes, the art on display documented war work, such as the exhibition of paintings by fireman-artists that Gwladys Cox and her husband attended at Piccadilly's Burlington House, on 29 August 1941:

> These artists are engaged in A.F.S. work and in their business-like navy & red uniform, some with beards, were much in evidence in the crowded galleries. The Exhibition was free, but the public were

Graham Sutherland's painting in gouache *The City: A Fallen Lift Shaft* (1941) renders the tangle of metal as if it is some great slain beast, limbs illuminated by the fire's glow. It is set in an area of London just north of St Paul's Cathedral. Like many of his contemporaries, Sutherland found the onset of war initially detrimental to his artistic career. But, as a prominent artist and friend of Kenneth Clark, Chairman of the War Artists Advisory Committee, Sutherland was soon employed as a war artist with the purpose of visually documenting London under attack.

expected to place a contribution in a fire man's brass helmet placed by the turn-stiles, in aid of the London Fire Service Benevolent Fund.

Having ourselves experienced the horror of fire-bombs, we appreciated to the full these artistic efforts to portray Fire in all its beauty and terror; apart from being a very necessary war record, the pictures themselves, as works of art, were very interesting, even if vermillion and yellow paint against indigo skies did somewhat pall.

Popular entertainment boomed during the war, and for much of it London was the engine. When war broke out, 'Tin Pan Alley' – London's Denmark Street, the unofficial headquarters of the songwriting business – immediately produced a glut of patriotic and topical songs including 'We're Gonna Hang out the Washing on the Siegfried Line', 'Adolf' and 'Somewhere in France with You', which enjoyed at least a brief popularity. Other songs tackled the loathed blackout with titles such as 'Till the Lights of London Shine Again' and 'They Can't Blackout the Moon', while the risqué topical songs 'Blackout Bella' by Douglas Byng and 'The Deepest Shelter in Town' by Florence Desmond were savoured by a sophisticated audience. Far more lasting, though, were those songs that dealt with wartime separation and eventual reunion. Outstanding in this respect was Vera Lynn's 'We'll Meet Again', but 'Room 504' and 'That Lovely Weekend' were also huge hits, as was 'I'll Be Seeing You', a 1938 song revived in 1944. The Blitz produced its own songs, such as 'The King is Still in London', while in an entirely different vogue, the popularity of South American-themed songs from the films of Carmen Miranda and American hits such as 'Long Ago and Far Away' from the film *Cover Girl* testified to a desire to be anywhere but here. More down to earth were songs like 'Roll Out the Barrel', 'Run Rabbit Run' and 'There's A Boy Coming Home on Leave'. George Formby and Gracie Fields, big stars of the 1930s, retained the public's affection with songs like Fields's enduring 'Wish Me Luck as You Wave Me Goodbye' (from the 1939 film hit *Shipyard Sally*) and Formby's repertoire from his wartime films.

In 1943, Hubert Gregg's song 'I'm Going To Get Lit Up When the Lights Go Up in London' (written three years earlier) was first performed, by Zoe Gail, in the revue 'Strike A New Note' at London's Prince of Wales Theatre. This was the show that catapulted comedian Sid Field to stardom. 'I Don't Want to Set the World on Fire' became the pointed unofficial anthem of both the National Fire Service and the civilian Fire Guard. Winston Churchill did not escape the attentions of

Leonard Rosoman's *A House Collapsing on Two Firemen* (1940) sprang straight from a scene he had witnessed as an Auxiliary Fireman, when two colleagues gave their lives battling fires in the City of London's Shoe Lane. The oil painting was exhibited in the Firemen Artists exhibition at the Royal Academy in 1941, attended by Gwladys Cox among others. Although Rosoman was later dissatisfied with the work as an over-literal interpretation, its capture of a dynamic moment between life and death is undeniably powerful and disconcerting.

Tin Pan Alley: the great comedian Max Miller penned 'The Grand Old Man', a tribute to the prime minister, who was also celebrated in 'The Man with the Big Cigar'. (Max Miller appeared with Vera Lynn at the Holborn Empire, before it was blitzed.)

In the spring of 1941, Noël Coward wrote the song that seemed to encapsulate all the best emotions and wistfulness of the Blitz – 'London Pride'. He had, he said, been standing on the platform of a London railway station after a particularly bad raid. Most of the station's glass roof had been blown out, and there was a constant smell of burning and dust everywhere. Watching Londoners still determinedly going about their business, he was overwhelmed by a sense of pride – and then noticed a small wild flower, London Pride, in a crack of the concrete. The symbolism became irresistible, producing an unashamedly sentimental hymn to the city, from its 'Cockney feet' that 'mark the beat of history' to 'Park Lane in a shimmering gown'. Most memorable was its chorus:

> London Pride has been handed down to us.
> London Pride is a flower that's free.
> London Pride means our own dear town to us,
> And our pride it for ever will be.

Taking entertainment to British and London war workers, as well as to troops, was the Entertainments National Service Association (ENSA). It was an enormous enterprise, driven by its director, Basil Dean, and would eventually employ about four-fifths of all those working in the entertainment industry at one time or another, including George Formby, Tommy Trinder, Margaret Rutherford and Vera Lynn. In London, every factory on an approved list had an ENSA party every week, often during the lunch break.

Instrumental and dance music was broadcast by the BBC, as in *Music While You Work*, aimed mainly at war workers, featuring orchestras conducted by the likes of Henry Hall and Sir Adrian Boult. In London, the Americans' Rainbow Corner hosted a number of US bands, including the always popular Glenn Miller and his Army Air Force Band. The capital's regular dance halls, such as the Hammersmith Palais and the Lyceum, were in great demand throughout the war, not only for the music and dancing but for the chance to meet London's latest arrivals. One keen attendee (as quoted by historian Norman Longmate) could count New Zealand Air Force officers, US soldiers and Canadian Fire Service volunteers among her dance partners on various occasions.

Classical music managed to navigate its way through London's war. In 1939, the members of the seven-year-old London Philharmonic Orchestra, founded by Sir Thomas Beecham, took control of the orchestra, and the cooperative company toured the country for the first time. On 10 May 1941, the last big Blitz raid, the Philharmonic was back in London, playing at the Queen's Hall, which was destroyed that night – along with many of the orchestra's instruments. The next year, the orchestra found a North London base at the Orpheum, in Golders Green. For about a year until its closure in 1943, the

Criss-crossing steel girders protrude from the ground like anti-tank traps, in R Vivian Pitchforth's watercolour *Post Office Buildings*, commissioned by the War Artists Advisory Committee. Pitchforth had been so successful in portraying the ARP and air raid damage that in December 1940 he was given a six-month contract with the Ministry of Information to cover subjects for the ministries of Home Security and Supply, including the headquarters of the General Post Office and surrounding area of London.

venue became quite a cultural centre, hosting opera, ballet, theatre, exhibitions as well as music, until location problems and travel difficulties meant that it was no longer a viable proposition. By contrast, the annual London festival of promenade concerts – the 'Proms' – was able to continue throughout the war with only limited interruption. In 1940, the traditional finale of the Last Night of the Proms was brought to a sudden stop by a bombing raid. The destruction of the Queen's Hall took away its usual venue, and only then did the Proms move to the Albert Hall in South Kensington, which would become its permanent venue, drawing wartime audiences of up to 5,000 nightly.

By far the biggest urban entertainment, before and during the war, was the cinema. After the initial closure period, cinemas had reopened in Greater London by 9 September 1939, and in some of the boroughs,

such as Cheam, Harrow and Sutton, programmes were hastily arranged. The Central London cinemas reopened on 15 September. Thereafter, most cinemas tried to stay open, despite the periods of bombing. Together, they sold about 30 million tickets every week, many of them to children – and a few of them to Londoners George and Helena Britton, who kept their transatlantic daughter informed of what they'd seen. On 27 November 1940, George related how:

> Last Thursday we went to the Odeon, Chingford Mount, and saw 'Earthbound' a very weird film in which the spirit figure of a man is super-imposed on the picture till the mystery of his death is unravelled; and 'Under Your Hat' with Jack Hulbert and Cicely Courtneige [*sic*], which is just a scream and [the] ideal picture to brush the times for a few minutes.

George Formby entertains Londoners sheltering in Aldwych Underground Station (28 November 1940). With his trademark banjolele (as here) or ukulele and his infectious, cheeky – and sometimes saucy – charm, Formby had risen from the variety stage through cinema to the peak of his stardom in the war years. He extensively entertained civilians and troops for ENSA.

Kenneth Rowntree's oil painting *CEMA Canteen Concert* (1941) depicts a scene in London's Isle of Dogs, and evokes the sort of lunchtime entertainments that were promoted in many factories and workplaces.

Under Your Hat, produced early in the war, was based on Hulbert and Courtneidge's successful stage show. Its musical-comedy plot was a throwback to pre-war England, involving an attempt to recover a carburettor from enemy agents and fly it back to London, but its songs delivered useful wartime messages such as 'Keep It Under Your Hat' and 'The Empire Depends on You'.

On 8 January 1941, George Britton could write that 'On Saturday we went to the Odeon and saw "Young People" with Shirley Temple and Jack Oakie, also "Money to Burn" both of which were very amusing without being uproarious which was just what we want.' It seemed to have served as the right kind of distraction from the Blitz. Two years later, on 4 August 1943, they were watching *The Life and Death of Colonel Blimp*, a film produced by the Powell and Pressburger team, which employed David Low's broadly sympathetic cartoon Blimp character and would be one

Popular comedian Tommy Trinder and actress Jean Colin do their bit for the Ministry of Information in a scene from *Eating Out With Tommy Trinder* (1941), a short MOI film extolling the virtues of the new British Restaurants. After a desultory episode of home cooking, Trinder (who plays himself) takes his hosts to experience his 'favourite' eating establishment.

of the best remembered films of the war – despite Churchill's attempt to block its production. Unlike the Brittons, who 'enjoyed it very much', the prime minister loathed the film.

Then as now, Hollywood provided the majority of the blockbuster films, which included *Gone With the Wind* (1939) and *Citizen Kane* (1941). In the early years of the war, films like RKO's *Gunga Din* (1939) and the three British films *Goodbye Mr Chips* (1939), *Four Feathers* (1939) and the comedy *Band Waggon* (a 1940 Arthur Askey vehicle, based on his BBC series) proved popular. Sometimes, film showings were accompanied by songs that spoke to the moment: 'The White Cliffs of Dover', 'I'm Going to Get Lit Up When the Lights Go on in London' in 1943, or 'Shine on Victory Moon' during 1944.

Although the public flocked to Hollywood films, the British cinema experienced something of a renaissance during the war. Nellie Carver enjoyed one home-produced hit, *Pimpernel Smith*, at a London cinema on 15 July 1941, finding its leading man, the matinee idol Leslie Howard, 'just as lovely as Ever!' In this contemporary drama, he played the absent-minded Professor Horatio Smith, who rescues the persecuted from Nazi concentration camps. It was a national calamity – and a blow for Nellie Carver – when this cinematic star, who had left Hollywood (where his major roles had included Ashley in *Gone With the Wind*) to help Britain's war effort, was shot down by the Luftwaffe in 1943. He had been flying back to Britain from Lisbon. The film critic Caroline Lejeune summed up the feelings of many when she wrote, not long after the war (in *Red Roses Every Night*):

> The death of Leslie Howard was a tragic loss to British cinema: for Leslie Howard, both as actor and director, was something of a symbol to the British People. He came home from America to help us when times were bad: his *Pimpernel Smith* and *The First of the Few* were the right films at the right moment. The public liked and trusted his quiet voice and whimsical judgement; he had, and always will have, a very special place in his country's affections.

Despite the loss of Leslie Howard, British film production continued to go from strength to strength. J. Arthur Rank and his Rank Empire financed many of films and encouraged new directors such as Carol Reed, David Lean and the Boulting brothers. Reed directed the *The Way Ahead* (1944), about the British Army, while other films with frankly propagandistic themes included Ealing Studios' *Next of Kin* (to discourage 'careless talk'; 1942) and Gainsborough Pictures' *Millions*

Like Us (1943), in praise of women working in aircraft factories. David Lean's directorial debut was the patriotic and Oscar-nominated *In Which We Serve* (1942), whose screenplay, by Noël Coward, was based on the true story of Lord Louis Mountbatten's command of HMS *Kelly*, sunk off the coast of Crete in 1941. The Two Cities Films production starred John Mills, and it marked the film debut of such actors as Celia Johnson and Richard Attenborough.

American dance-band leader Glenn Miller at the microphone during a London radio broadcast. With hits such as 'Pennsylvania 6-5000', 'Chattanooga Choo Choo' and 'Tuxedo Junction' under his belt, Miller and his swing Orchestra, with their clarinet-led sound, acquired an international audience in the early war years. Commissioned into the US Army Air Force in 1942, he, and the service band he now led, were performing in London in 1944, just months before his plane disappeared in a fatal flight to Paris.

Cinemas themselves did not escape the ravages of wartime. Out of 4,000 operating in Britain, 160 were destroyed by bombing, 60 of them in London. The first London venue to be hit was the Kinema in West Ham, which was showing the musical *On Your Toes* and the 1940 comedy *Tilly of Bloomsbury*. The bomb hit the back of the cinema, destroying three dressing rooms. On this very first day of the Blitz, the startled audience, once they had recovered from the shock, began singing. The

Queues snake past the Dolcis shoe shop for admission to the Empire and Ritz cinemas, in London's Leicester Square (March 1941). The Empire was showing *The Philadelphia Story* (1940), which ran for four weeks, while at the Ritz *Gone with the Wind* (1939) was playing, as it would do for most of the war. Aerial bombing only seemed to increase Londoners' appetite for films.

cinema's secretary, though buried in the wreckage, still managed to turn up for work the following day; but the venue itself was closed for several months, until it reopened on 20 November.

Sometimes audiences stayed on inside the cinemas after the last showing, as raids continued outside; and sometimes the film showings just kept on running, as when the Granada cinema in Clapham Junction showed five feature films over one night. On 20 September 1940, the air raid warning sounded at a different Granada cinema, in Sutton, South London, just before the end of the American musical *It's a Date*. Most of the audience had already left, save six who had fallen asleep at the back of the stalls. The cinema assistant recounted the story:

> I took cover and waited, and just as I got up an oil-bomb hit us. It came through the roof, but hit a girder and exploded in mid-air in the auditorium.

The heartthrob Leslie Howard (right) in a BBC studio for a wartime broadcast with the writer J B Priestley. The death in December 1943 of this star of such films as *Pimpernel Smith*, *Berkeley Square* and *Pygmalion* was a much-mourned tragedy.

> All I could see was a sheet of flame up to the ceiling completely blocking out the stage. Apart from a loud crack, there was very little noise.
>
> The blast blew the front doors and bent the iron bars and padlocks like hairpins. The A.R.P. man found himself with a padlock and chain round his neck outside the cinema against the wall, with the exit door closed behind him. The six customers just vanished into the night over the flattened front doors.

The following day also brought a false alarm about an unexploded bomb, which cleared the high street. It was a month before the Sutton Granada reopened – with 350 new seats.

Despite all the challenges, the arts and entertainment scene weathered the war, and in many cases even prospered. London's – and the nation's – sporting scene was, by contrast, severely affected. Arsenal Football Club, in common with other football clubs, had encouraged its regular players to volunteer *en masse*, and as a result was left with just two professional footballers out of forty-two. Their ground at Highbury was turned into a public shelter, and the club – its players now part-timers – was forced instead to share a ground with their local arch rivals Tottenham Hotspur. Similarly, the English Rugby Union Headquarters at Twickenham became a shelter (as well as allotments), Surrey's cricket ground at the Oval was requisitioned as a prisoner of war camp, and the RAF began using the Lords' pavilion and practice ground. Despite the depredations, football did manage to continue in London, where sixteen clubs broke away from the Southern League (because of the difficulties now involved in travelling) to form their own, more localised league during the 1941–2 season. But crowds were down, not only because of the limits placed on capacities, but because in wartime so many people were either working on Saturdays or trying to visit their evacuee children. Some of the matches that did take place were war fundraisers, in which the Football Association and English Football League were instrumental, such as the game organised by the League at Chelsea in May 1943, which raised £8,000 for the Navy Welfare Fund.

By 1943, interest had revived sufficiently – and the circumstances were more propitious – to deliver a 60,000 crowd for an England–Scotland football international. This revival in interest was mirrored in other sports, and saw amateur Rugby Union players lining up alongside their professional Rugby League cousins for the first time in history. In 1943 also, and despite its wartime use by the RAF, Lords witnessed a quarter of million spectators to attend the cricket there. Although the traditional three-day county games had been abandoned, new cricketing teams were formed representing Army and Civil Defence units, and new sides were put together, such as the London Counties and British Empire teams.

War had transformed much of Britain's coastline into out-of-bounds or thickly defended areas, so unsurprisingly one form of traditional leisure pursuit for city dwellers declined markedly: a seaside holiday. And travel was, in any case, not at all easy. Instead, from 1943 London boroughs encouraged people to 'holiday at home'. The Borough of Barnes in West London, for example, issued a *Programme of Events for Holidays at Home*, which advertised a band concert, a Punch and Judy show, a fair, cricket matches and a concert in aid of Anglo-Soviet Friendship. London swimming pools held galas, while open-air theatre events took place in London parks such as Clapham Common and Victoria Park. In an exception to the rule, there were schemes for free or assisted holidays for exhausted London Civil Defence workers to visit the coast, but this evolved into stays at more easily manageable holiday hostels in the countryside, where food was more freely available and people could at least relax away from sirens and air raids. Seaside resorts only really became holiday destinations again at the end of the war.

At least there was alcohol with which to unwind. Unfortunately, even this became increasingly hard to get during the war. Quite often in crowded London pubs there were no spirits to be had and little beer, which cost a shilling a pint and was often watered down. In Anthony Powell's novel *The Soldier's Art*, set in 1941 and part of 'A Dance to the Music of Time', a character sadly observes: 'The wine outlook becomes increasingly desperate since France went. One didn't expect to fight a war on an occasional half-pint of bitter, and lucky if you find that.'

In London, pubs and the bohemian set formed a natural nexus, particularly in the Central London hubs of Soho and Fitzrovia. Theodora FitzGibbon remembered drinking through the first raids with her then partner Peter Rose Pelham (a photographer and painter) and poet Dylan Thomas at the King's Head and Eight Bells in Chelsea. As she remembered, generally you could get a few glasses of beer or Guinness, but spirits were only available to regulars, and at one pub you had to bring your own glass. Nevertheless, she thought that London's pubs during the war represented the only places where people could entertain, or be entertained, cheaply, and of course they provided much needed companionship.

Later, Dylan Thomas also drank with the short-story writer and fellow scriptwriter Julian McLaren-Ross, who arrived in London in 1943 having been discharged from the Army. However, a woman accused McLaren-Ross of being a 'Soho non-blitzer'. It was a double insult: the experience of going through the Blitz had become an important marker of identity for a Londoner, while – as the editor of *Poetry London* magazine explained –'Sohoitis' could be a charge levelled at both writers, for it stood for staying in the pubs and getting no work done.

The two writers drank in the Fitzroy Tavern and Wheatsheaf pubs among others. One of the virtues of the Wheatsheaf was that it sold Younger's Scotch Ale, which was stronger than the English ales. Run by Mona Glendenning and her brother Redvers and his wife Frances, the Wheatsheaf was generally considered to be more rowdy and boisterous than the neighbouring Fitzroy Tavern. As it was some distance from central Soho, there were also fewer foreign servicemen and prostitutes. Its regulars included the elderly Wilf, a member of the Home Guard, and the equally elderly Mrs Stewart, who did the crossword while nursing a bottle of Guinness and who didn't take to anyone who tried to help her. The pub was also the favourite haunt of artists such as Augustus John, John Minton and the ostentatiously bohemian Nina Hamnett. She would tell stories of modelling for the sculptor Henri Gaudier-Brzeska, of meeting Picasso and James Joyce, and of having

Soldiers, sailors and civilians down their last pints, in this design for a wartime scarf entitled 'Time Gentleman Please', as produced for Jacqmar of London. Around the borders are the names of London pubs. Their trade increased in wartime, especially during certain short periods of alarm, as at the beginning of the Blitz, when other social venues closed. But the shortages, and rising prices, threatened to dampen the spirits of committed drinkers.

affairs with Rodin and Modigliani. To add to the merriment, she would reveal her breasts at the slightest provocation. The literary men Stephen Spender, John Lehmann and George Orwell were all known to pop in to the Wheatsheaf, but it was not their natural habitat.

For determined drinkers, the Wheatsheaf offered one particular asset. Its location was on the boundary of Holborn and Marylebone boroughs, which had different closing times. So, when 'time gentlemen, please' was called at 10.30pm, a customer could just step out for an extra hour's drinking at the pubs on the opposite side of Charlotte Street – if they hadn't run out of beer already – or head south into the centre of Soho proper.

For drinkers of all kinds, the end of the war seemed to bring little relief. In the April 1945 budget, a cheap bottle of whiskey had gone up to twenty-five shillings and ninepence – more than double the 1939 price. 'Sohoitis' might involve little work, but it seemed to require increasingly deep pockets.

IN FOCUS

LITERARY LONDON

Wartime brought about an increase in the habit of reading – as a way of gaining information and news, and perhaps because, after all, there was sometimes little else one could do amid the enforced leisure or cramped spaces when taking refuge after the sirens went. The classics – Jane Austen, Charles Dickens, and Anthony Trollope – were popular, and certain titles from earlier in the century, for example Hugh Walpole's *Rogue Herries* and John Galsworthy's *Forsythe Sage*, enjoyed a resurgence. After the Soviet Union became a war ally, Britain's interest in all things Russian increased, and Tolstoy's *War and Peace* became the favourite foreign classic of the war, particularly after it was recommended on *ITMA* and serialised on the radio.

However, while the demand was there, the means to supply it was endangered by the depredations of war. For a start, there was a shortage of paper, which, Gwladys Cox remarked, 'is becoming a real hardship, not only just for newspapers'. And what there was, was declining in quality. George Orwell thought that 'Writing paper gets more and more like toilet paper while toilet paper resembles sheet tin.' In fact, publishers were reduced to just a quarter of their pre-war paper supplies initially, and later on in the war they were still below 50 per cent of what they had been used to before. Added to the paper problem was the Blitz, for London, then as now, was the centre of the British publishing industry, and its offices, warehouses and printing works could not hope to escape the ravages of the bombs. In the 'second great Fire of London' on 29–30 December 1940, storehouses and 27 publishers' premises were hit, destroying 5 million books.

Unsurprisingly, the number of published books declined from around 14,000 in 1939 to just 6,700 in 1943, remaining at that low level until the end of the war. But relative scarcity seemed only to add to the desirability of books, for at the same time the reading public's expenditure on them rose dramatically, from £9 million in 1939 to £23 million in 1945. New books were selling out quickly and going out of print in a matter of weeks. Libraries, too, were in greater demand, and the sale of second-hand books was booming.

This appetite to read spurred on the appearance of new publishing houses, which thrived in wartime. Founded in the 1930s, Penguin Books, based in Harmondsworth, west of London, had helped democratise reading through the innovation of the affordable paperback, and wartime played to the company's strengths. There was a huge demand for the 'Penguin Specials', the paperbacks priced at sixpence and covering recent history and current affairs. For the 87 titles produced in 1941, Penguin sold over 100,000 copies collectively. An earlier title, Harold Laski's *Where Do We Go From Here?* (1940), sold more than 80,000 copies alone – quite an achievement for a work on left-wing political theory.

Among the mass-market publishing genres, thrillers, crime fiction and detective stories remained popular, from the American hard-boiled detective fiction such

Opposite A surprising number of books still cling to their shelves in the otherwise bomb-shattered library of Holland House, Kensington (1940). Unfortunately, the damage at some other libraries, such as the London Library, was much more severe – and the premises of London's publishers, booksellers and printers suffered badly during the war.

Some of the 180 workers and volunteers at the Services Central Book Depot in London (1944), who repaired and rebound books for readers in the services. Through these efforts, 130,000 books had been given a second life by July 1944 – in its own way, a method of 'make do and mend'.

as Peter Cheyney's Slim Callaghan series to James Hadley Chase's violent thrillers, or the novels and London characters of authors like Agatha Christie (Hercule Poirot), Margery Allingham (Albert Campion), Ngaio Marsh (Inspector Roderick Allen), 'Nicholas Blake', pseudonym of Cecil Day Lewis (Nigel Strangeways), and Georgette Heyer (Inspector Hemingway).

In this fertile literary environment, new and important literary periodicals also appeared. These weren't solely in London, for Wales, Scotland and Ireland also had their literary effusions (and indeed so did other parts of the Empire, such as Cairo and India); but London remained the heart of literary life. The poet and critic Stephen Spender helped edit Cyril Connolly's literary journal *Horizon*, which first appeared in 1940 and continued throughout the decade, as did John Lehmann's *Penguin New Writing*. Lehmann, who was in the Home Guard and worked for various newspapers and periodicals as well as the BBC and the MOI, had founded *New Writing* in 1935, before persuading the Penguin founder Allen Lane to put it out as a monthly renamed *Penguin New Writing* – thus preventing its demise because of the paper shortage. However, a lack of paper did force the journal to become a quarterly in 1942. For a relatively rarefied literary periodical, it had unprecedented popularity, selling out a print run of about 75,000 for each issue. It published new work by nearly all the leading authors, essayists, critics and poets of the time. Many of them drew on their experience of living and working in wartime London.

The literary editor John Lehmann, who started the important periodical that evolved into *Penguin New Writing* during the war. He is in his Home Guard uniform and striking a pose outside the University of London's Senate House, which was taken over by the Ministry of Information.

George Stonier, for example, wrote wry, humorous sketches about the character 'Fanfarlo', which later appeared in book form as *Shaving Through the Blitz*. This was not quite the uplifting MOI-type view of the world:

'I think the Blitz makes people better somehow, don't you?' She says.

No, I don't. I think it kills a lot of people; I think it makes a few brave and others mad, and the rest more interested, forthcoming and sly. Do I like that? In a way (and this distresses me), I do.

As Lehmann pointed out in his autobiography *I Am My Brother*, 'Fanfarlo' was one of the most popular features of *Penguin New Writing*, and if the character missed an issue, Lehmann would receive anxious letters. It was Lehmann's view that he would rather have been in London during the war than anywhere else; that feeling was echoed in the work of many who wrote for his periodical, such as Henry Green, whose short stories 'The Rescue' and 'Mr Jonas' reflected the author's experiences in the London fire service.

Horizon was slightly more highbrow than *Penguin New Writing*, its aim to maintain cultural standards despite the war. Connolly, assisted by Spender and backed by a rich patron, Peter Watson, did not see *Horizon* as a vehicle for first-time writers. But the journal also rejected the writing of some of the more popular authors, such

POETRY

(LONDON)

A BI-MONTHLY OF VERSE AND CRITICISM

HERBERT READ: A SALUTE

PIERRE JEAN JOUVE

TWO POEMS BY **WALTER DE LA MARE** ● ON A WEDDING ANNIVERSARY BY **DYLAN THOMAS** A WARTIME DAWN BY **DAVID GASCOYNE** ● TWO WAR POEMS BY **GEORGE SCURFIELD** ● THE DYKE-BUILDER BY **HENRY TREECE** ● IN A TIME OF CRISIS BY **LAWRENCE DURRELL** ● RICHARD EBERHART BY **NICHOLAS MOORE** ● EAST COKER BY **JAMES H. KIRKUP** ● EN PARTANT POUR SYRIE BY **G. S. FRASER** ● FOUR LYRICS BY **TAMBIMUTTU** ● ALSO POEMS BY **ANNE RIDLER, GAVIN EWART, PETER J. LITTLE, G. S. FRASER, JOHN MALCOLM BRINNIN, J. C. HALL** and **NICHOLAS MOORE.**

No. 4 JANUARY-FEBRUARY ONE SHILLING

Volume 1, Number 4 of *Poetry London* (1941). This publication, describing itself as a 'bi-monthly of verse and criticism', brought together many poets and critics under the eccentric editorship of 'Tambi' – Meary James Tambimuttu.

Poetry London also featured cover designs by prestigious artists, as in these two interpretations of the 'lyre bird', by Henry Moore for Volume 2, Number 8 (*above left*), and by Graham Sutherland for Volume 2, Number 9 (*above right*).

as W Somerset Maugham. The historian, biographer and MP Harold Nicolson read the first issue, and was rather underwhelmed: 'The editorial note says that in this war we are inspired by "pity or hope" as in the Spanish war. No pity. No hope. Glum. Glum. Glum.'

A question posed in the literary journals at the beginning of the war was: 'Where are our war poets?' The war poets of the Second World War were civilians as well as servicemen, and the journals sought to give them a platform. As well as *Horizon* and *Penguin New Writing*, there was *Poetry London* and *Poetry Quarterly*, the latter also London-based.

Poetry London was edited by Meary James Tambimuttu, a poet originally from Ceylon (Sri Lanka). 'Tambi', as he was known, was a charismatic figure, who led a sort of underground literary scene in Soho. He published both established and first-time poets, and his roster included Idris Davies, Keith Douglas (d.1944), Lawrence Durrell, Glyn Jones, Alun Lewis (d.1944), Dylan Thomas, Kathleen Raine, Herbert Read, Keidrych Rhys, Lynette Roberts, Spender and Vernon Watkins. However, the periodical, with covers drawn by Henry Moore and Graham Sutherland, appeared erratically, in just ten wartime issues, though its circulation rose to 10,000 copies in 1942. 'Tambi' seems to have been a rather elusive character, who had the knack of raising money and impressing patrons, while dodging creditors. He held court in Fitzrovia, until he left for Ceylon in 1949, leaving *Poetry London* under a cloud and having acquired a lasting reputation as a charlatan from poet Julian McLaren-Ross's *Memoir of the Forties*. He did, though, publish Henry Moore's *Shelter Sketch Book* in 1945.

Poetry Quarterly was edited by Wrey Gardiner, who published the work of many of the writers already mentioned, as well as others of the likes of Brenda Chamberlain, Sidney Keyes and Henry Treece. The periodical also featured reviews by Spender and Orwell. Although Spender did a lot of reviewing, his own poetic output was actually somewhat stunted by the war, as he acknowledged much later, in 1990:

I did write a bit during the war but you felt that everything, and ideas that we stood for in 1930, had been taken out of our hands. A kind of huge machinery of armies and democracy replaced them, which one supported, as we were after all in a democracy, and had good aspects – but entirely negative for writing as far as I was concerned.

However, Spender did a lot for other poets' careers. According to Connolly, as co-editor of *Horizon* Spender was responsible for the good war poetry that was published in the journal in 1939–41 – work by writers such as John Betjeman, Cecil Day Lewis, Louis MacNeice and Dylan Thomas.

An issue faced by poets, though not just poets, was that war made it difficult to be a *full-time* writer. Just like other civilians, writers were required to contribute to the war effort. That took its toll on their creative efforts, according to Mollie Panter-Downes in the *New Yorker* (11 March 1945):

During the war years, more and more Londoners have taken to reading poetry, listening to music, and going to art exhibitions, although there is less and less of all three to be had in this shabby, weary capital. Most of the poets are too personally involved in the war to have attained that state of impersonal tranquillity which generates good poetry. Louis MacNeice, whose most recent collection, Springboard, *was quickly sold out, is working at the BBC, C. Day Lewis has a job at the Ministry of Information, Stephen Spender is a full-time fireman, and most of the younger poets are in uniform. Several have been killed, among them Alun Lewis, who was considered one of the most promising. The output of good poetry is small, but the public hunger for it is pathetically great.*

Nevertheless, the period – and the London Blitz in particular – did produce some stand-out poems that reflected the times: David Jones's 'Prothalamion', written during the Blitz, which appeared much later in the volume *Wedding Poems*; T S Eliot's 'Little Gidding' in *Four Quartets*; and Dylan Thomas's 'Ceremony After a Fire Raid' and 'A Refusal to Mourn the Death, by Fire of a Child in London'.

As Panter-Downes suggested, writers easily found work during the war. Sometimes this involved redirecting their writing skills in some 'useful' direction, as with George Orwell, who worked at the BBC, or the raft of writers who worked for the Ministry of Information. Other writers joined the services. Elizabeth Bowen and Graham Greene were Air Raid Wardens, and both Bowen's *The Heat of the Day* (1948) and Greene's *Ministry of Fear* (1943) and *The End of the Affair* (1952) were set during the Blitz. T.S. Eliot was a fire watcher at his publishers, Faber & Faber. Even Dylan Thomas, who was in London for long periods during the war and who declared 'I want to get something out of the war, & put very little in (certainly not my one & only body)', ended up writing film scripts for the Ministry of Information.

Henry Green, William Sansom and Stephen Spender all served in the fire service. Green, pseudonym of Henry Yorke, took literary advantage of his own experiences for the novel *Caught* (1943), in which he captured the tensions between professional firemen and the amateur Auxiliary Fire Service personnel in the early days of the war and the Blitz. It shows up class tensions between the two services, and details the lives of men and women living in close proximity for too long, with little to do but gossip and become suspicious of each other, until the Blitz arrives. Another author–fireman during the Blitz, William Sansom, vividly portrayed the civil defence services in Central London in his fiction, notably in the short-story collection *Fireman Flower* (1944). Sansom served alongside the artist Leonard Rosoman, and Sansom and Henry Green were responsible for Stephen Spender joining the fire service.

London's literary men and women played their own part in the artistic and social scene that existed, at various levels, throughout the war. The more established editors and writers such as John Lehmann and Cyril Connolly hosted lunch and dinner parties, as did, for example, Eliot and the Sitwells. And literary London could get a look-in, too, at the gatherings hosted by the cultured Lady (Emerald) Cunard at her Dorchester suite. James Lees-Milne was a regular at these get-togethers, as on 30 May 1944:

Dined at Emerald's. Nancy [Mitford], Joan Moore and a don called Denis Rickett, terrifying incisive, intellectual and All Soulish. Emerald was in sparkling form. Venetia Montagu in at 11.30. She is a very clever well-informed woman, with a masculine and independent mind. Denis Rickett told Emerald that she had an astounding knowledge of the classics. It is true. Talk was of George Eliot and English novelists. There seems to be no novel that Emerald hasn't read, and what's more, remembered.

Another attendee was Field Marshal Archibald Wavell, who was taken to the Dorchester by the great socialite 'Chips' Channon in 1943. The MP reported the occasion:

As soon we got back to London the FM changed from his blue flannel suit back into uniform and we drove to the Dorchester to dine with Lady Cunard. I had proposed ourselves, and was rather apprehensive lest her party would be more than usually ill-chosen, and it was a scrap Sunday collection of boys and girls. Bridget Parsons, Enid Paget, Jim Lees-Milne and James Pope-Hennessey. However, Wavell was in high spirits, and as he was treated like royalty, soon dominated the dinner and made it hilarious. Afterwards we were joined by Francis Queensberry and before long Wavell was quoting from Keats and Kipling, and it became a duel between him and Queensberry. Then we [were] interrupted by General Nye, the Vice-CIGS telephoning, and I had to escort him to King's Cross, where he was to board the special train to take him to an exercise in the North.

It was a decidedly aristocratic gathering, though there were two writers present, in the shape of James Lees-Milne and James Pope-Hennessey; the latter collaborated with Cecil Beaton on the illustrated book *History Under Fire* (1941), about the Blitz. John Lehmann remembered these gatherings as decidedly right-wing, comprising Conservatives such as Duff Cooper and his socialite wife Diana, where only the most established writers were admitted; whereas 'the attitude towards my own contemporaries, with few exceptions, [was] one of revulsion and rejection', The guests were, in his opinion, 'almost at times a caricature of the conventional aristocratic class-consciousness, though sustained with a wit and a vigour of mind that were delightful to anyone with an ear for dialogue'.

Lehmann thought the 'Ordinaries' of the interior designer Sybil Colefax to have a broader clientele – from Cabinet ministers, novelists and poets to theatrical stars, European royalty and American celebrities. But Harold Nicolson attended one in December 1942, and was not impressed: 'Everybody loathes them, and one feels a sort of community of dislike binding together what would otherwise be a most uncongenial company.'

Meanwhile, in Soho and Fitzrovia, but also in Chelsea, writers and artists continued to gather at the favoured pubs of bohemian London. It was in Chelsea that local resident, the Welsh artist-poet David Jones, spent time in either the Six Bells or, less frequently, the Eight Bells, meeting up a couple of times a day with writer-illustrator Mervyn Peake and painter Augustus John, and trying to ignore the inconveniences of the 'fucking sirens' that 'go just when you want to get somewhere'.

The gifted novelist Henry Green, pseudonym of Henry Yorke, in his Auxiliary Fire Service uniform outside the Ministry of Information. His service during the London Blitz inspired his novel *Caught* (1943). Its title was typically concise; other novels included *Living* (1929) and *Loving* (1945). Just before the outbreak of war he published what many came to regard as his masterpiece, *Party Going*.

A bewildered woman, wrapped in a blanket to keep out the winter cold, knows all too well what it means to be bombed out during the phase of bombing known as the Little Blitz (24 February 1944). Behind her, on the pile of mattresses, are what few possessions she and her neighbours have so far managed to salvage.

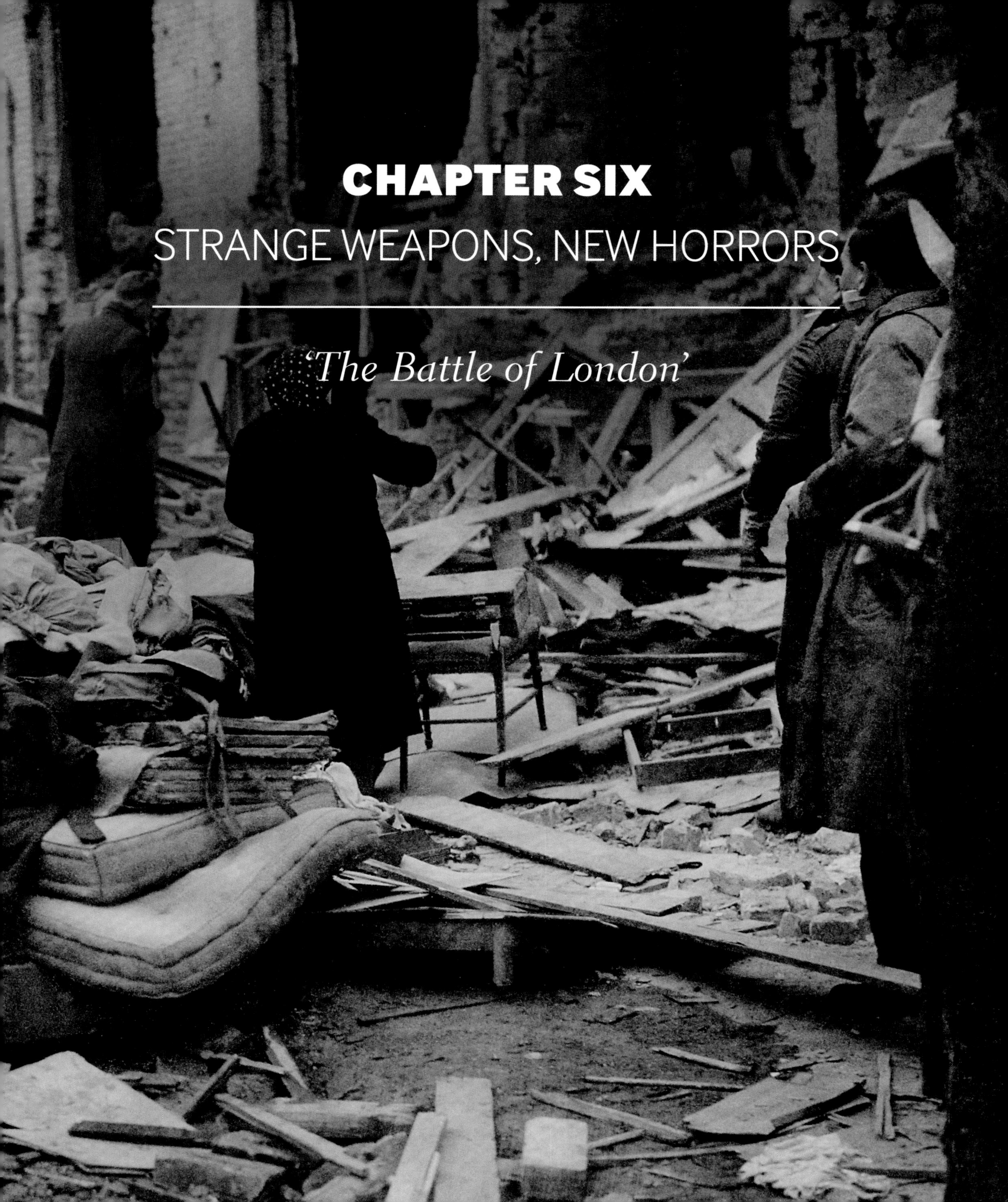

CHAPTER SIX

STRANGE WEAPONS, NEW HORRORS

'The Battle of London'

Following the intensity of the Blitz in 1940 and 1941, Britain was not entirely free from aerial bombing in 1942 and 1943. In the spring of 1942, in retaliation for an RAF raid on Lübeck, the Luftwaffe targeted England's historic and cathedral cities in the so-called 'Baedecker Raids' – named after the renowned German travel guides. Exeter, Bath, Norwich, York and Canterbury were all on the receiving end.

As for London, occasional daylight raids continued. One of the worst occurred on 20 January 1943, when Catford Central School for Girls and the adjoining primary school suffered a direct hit. The girls had been evacuated to Smarden and Charing in Kent, in 1939, but had, like so many other Londoners, drifted back to the city in the aftermath of the Blitz. In this incident, 38 children and 6 adults were killed, and pictures of the distressing scenes were banned by the censor. Towards the end of 1943, there were night raids on London, such as that of 7 November in which Putney Dance Hall was wrecked, killing 79 people in the process. The press, unable – as ever – to give specifics, described 'a Dance Hall above a Milk bar, in a High Street', in a 'London area'.

The authorities and Civil Defence services had learned valuable lessons during the Blitz, which had highlighted three main issues in particular: the poor provision for the homeless, the necessity of clearing debris, and the need for more, and better, air raid shelters. For the fire services, nationalisation had been completed by August 1941, bringing standardisation of equipment and drill. Fire prevention was aided by the formation of the Fire Guard Organisation – although unfortunately the experience of the Baedecker Raids exposed it as undermanned, badly led and ill-equipped. However, the end of the Blitz also pulled the authorities' attention away from Civil Defence, which consequently suffered a depletion in manpower. Its regional commissioner for London, Sir Ernest Gowers (author of the classic *Plain Words* writing guide), reported that morale within its various services had dropped dramatically.

The raids during 1942–3 turned out to be a kind of interlude, nothing like the Blitz – nor what was to come. The next phase of attacks on London acquired the name 'Baby Blitz' or 'Little Blitz', though this perhaps underplays its relative costliness. Called Operation 'Steinbock' by the Luftwaffe, this campaign was mounted in retaliation for RAF raids over Germany, and Berlin in particular, during late 1943. Thus, in the first months of 1944, a series of generally short attacks, each lasting just over an hour, targeted London, using new steel-nosed incendiaries (that could penetrate roofs) as well as incendiaries that

Ruskin Spear's *Scene in an Underground Train, 1943: Workers Returning From Night Shift* is a self-explanatory commission for the War Artists Advisory Committee. At this time in the war, the Underground was reasserting its primary role of transporting people across the city rather than sheltering them from danger, since the Luftwaffe attacks were isolated and intermittent.

exploded after a time delay, usually seven minutes after ignition. From mid-February particularly, the raids found their mark in a city again full of children, and swelled with service personnel.

For Gwladys Cox, the attacks that occurred on 18 February 1944 were 'So far, for us, one of the most terrible nights of the war!' Two days later, in Notting Hill, Vere Hodgson showed both great curiosity and a certain insouciance when raids hit again:

> Finally we decided to go up on the roof. Very cold as we climbed by the fire escape. Firewatchers were like ants below. White frost on all the roofs, and in the direction of Portobello Road there was

Bruised and battered, but flying the Union flag and gesturing 'V' for Victory, Mr and Mrs Jack Benady even manage a smile in front of what used to be their home (21 February 1944). The location is Gwendwr Gardens, Fulham, although it was described in 1944 as being in West Kensington.

> the sound of a crackling fire. We knew it was near. Other fires round about. We well deserved pneumonia, but could not resist such an amazing sight from the roof. We then had a cup of tea, refilled our hot water bottles and returned to bed, but it was long before I slept. Heard the fire engines clanging through the streets. Finally dropped off, thinking – Well, saved again.

The following day, she could see that 'Huge fires reddened the sky in all directions… Then all went quiet and we ventured into the Street. Pembridge Square seemed to be on fire.' She and her neighbours rushed to help, but 'We could do nothing and returned to our beds. I have never seen such a horrifying fire.' Nellie Carver was impressed by the barrage put up by the anti-aircraft guns, more than she had been during the Blitz. She wrote in her own diary for 22 February 1944:

> This was the most concentrated [raid] so far – guns nearly tearing the roof off – Rocket guns (like express trains) roaring overhead. How long the doors and windows will stand this – I don't know – or ourselves for that matter! I can't imagine what it must be like amongst those shells. London is hitting back with a vengeance! In 1940 we had to sit undefended almost for 7–8 hours & listen to bombs drop but now it's all over in an hour or so, if one can survive the bombardment.

When the Little Blitz struck, Londoners had got out of the habit of going to the Tube stations for shelter, and their Anderson shelters had often fallen into disrepair, while, by the end of February, only about 9,000 Morrison shelters had been dispensed in the London region. (In the end, 25,000 of the 100,000 ordered for Londoners were cancelled anyway, because of the steel shortage.) Moreover, of ten deep shelters planned in 1940 for construction underneath Tube stations, none were yet available for public use. However, as the raids intensified in February, the Underground was filling up again. Vere Hodgson noticed that the queues started at 4pm. She added that 'At Holland Park there are bunks for 500. They had had 1,500 people there this week. They sleep on the platforms. One night they had to send the train on as passengers could not alight among the sleepers.'

On 23 February, Central London was targeted. Chelsea, Fulham, Westminster were all hit badly, as was St James's Palace and the new wing of the private London Library in St James's Square. 'They think about 20,000 books are lost,' lamented James Lees-Milne, who worked for the National Trust and helped to salvage the damaged volumes. 'It is a tragic sight… The books lying torn and coverless scattered under debris and in a pitiable state, enough to make one weep.'

The suburbs were hit as hard as Central London. On 24 February in South London, West Norwood was struck by a large number of incendiaries resulting in one of the biggest fires of the Little Blitz and, accordingly, much damage. Yet still a 'business as usual' mentality was in evidence. One local shopkeeper placed a few bits of salvaged furniture and a huge Union Jack in the gaping hole where his shop window had been. The staff of the Post Office, who had had to leave their own building, established themselves in an empty wool shop, and, according to Nellie Carver, were 'working away as if nothing has happened'. It happened to be the beginning of 'Salute the Soldier' week which continued as planned and saw processions of tanks and armoured cars through London's streets. Even in the suburbs further south, in Coulsdon and Purley, 6,000 incendiaries fell during these attacks.

In March, the raids prompted Vivienne Hall to take shelter in an Underground station for the first time. It was a salutary experience:

> Ah well, what of this week – nothing, nothing at all! Just existence, with a raid on Wednesday to make the week seem like any other week – we were caught just as we were at Gloucester Road Station and as neither Cynthia nor I had been down to the a tube during a raid we thought we'd go. No, I shouldn't choose it, despite the fact you can hear nothing of the noises going on above. The long rows of people, young and incredibly old, huddled in all manner of rug, blanket, or coat on the bunks and on the platform itself, babies and youngsters sleeping muffled up in clothes and shawls; an array of bottles and jugs and tins of drink and food and parcels – parcels and bundles everywhere! These are the 'regulars' who come down night after night and stay until morning – the rest of us – hundreds – stood about the platforms, the wardens marshalling us hither and thither in an endeavour to keep clear lanes to the exits and every now and then a train screamed into the station and disgorged another crowd of people. Oh no, give me the risks above ground thank you, the mass of humanity and the total absence of knowing what is going on is, to me at any rate, most unpleasant.

The bombs continued to fall. Croydon was hit by as many as 3,000 incendiaries. Kathleen Church-Bliss and Elsie Whiteman were witnesses to some of them. They had run a restaurant in the Home Counties but volunteered for work at Croydon's Morrisons aircraft components factory, and they kept a joint diary. On 19 April 1944, 'An alert last night 1 a.m. Spasmodic firing and one very heavy bomb shook the house. The noisiest we have had here. A huge fire could be seen over Purley Way, near enough to see the flames.' A week later, a Morrisons factory inspector and his wife were 'both suffering from blast shock' after their house had been demolished by the bombs: they had both been in their shelter at the time.

The raid of 18–19 April turned out to be the last London raid of the Little Blitz. But Operation 'Steinbock' continued across Britain – targeting Hull, Bristol, Falmouth and Portsmouth – ending only at the end of May 1944. Although it had proved ineffective as a strategic attack on London, it had brought home to Londoners the evolving and ever present dangers of aerial attack. The campaign had also left 1,500 dead, of which the vast majority – 1,178 – were in London.

The next phase of aerial attack, over a longer period than the Little Blitz, was to prove deadlier still – and shocking to the people of London in many ways. One surprise was that Germany was even capable of mounting a renewed campaign. The Allied landings in Normandy on D-Day, 6 June 1944, appeared to herald the beginning of the end of a long and hard-fought war; it even eclipsed in the national press the capture of Rome just two days before by forces under US General Mark Clark. It was a time of excitement and a (sometimes disappointed) hunger for news, in which, on 10 June, Kathleen Church-Bliss and Elsie Whiteman 'chased all over Croydon to find a Cinema with Invasion news and finally pedalled all the way to Purley in order to get a decent film as well as the news. To our utter disgust there were no invasion pictures, not even Rome, and we felt completely swindled.' Three days later, Germany deployed a completely new weapon against London and other British targets: a flying bomb.

Back in April 1943, Duncan Sandys, Parliamentary Secretary to the Ministry of Supply and Churchill's son-in-law, had been appointed to investigate the threat of German rocket technology, which had been discovered through intelligence reports. Subsequent photo reconnaissance over the Baltic peninsula of Peenemünde revealed the development of German missiles – and prompted raids by Bomber Command, which slowed, but did not halt, the programme. Although the first of the new German weapons could not be deployed at the time of the Little Blitz, and although by February 1944 around three-quarters of the launch sites had been destroyed by British and US air attack, the threat remained. It became real on 13 June 1944.

On that day, the first *Vergeltungswaffe Eins* – 'Revenge Weapon No. 1' – hit London, one of four sent over early on 13 June. The V1, as it became known, was a small pilotless aircraft filled with high explosive, which made a sinister buzzing noise that stopped only when it was about to plummet to the ground. The jet-propelled weapon could reach up to 400 miles per hour, and could, on a 'good' day, travel 200 miles on a pre-set course, so that London and southern England were – for now – in range from the remaining bases across the Channel. On 13 June, the first strike hit a bridge in Bow, East London, destroying the nearby houses and killing six people.

Very soon, the attacks came with greater intensity. On 15 June, 244 missiles were fired, but 45 crashed after launching, and only 73 got through to London. Struggling to make sense of this new type of aerial attack, Nellie Carver wrote of that day:

> Had 'Red' [alert] at 11.35pm, such a strange noise the planes made – we were very scared, they sounded different & much quicker than usual & when our gunners fired at them it was after they had passed. There was no 'clear' given all night but long intervals of calm then planes again & loud bangs. We got up several times & had very little sleep. Something unpleasant was happening we know.

On 16 June, the strange new weapon had acquired, she noted, a name: 'pilotless planes' (PPs), a term used in a number of Londoners' diaries of the period, though other descriptions also sprang up – 'flying bombs', 'robot planes' or 'rockets'. They would become much better known by the strange sounds they made, in the US descriptions 'doodlebugs' or 'buzz bombs', though an even more inventive phrase was 'Bob Hopes', after the popular comedian: you bobbed up and down, and hoped they would fly over.

The very next day, Nellie Carver got to see her first 'PP' for herself:

> At about 6pm during another alert I looked out of the window & saw two of these brutes quite near sailing along together. They are like small planes, but with fire coming from their tails. A shot from a gun caught one & it exploded in the air with a tremendous bang. All our balloons have vanished, they have been taken to green spaces outside the city to try and trap the flying bombs. I suppose they are Hitler's Secret Weapon. They must be costly to produce & fire, but they save pilots' lives of course. Expect we shall think up an antidote in time. Sat night was noisier & more alarming than Friday, we were dazed with the row & had no sleep again. We certainly cannot stand too much of this.

Vivienne Hall was just one of many trying to acclimatise to the new circumstances:

> We little people are once more the target of an unpleasant 'secret weapon'. We waited patiently in our shelters for five hours last night and all that seemed to be happening was a burst of gunfire

Right and below In the V1 campaign, just as in the Blitz, it was the East End that was on the receiving end of the first strike, this time in Grove Road, in the Bow/Stepney area (now Tower Hamlets), on 13 June 1944. Here, Civil Defence workers, aided by a mobile crane, attempt to clear up the debris. All that remains of the railway bridge are the thin slivers of the rail tracks still connecting the two sides.

Not far from where Nellie Carver lived, PC Frederick Godwin (Stationed at Gypsy Hill) offers a consoling cup of tea to a man who has been widowed by a V1 hit on Upper Norwood (1944). As is evident from the wreckage, the unfortunate victim was also left homeless.

about every half an hour and in some cases, wrecked homes and casualties. This continued into the morning and I find that the Germans are now firing some sort of jet propelled missile from France straight over to London! It's most unpleasant and for the moment at any rate seems to be without redress. We have already been down the office shelter three times this morning. The balloons are down and one presumes that the gunners are trying to hit the things as they hurtle through the air for there are bursts of gunfire every now and again. The actual damage to the war effort seems to be negligible and so far at any rate it seems to be a colossal and hideous game of spite; just to send these things over haphazard to make life a chancy unpleasant thing for we miserable and long-suffering Londoners.

Croydon would have the misfortune to become the most frequently hit target area of the V1s. Kathleen Church-Bliss and Elsie Whiteman registered the strangeness of an early attack there, on 16 June:

> On firewatch last night and to our surprise the alert went at 11.30 and we rushed out to Duppas Hill. A very peculiar raid which we couldn't understand. No fighters were up and no gunfire, but a good many very heavy explosions were heard and several planes roared overhead very low. It went on for hours and we got colder and hungrier every minute, as we have to stand on the steps of the shelter, with nothing to sit on and no cover over our heads. Hour after hour went by and still no all clear. Finally the dawn came and still there were gun-flashes and intermittent firing. At about 4 a.m. what seemed like a very low plane swished overhead and released a bomb about ½ mile beyond Waddon station. Terrific explosion and a great flash and sparks and debris flew up in every direction... At 6 a.m. we came in even though the all clear hadn't gone. We cooked breakfast with frequent interruptions caused by heavy gunfire and low flying machines. We finally went off in our tin hats and on arrival were sent straight to the shelters. The factory Home Guard had been on duty all night and the first person we saw was our dear Joe Phillips [with whom they spent lunchtimes] looking very tired and green. He is highly excitable and was obviously very much worked up. We soon learnt that this peculiar raid was not being made by bombers, but by pilotless aircraft, fired from France. This information was startling, and as the weather was very stormy and lowering, the feeling of tension was acute. When the all clear went at 8.30 a.m. Mr Proctor [Managing Director and Captain of the factory Home Guard] addressed us over the microphone and explained that these raids were expected to last all day and might be continuous. The factory siren would give warning and we were then to go at once to the shelters, unless the 'crash' warning was sounded, in which case we were to throw ourselves on the floor immediately. Everyone was very excitable... The rest of the day was spent in bobbing up and down to the shelters a great many times.

One V1 fell about 150 yards (140 metres) from their house, but luckily it only damaged the front door.

Worried at the possible effects on morale, the authorities responded to these early V1 attacks by trying to shroud them under a veil of secrecy. Home Secretary Herbert Morrison ordered that they not be reported in the press, and tried to reassure his Cabinet colleagues that the effect of a V1 was little greater than a parachute mine and less than a 2,000-pound bomb.

The assault continued. On 18 June, the third V1 attack on Westminster hit the Guards Chapel at Wellington Barracks. It proved to be one of the worst incidents of the whole V1 campaign, killing 119 people – mainly servicemen – and seriously injuring another 102, some of whom later died. James Lees-Milne wrote in his diary:

> In St. James's Park crowds of people were looking at the Guards Chapel across Birdcage Walk, now roped off. I could see nothing but gaunt walls standing, and gaping windows. No roof at all. While I watched four stretcher bearers carry a body under a blanket, the siren went, and everyone scattered. I felt suddenly sick. Then a rage of fury against the war welled up inside me.

The attack had also blown in most of the windows at the War Office, as noted by General Alan Brooke in his own diary. Two of his friends had died in the chapel, and he could not get them out of his mind. The King and Queen, too, lost many friends to this V1.

The V1 campaign heralded a new round of damage to London's landmarks. The Tate Gallery, Natural History Museum, British Museum and Royal Observatory in Greenwich were all struck, as was Buckingham Palace – twice, on 21 and 26 June. The latter V1 destroyed the King's tennis court and shattered many windows in the palace. Yet the Royal Family remained there throughout. As a concession, King George did move his weekly Tuesday lunchtime meeting with the prime minister to the palace shelter.

Although Londoners were well aware of what was happening, there was still no official reference to London being targeted by these new weapons. George Britton was under no illusions, writing to his daughter on 21 June 1944 about 'the thing which everybody is talking and thinking about… the new German secret weapon':

> Of course, it is neither new nor secret. We knew about sort of thing long ago but the brass hats, the Colonel Blimps, couldn't see its possibilities. People, and more than one, have said to me, 'It is a dirty way of waging a war.' Just as if there was such a thing as a 'clean war'. War's a dirty business and everybody and everything connected with it gets more or less smudged.

Above and above right
Interior and aerial views of the destruction wrought in one of the most deadly V1 strikes, at the Wellington Barracks' Guards Chapel on 18 June 1944. It was a Sunday, and the chapel had filled with hundreds of service personnel, including senior officers, and civilians for the morning service. More than 220 of them lay dead or injured afterwards.

> Of course, you know quite as much as we do about this new 'Bumblebomb'. Maybe a good deal more. Besides, if you don't, by the time you get this information [anything] I might write would be ancient history by the time it reached you, even if the censor allowed it to reach you at all. I only know that the bang is very loud and the blast seems to wipe out everything in its path but it doesn't seem to make craters in the grounds that the bombs did. The uncertainty as to when we shall hear 'Wailing Winnie' next and how long the 'Alert' will last is very disturbing. I must admit that if the object is robbing people of their sleep there is a large measure of success.

He was right in that the sheer unpredictability of attacks from individual V1s created a new kind of stress for Londoners. He added on 28 June 1944 that 'The sound of the flying bomb, buzz bomb, or as the Americans have christened them Doodle Bugs, is rather terrifying and even when the engine stops and you are waiting for the bang it can be quite nerve racking'. Author Evelyn Waugh, no stranger to danger from his Commando service on Crete, recorded on 24 June: 'I heard one flying near and low and for the first and I hope the last

Shattered exhibition cases in the Natural History Museum, South Kensington. On 11 July 1944 a V1 exploded on Cromwell Road, outside the museum's West Wing. The greatest damage was sustained by the museum's Bird Gallery.

time in my life was frightened'. Vivienne Hall 'thought the blitzes frightening enough but this horrible machine is worse, you are always listening, always waiting for the drone of machinery which drives the pilotless plane nearer and nearer – oh hell, its a hateful business!' The YMCA canteen at Victoria where she worked witnessed one of the V1 strikes, causing 17 fatalities. She tried to cheer herself up with some 'wonderful' war news from the fighting fronts:

> ... gains everywhere, Cherbourg ours, the Russians surging forward toward Poland and Germany, the Germans being pushed back in Italy, the Japanese suffering heavily on all sides – it is just a question of time I think and if we can only survive these flying-bombs and any other 'secret' weapon which will no doubt be hurtled at us, we shall see the end of the war....

A V1, identifiable by a shadowy outline and fiery glow, streaks across the London skyline as searchlights try to penetrate the darkness, in Frederick T W Cook's oil painting *A Flying Bomb Over Tower Bridge* (1944).

Despite new realities, life had to carry on, and people had to get used to seeking shelter again. During the V1 attacks, about 75,000 people took to the Underground stations, while at the end of June 1944, Ellen Wilkinson was informing the Civil Defence Committee that 20,000 Morrison shelters had been issued, and another 4,000 per week were being distributed. During July, the first of the deep shelters were opened, and eventually there were eight, each catering to 8,000 people, and lying 80–100 feet (up to 30 metres) underground. By the end of June's V1 attacks, London had seen almost 1,700 people killed and another 5,000 seriously injured. In addition, 270,000 houses had been damaged, 7,000 of them completely destroyed. At least the rest centres were holding up.

But Londoners were exhausted. The constant threat meant very little sleep, as Vivienne Hall confided to her diary: 'Tiredness is on us again and it seems we shall never really enjoy life again, but we just live on from day to day, week to week, heaven alone knows what for?!'

It was not until 6 July 1944 that the first statistics about the attacks were released and Churchill spoke in Parliament about the V1 menace. Nellie Carver noted that although it was one of the prime minister's fighting speeches, 'we in London feel very depressed'. She thought the lack of sleep hit morale harder than anything else. Two weeks later, on 20 July, she was herself caught up in a V1 strike, which hit her workplace, the Northern Assurance Company in Moorgate:

> On Wednesday morning I got to the Bank station and as I walked up Princes Street I heard the danger overhead warnings from the Banks – I didn't know there was an alert on even, but quickened my pace and arrived at the Northern and was waiting for the lift when all hell was let loose about me. A deafening roar and a sickening thud, followed by our huge eight-foot windows crashing in, frame and all, plaster and glass careering down the lift shafts. I crouched under a counter and waited for the ceilings to come down but after a few seconds things stopped falling and we who were in the department slowly got up to survey the damage. A thick cloud of dust obscured our view for a bit but as this cleared we saw that the windows and doors and fittings were all over the place and the building opposite was a horrible sight. The bomb had struck there and the inner roof had collapsed. Almost immediately the Civil Defence services and police started getting out casualties, poor dirty bleeding people. I wondered if our top floors had gone and dashed to the first aid room to get to work there. By a miracle we had no bad casualties in the 'Northern' – about twenty cases of cuts, not bad ones and a few cases of shock – that's all. Had it been after instead of just before 9.30 we should of course have had many more people in the office – but all morning we had a steady stream of girls and men wanting tea and attention for cuts, for our men and a number of the younger girls set to at once and with every available weapon cleared the glass and broken wood from the departments and stairways, and even got up the carpets! All this despite the fact that alerts and danger overhead signals were going all the morning! The coolness and bravery of these people is wonderful really. Stayed at the office until 3.45 on first aid duty and then as everyone had gone home we also went home – oh I was tired and I suppose it was a bit upsetting. When I began to think of those heavy windows and the lumps of glass and stuff that had fallen around me as I crouched under a most inadequate counter I realised what an amazing escape I had had.

In the aftermath of a V1 hit on St John's Hill, Battersea, South London (17 June 1944), a casualty is stretchered away as crowds look on. A pub, several houses and at least one trolleybus were damaged, and there was one fatality: a 14-year-old girl. The unpredictability of when or where a V1 incident would happen played on the nerves of exhausted Londoners.

HR

Opposite A pall of smoke rises in Central London from a V1 incident in Drury Lane, near the Aldwych (30 June 1944). Some people rush to get a better view, but others scurry away anxiously. By this time, in just over two weeks of V1 strikes, the death toll had reached 1,700, with three times that number seriously injured.

As if that wasn't enough, on 29 July a V1 landed in Nellie Carver's street. Luckily, her house was declared safe by the Wardens and surveyors, although it took four days to clear up the damage, during which time she slept in a friend's shelter. The experiences had done nothing for her nerves: 'Am more scared than ever I'm afraid – oh dear, oh dear.'

'Blitz spirit' was harder to come by during the V-weapons attacks – the lack of a pattern or routine to the attacks frayed people's nerves. To try and get sufficient warning, many houses used their own private roof spotters. Quite often these would be teenagers, who blew a whistle to warn neighbours of an impending attack. One Warden in Carshalton even employed the services of her two-and-a-half-year-old daughter who would shout 'Doodlebug, Mummy!' when she heard the familiar drone – before rushing inside to the Morrison shelter.

There were fewer children in London now, because – once again – an official evacuation had got underway. By September 1944 there were just over a million official evacuees, and an even larger number of unofficial ones who headed out of town under their own steam. Among older children who remained in London, the flying bombs were a source of fascination as well as fear, and some avidly collected V1 relics (identifiable via *Aeroplane Spotter* magazine). For John Simonson and his brother, at Highgate School in North London, 'one wet dull June morning' became considerably more interesting when:

> ... a V1 came down just inside the playing field, but we all mostly had lucky escapes. The morning break had just started, so that there was a lot of noise and chatter. Suddenly above this we could hear a very loud noise of the V1, the engine did not cut out, and there was a brilliant orange flash, but strangely no noise other than local sounds of glass and plaster and things falling around. A few minutes earlier my class had been sitting with our backs to large windows that opened out on the field, and of the windows there was nothing left. My brother was in another building and he can remember the linoleum on the floor being whipped up by the blast to give some sort of protective wall!

Islington school-leaver Harry Atterbury, now an engineering apprentice, had an even narrower escape from his Queensbury Street home:

On a quiet Sunday morning [18 June], after a warning had sounded, and after I had promised to leave my bed to follow my parents who had left the house to take shelter in the brick street shelters, a V1 crashed at the corner of the street about 200 feet away. My parent's home was completely demolished with me underneath. I was still alive because my bedroom door had blown inwards, twisted in the air and somehow fallen over the bed, resting on the top and bottom bed frames, creating a space in which I was saved from being crushed. The door held the debris off me. I soon regained consciousness, choked with the soot, dust and smoke; terrified by the noises, shouts and screaming. My reaction was to struggle and shout until I suddenly noticed a chink of light to one side above me through which I eventually pushed my hand. This action led to a frantic effort to get to me by some rescue workers who had seen the movement and as I was pulled out quite naked and bleeding from the numerous abrasions caused mostly by flying glass and scratches from jagged wood, I had a coat or a blanket around me and was carefully carried in the arms of one of the rescuers, up and over the debris of my home.

At the same moment of time I saw my mother and father framed by what was left of the front door jambs, standing crying and in a state of shock, hardly believing that they could see and hear me again. After they had been reassured that I was not seriously hurt, we were led through the smoking rubble and past so many people tearing at and digging into the ruins of other houses, where other people were still buried.

The three were led to the Underground Station at Essex Road for emergency help and then went to stay with Harry's sister Ada, who lived in Hackney.

Complicating the care of the injured was the fact that V1s struck a number of London hospitals. St Helier Hospital in Carshalton was unlucky enough to be hit twice, on 21 June and then again on 27 June. In the first attack, 12 nurses were injured, the medical superintendent's house was demolished, and the doctor on duty was nowhere to be found. It turned out he had crawled to the operating theatre while seriously injured and needed an operation to his head. At least there were no fatalities. Mrs Ingeborg Samson, a refugee from Germany in 1939 who was now working as a St Helier nurse, witnessed both attacks. During the first, together with her two best friends, she thought her number was up: 'The bombing was so heavy during the night that we slept part of it in the corridor when we heard the motor of a flying bomb cut out above us prior to crashing. We said to each other, "Good-bye, it was nice knowing you."'

The second attack landed between the two wings of the hospital. As she remembered:

> I went off duty at 9 p.m., rang the bell for the lift, changed my mind and started to walk down the four flights of stairs. I heard a doodlebug, then it crashed with engines still running onto our roof. The building shook as if in an earthquake. I heard terrible screams and crashes, plaster crashed down and I bruised my shoulders. The lift which I had nearly taken crashed from the fourth floor down into the basement.
>
> I ran to the ground floor ward, the air raid casualty ward, which was on fire. I could scarcely see or breathe for smoke. I put a damp handkerchief over my nose and mouth.
>
> There were already soldiers and fire fighters on the ward. At the entrance of the ward I saw a dead 12 year old girl lying on the floor.

The little girl was not the only fatality. A male nurse, identifiable only by his watch, had also been killed. On 9 July, two wards at St Helier were reopened. But two days earlier, Ingeborg Samson found 'the whole district was devastated by flying bombs. 90% of the houses were damaged or destroyed.'

Despite the fear and unpredictability that the V1s brought to London, the weapons had vulnerabilities that could be exploited – and they were brought down in increasing numbers during the summer of 1944. London was better defended than in 1940, and London's civil defence infrastructure was now much better equipped to cope with aerial attacks. For daylight attacks, standing RAF patrols flew at 12,000 feet over England's south coast, and when an attack was imminent further aircraft would patrol at 6,000 feet. With better technology, night attacks were countered by fighters under various forms of radar control. On the ground, London was reinforced with 192 heavy and 246 (later reduced to 192) light anti-aircraft guns and 480 balloons. Protecting London too were 376 heavy and 392 light guns (by July 1944) in southern England, along with 1,750 balloons and nearly 600 light guns manned by the Royal Air Force Regiment on the south coast.

A somewhat grainy photograph reveals a V1 mid-flight, moments before its destruction by the cannon of an RAF fighter (July 1944). The image was captured by the fighter's gun camera. The Royal Air Force became increasingly adept at bringing down the V1s, as did the anti-aircraft guns below.

In action against the V1s were thirteen squadrons of single-engine fighters and nine Mosquito squadrons, which were able to destroy about one in three V1s. The guns were less successful, accounting for about one in ten, but their effectiveness was improved after they were moved nearer the coast and could make better use of radar technology. In late July 1944, therefore, 23,000 personnel went to the south coast to man the quantities of heavy and light guns, which augmented those of the Royal Air Force Regiment (and 28 from the Royal Armoured Corps). By August there were 800 heavy guns, 1,800 light guns and more than 700 rocket-barrels deployed against the flying bombs, with increasing success. The statistics for just one day, 28 August 1944, are telling: out of 97 V1s sent over, the guns destroyed 65, fighters intercepted 23, balloons stopped 2 – and only 4 reached London.

For those that got through, London was better adapted to cope. Anderson and Morrison shelters proved very effective against V1s – indeed, historian Norman Longmate called the summer of 1944 the 'finest hour' of the Morrison shelter, which saved people as their houses collapsed around them. The surface shelters proved popular, too, because they could stand up to the blasts.

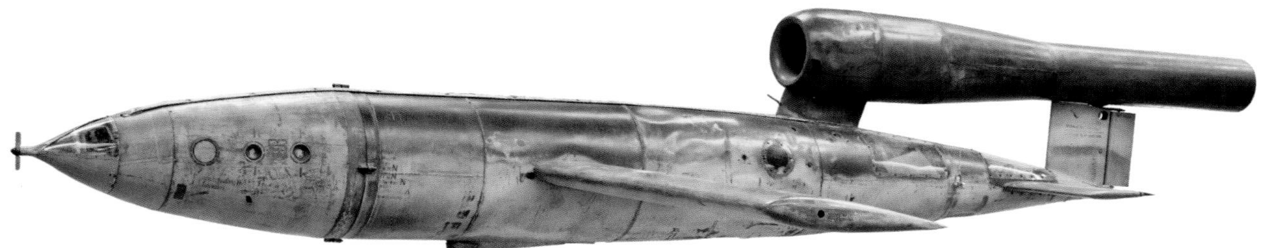

This surviving example of a jet-propelled Fieseler Fi-103 *Vergeltungswaffe Eins* – the V1 – clearly did not fulfil its destructive purpose. It was acquired by the Imperial War Museum in 1946, and it still bears its wartime paint.

Similarly, the Civil Defence services were more than capable of dealing with all that the V1s brought. The old Rescue and Stretcher Parties were formed into a rescue service; Civil Defence Warden's Posts were continually manned, as the V1s could come at any hour. Wardens who had been working in industry were recalled, part-timers went full time, and volunteers were drafted in from outside London – more than 1,000 Wardens were reallocated to London. The unified and streamlined National Fire Service used its own elevated observation posts (complete with field telephones and floodlights), which meant that its personnel were often at incidents before the local Wardens. Five thousand labourers toiled to clear the rubble and bomb sites created by the V1s, and to keep traffic flowing. All these services were augmented by the WVS, who staffed a system of Incident Inquiry Points: there were 778 of them in London by the end of August 1944.

One difference from the Blitz was that families were moved back into their houses as soon as possible after attacks, to prevent looting. The Queen's Messenger Convoys, funded by the United States and Commonwealth countries, and helped by the WVS and other voluntary charities (such as the Salvation Army), provided sustenance to Londoners bombed out of their homes; they were now split into smaller units to distribute to those affected. In Beckenham, South-East

The British Restaurant on the St Helier Estate, Carshalton, Croydon, shows its damage from a V1 that struck on 6 July 1944. Croydon was not called 'Doodle-bug Alley' for nothing.

London, the WVS served no less than 101,407 cups of tea during the V1 campaign – nearly 1,500 cups per flying bomb.

At the same time, social life carried on. During the V1 attacks, most London theatres and cinemas remained open, including all 15 West End cinemas, showing films such as *The Way Ahead* (1944; starring David Niven) about the British Army, and the always popular *Gone With the Wind*. The highest grossing film of 1944 was the David Lean-directed *This Happy Breed*, adapted from Noël Coward's drama tracking the lives of a lower-middle-class family over the interwar years. All the theatres escaped V1 damage. The Granada cinema in East Ham was somewhat less fortunate, suffering damage from three hits on the night of 28 July – but it reopened three weeks later.

The V1 campaign petered out from September 1944. Herbert Morrison, in a speech of 6 September, declared that 'Hitler has already lost the Battle of London' a verdict later confirmed by Duncan Sandys in a press conference. By October 1944, the last French launch site within range of Britain had been captured. But, despite the recent successes in interception, the campaign had taken quite a toll. Out of the 6,000 deaths across the country, more than 5,000 (5,126 to be exact) were in London, where in excess of 2,400 V1s had fallen. Almost 15,000 Londoners had been seriously injured, with another 25,000 hurt. London's hospitals had lost 2,600 beds permanently, 6,000 temporarily.

Croydon was hit by more V1s (140) than any other London borough, giving it its nickname – according to Kathleen Church-Bliss and Elsie Whiteman – of 'Doodle-bug Alley', although its casualty rate (215 dead, 705 badly injured) was disproportionately low. Other South London boroughs hit hard were Wandsworth (126), Lewisham (117), Camberwell (82), Woolwich (82), and Greenwich and Lambeth (73 each), while suburbs such as Coulsdon and Purley (58) and Mitcham (46) suffered too. And yet, Londoners had again got used to things. The V1 campaign had – after the initial scares and shocks – not destroyed morale. By the end, Vivienne Hall, for one, could remark on the absence of 'panic of the Londoner' and was taking it all in her stride: 'damn, there goes another beauty – more homes are being wrecked and more people are homeless but we're still all here and working!'

This was not quite the end of the V1s. After a time, German forces managed to carry on V1 operations from the Occupied Netherlands, including mid-air launches from bombers. But the sting had gone from the tail. Moreover, it was replaced almost immediately by something more sinister: the V2 rocket. This would prove an altogether more serious threat, and it arrived without missing a beat, and without any warning drone, at 6.45pm on 8 September 1944. The new *Vergeltungswaffe* was a 46-foot-long (14-metre) rocket-propelled ballistic missile. It could be launched more than 50 miles up into the stratosphere from mobile vehicles, and could deliver a ton of explosive at supersonic speed to a target up to 220 miles away, taking around 5 minutes to get there. Both the RAF and anti-aircraft guns were impotent in the face of the V2.

Three people died when that first V2 hit Staveley Road, Chiswick, and another ten were seriously injured. Seven houses were immediately demolished, another five wrecked beyond repair, and there was a 40-foot (12-metre) crater. Blast damage also affected another 600 houses within a 600 yard radius. It was fortunate that many of the inhabitants had not yet returned from work, otherwise the death toll would surely have been much higher. Just sixteen seconds later, another V2 landed on the other side of London, in Epping. The explosions were heard for miles around, including by Vere Hodgson, though she clearly didn't realise what they signified:

> Tonight, however, at a quarter to seven, a Terrible Explosion rent the air, followed by a low rumble. I nearly leapt out of my skin. No

> Warning on. So it could not be the new secret weapon. Perhaps it was an explosion at the munitions factory, or a bomb of long delayed action. All the Old Dears much upset...

This was the beginning of a campaign that would see more than a thousand V2s launched towards London.

Herbert Morrison, Ellen Wilkinson and the Regional Commissioner of Civil Defence, Admiral Sir Edward Evans, immediately visited the Chiswick site. Once again, the government, worried about morale, was secretive and quickly adopted a 'silence' policy. It proved remarkably successful, with many Londoners not realising how serious and widespread the scale of the V2 attacks actually was – they were usually reported in the press as 'gas main explosions'. Not everyone was fooled, though, and London remained abuzz with, as Vivienne Hall put it, 'Great Talk of the secret V2 which is said to be a rocket weighing 2 ton which hurtles down on us quicker than sound and leaves a crater 25ft deep... most of us in London think the mysterious bangs have been these same V2s.'

Ten days after the Chiswick attack, on 18 September, a V2 fell quite near to Nellie Carver's West Norwood home on Tulsemere Road. It was her birthday and four years to the day since she, her mother and her aunt had been bombed out of their home on Idmiston Road. Come October, Vivienne Hall's office was hit too: 'we are once more being patched up and managing to carry on somehow'. At least there was one piece of good news. In September 1944, the blackout was relaxed into a 'dim out'. After all, it didn't make any difference to a V2 rocket whether it was dark or light.

From November 1944, between three and five rockets a day were launched. Not every one reached its target – about one in ten exploded in the air, and many went astray. On 2 November, one stuck in the trees outside a hospital in Banstead, killing three and seriously injuring eleven. But nearly all of the worst incidents occurred in London.

Finally, on 10 November 1944 Churchill acknowledged the reality of the V2s in the House of Commons, justifying the earlier silence on the grounds of not giving information away to the enemy. The real reason was that the cat was already out of the bag, following coverage of the V2s in the German press. Mollie Panter-Downes told her *New Yorker* readers on 16 November 1944:

A V2 missile, as preserved in the Imperial War Museum, London. Its rocket and warhead had a combined height of more than 14 metres, and its warhead weighed as much as 1,000kg out of an overall launch weight, including fuel, of 12,650kg (around 13 tons). It could travel at 3,500 feet per second to drop silently on its target.

> Prime Minister Churchill's statement, which made it all right to talk out loud about V-2 instead of cautiously referring to it as if it were something supernatural which had dropped in somehow and made a big hole in the back yard, came as a relief to the inhabitants of southern England. The Government's secrecy and the ordinary public's silence since the first of 'those new things' arrived have both been amazing. The new bombs had been expected for so long that by the time they did turn up a lot of people had reached a state of scepticism and for a while they thought the distant, unheralded explosions were anything from a stray robot to a thunderstorm. Even when it became apparent that the V-2 was a reality, nobody mentioned the thing by name in public. Perhaps because of deliberately planted rumours, the first big, mysterious explosion was ascribed to a bursting gas main, and that fiction was solemnly maintained for days by people who must have known better but who wagged their heads and said that it was extraordinary how many gas mains had been reported going up lately. This conspiracy to gloss over a topic which everybody was naturally longing to discuss gave most people's faces a taut look which suggested that they themselves were on the verge of exploding. To the strain of this self-imposed censorship was added a flood of anxious letters from relatives in other parts of England who had heard the usual elaborate stories of disaster.

She then considered the relative hazards of the two V-weapons:

> Now that the secret is out, the great question is whether the rocket is worse than the robot bomb. Jumpy folk are inclined to believe that they prefer the robot because it could at least be detected by the defences in time to sound a warning. The V-2, with nasty abruptness, just arrives. 'If I'm going to be killed,' one lady remarked, 'I would like to have the excitement of knowing it's going to happen.' However, the majority of Britons philosophically declare that nights without sirens are worth the hazard of unpredictable blots from the stratosphere. So far, morale has stood up well under the V-2s, and there has been nothing approaching the dismay that the flying bombs created. There has been little or no precautionary evacuation of people from London. The city continues to be jammed with cheerful crowds who you might think that never heard of any rockets more deadly than the ones shot off on Guy Fawkes Day.

'Practically all the grumbling during the period of censorship,' she added, 'was directed at the Government's policy of silence, since the British always feel aggrieved if bad news is withheld.'

Mollie Panter-Downes was, perhaps, a little too sanguine about morale. The V1s were not quite over, and the V2s continued to fall on London – 26 of them between 15 and 22 November. In Bethnal Green, 25 people died in a single attack. At the same time, Britain was entering an unbearably cold snap. Gwladys Cox confided she was:

> Colder than ever! I am writing this lying on my bed, fully dressed. The V-1s and V-2s are so frequent we never know! However, if a rocket bomb did hit this block we should simply disappear, together with all our possessions. We Londoners are certainly going through a time of terrible strain.

On 20 November, Helena Britton wrote to her daughter: 'I just can't concentrate these days, everything is so unsettled, and I am very nervy,

A scene of devastation, which the press described as a 'mystery explosion' somewhere in 'Southern England' – and the censor's cross tries to keep it mysterious. In reality, this was the first V2 strike on London, in Staveley Road, Chiswick (8 September 1944), the beginning of yet another phase of aerial attack on the capital. Only Antwerp was targeted with V2s in a similarly sustained way.

in fact I feel things are getting me down, I don't think I could carry on if Dad were not at home.' The lack of warning as to when or where a V2 might strike was taking its toll. Two days later, her husband George could report:

> We've just had a 'big bang'. One of the rockets which you have heard about. When a fly-bomb is on its way we have an air-raid warning and dash for the shelter, but with these things you get no notice. They just come like bolts from the blue, or bolts from the black according to whether the visitation is in the day time or night time. A peculiar feature of these particular machinations of the devil is that owing to the fact that they travel faster than sound you hear the noise of its progress through the air 2, 3 or 4 seconds after you have had the noise of the explosion. It is no good worrying about them. If you hear the bang you are out of danger.

A V2 is prepared for launch, perhaps against London, from somewhere in Europe. The photograph gives a sense of the sheer size of the rocket and warhead when set against the technicians preparing it .The missile's engine used alcohol and liquid oxygen as propellant, but the fuel demands of the V2s were a drain on the dwindling resources of the German war effort.

Gwladys Cox echoed this description of weapons whose 'entirely silent approach cannot be heralded by sirens and [it's] clear weather does not deter them. Travelling faster than sound, they are well-nigh impossible to stop.' The following week, 40 more V2s targeted London, including one that hit a Woolworth's store in New Cross (25 November) and killed 160 people.

Randolph Schwabe's sketch depicts the Royal Hospital, Chelsea, in the aftermath of the V2 incident there on 3 January 1945, which killed the Captain of the Invalids. The artist was under commission to the War Artists Advisory Committee; he was paid 12 guineas for this particular drawing.

The festive season brought little relief. On Boxing Day evening, a V2 struck near the Prince of Wales pub on the corner of Mackenzie and Holloway roads, Islington. The cellar of the pub was being used as a bar, and 165 of the customers – nearly all of the number present – were killed or badly injured from the debris crashing down. The landlord, his wife and the barmaid, who were on the ground floor, were lucky enough to escape with minor injuries, but around the pub more than 40 shops and houses were destroyed or damaged beyond repair. New Year's Eve brought more misery when a V2 landed on Crouch Hill, North London, killing 15 and leaving 34 seriously injured. Gwladys Cox, who was listening to the wireless, registered the impact: 'After the watch-night service at St. Paul's, I felt the familiar vibration of a rocket bomb and could swear that during the pealing of the bells I also heard an explosion.' It was, she later discovered, 'A disastrous New Year for our old friend Miss G. of Crouch Hill! She sits today shivering in the kitchen, with all the windows in her house blasted and the top floor uninhabitable.'

On 3 January 1945, it was Chelsea's turn, when a V2 hit the Royal Hospital, killing two members of staff and three Chelsea Pensioners. It was the only V2 to fall on Chelsea, but it happened to land in the same place as a German bomb dropped in 1918. On that earlier occasion, the Captain of the Invalids had escaped death, but this time the holder of that position was not so fortunate. A couple of days later, James Lees-Milne, who lived nearby in Cheyne Walk, remarked on this rocket, which:

> ... fell on Tuesday morning with a terrific explosion and roar on the eastern wing of Wren's Chelsea Hospital, completely wrecking it and breaking windows for miles around... The V2 has become more alarming than the V1, quite contrary to what I thought at first, because it gives no warning sound. One finds oneself waiting for it and jumps out of one's skin at the slightest bang or unexpected noise, like a car backfire or even a door slam.

It was to be the coldest January for more than fifty years, during which time the hands on Big Ben froze. Adding to the problems was a fuel crisis, so it was harder to keep warm, as James Lees-Milne felt acutely: 'The cold persists. It is appalling, and I have run out of anthracite.' Morale could have plummeted, but, after several months of V2 attacks, Londoners were grimly learning to live with them – as best they could.

As during the main V1 campaign, theatres and cinemas remained open – though the East Ham Granada suffered the misfortune of more damage to its doors and windows from a V2 in late 1944. At three in the morning of 1 February 1945, it was the turn of the West Ham Kinema to be hit: it happened to have been the first London cinema damaged in the Blitz, and it would turn out to be the last to be hit during the V2 campaign. On this occasion, after the doors, windows and roof were all blown out, the manager and two helpers stayed up all night trying to make repairs; the cinema reopened the next day at 1.30pm, just an hour later than usual, and even though the V2s kept coming: one exploded in the air over nearby Barnaby Street, killing 48 people. The film being shown was *Tender Comrade*, starring Ginger Rogers. Noting that the takings were down, the seemingly imperturbable manager could 'only put this down to the V.2s we are having here, though our patrons were a bit disappointed Ginger Rogers did not dance in this film.' Overall, although London cinema audiences did dip during the Blitz and the V1 attacks, numbers remained as high during the V2 campaign as they did in 1943.

If some people chose no longer to venture out to the theatre or cinema, others were taking their place; and a younger generation of service personnel continued to party in London. Mollie Panter-Downes painted a generally upbeat picture for her American readers:

> Outwardly at least, the London crowds seem to be not especially troubled by the danger, although the tubes are again filled up every evening with shelterers who feel happier if they are sleeping deep. The theatres and

> cinemas are losing the business of customers who feel that it's better to take precautions than be sorry, but the V-bombs have not affected such established sellouts as the Lunts, who have opened at the Lyric with their usual much-admired performance in a not much-admired play called *Love in Idleness*. The big funny-man shows starring the English comedians Tommy Trinder and Sid Fields [*sic*] are also booked for weeks ahead. Even the audiences at the musicals appear to have come out dressed to meet any emergency, from bombs to a long tramp home. It is rumoured that in the Midlands and the North the prosperous manufacturers' wives are regularly putting on long evening dresses, but the women in the London theatre audience usually look as if they had come straight from their jobs. The young things who go out and dance at night get themselves up rather more festively and every dance place in London is jammed with boys and girls on leave. If they have money to burn, they dance at the Mirabelle, Manetta's, the Four Hundred, or one of the big hotels. Those who can't afford such places dance at the Stage Door Canteen or at one of the big dance halls, where you can have hours of swing for about half a crown. Dancing is having a healthy boom right now despite the menace in the stratosphere.

The menace was indeed ever-present. March 1945 witnessed further devastating attacks, as when 129 died in Smithfield Market (8 March). One V2 struck the Finchley Road on 17 March, very near to Gwladys Cox's home, although she and her husband were away on holiday. By 20 March she was back, and:

> After tea, we took a walk along the Finchley Road and saw the bomb damage to the public library. The building had been cut clean in half and there is a huge crater, like that of a small volcano, in the adjoining gardens. There was a notice posted up in the library gate as to the latest V Bomb casualties.

Those casualties numbered a hundred-and-twenty-eight. One of the last V2 incidents was also one of the most catastrophic, when, on 27 March, a block of flats in Stepney – the borough that had suffered so much in the Blitz – was destroyed, causing more than 130 deaths.

The last V2 to hit Britain fell short of London, landing in Kent on 29 March 1945. Just the day before, the last V1 had landed in Hertfordshire. Indeed, over that month only 13 of the V1s had managed to penetrate to London, out of more than 270 launched. By this time, the Allied advance had crossed the Rhine had overrun any remaining

V1 facilities as well as the V2 storage sites and areas for the mobile launchers, which were often in forests. By April, Allied bombers were destroying the V2 production site at Nordhausen, where the weapons had been manufactured by forced labour in appalling conditions. In London there was a palpable sense of relief, as expressed by Vere Hodgson on 9 April:

> No more bombs for more than a week. No one knows what it means to us to go to bed in peace, and not take leave of all our possessions, and wonder if we shall wake up in pieces, or with the roof collapsing on our heads, unless they have lived with it.

Since September 1944, London had survived 517 V2 rockets, and the price had been another 3,000 dead, with about twice that number seriously injured. Another 537 V2s had missed the city, falling mostly in Essex and Kent, where a low density of population and buildings had limited the death and destruction. (One distinct flaw in the V2 was its accuracy, not only because of technical problems, but because of a notably successful covert operation to feed inaccurate targeting data into the German war machine.) Accordingly, 90 per cent of the V2 casualties were in London – though not in the outer boroughs and suburbs such as Croydon, which received relatively few V2 hits, contrasting with their punishment from the V1s.

Helping Londoners get through the V-weapons onslaught was the now efficient set of support services. At the scenes of 260 incidents were the Queen's Messenger Convoys, providing the much needed refreshments from their canteens. In addition, the Londoner's Meal Service provided its travelling service to the owners of damaged houses. There were mobile bath and laundry services, too. And between December 1944 and March 1945, more than 8,000 people were admitted into rest centres, which were now a very well run operation – though two of them were themselves victims of V2 attacks, on 17 and 28 March, killing five people.

Londoners' relief at the days of quiet, added to by reports about Russian advances, was tempered by news of President Roosevelt's death on 12 April. 'It is,' wrote Vere Hodgson, 'a Black Day for all of us':

> President Roosevelt died yesterday very suddenly. What a shock when I hopped out of bed this morning, and found the *D.T.* [*Daily Telegraph*] all in Black, and the terrible announcement. I shed tears. It will make it harder for Mr Churchill. They got on so well and Stalin is of a different mentality, and a hard nut to crack.

The V2 strike at London's Smithfield Market on 8 March 1945 was one of the last, and one of the worst, incidents of the V2 campaign, killing 129 people. Here, mobile cranes begin the enormous clear-up job. Such was the devastation that the photograph was not released by the censor for nearly three weeks.

> Anyway, so many thanks to you, Mr Roosevelt, for all the help you gave us, and the way you worked to save us all in those dark and lonely days of 1940. The House of Commons adjourned today on Mr Churchill's suggestion – the first time in English History it has done this for a foreign statesman. That shows the debt we owe him.

Nevertheless, even Roosevelt's demise could not dim the reality that the Battle of London was now *truly* over – and won. Against everything, London had come through.

IN FOCUS

LONDON ON FILM

Inevitably, London's travails and Londoners' lives, especially during the periods of intense bombardment, became fertile territory for contemporary filmmakers, and a number of notable films emerged from both British and Hollywood studios.

Some 1,400 official short films were produced under the auspices of the Ministry of Information, mostly by the Crown Film Unit. They were only about five minutes in length – because Kenneth Clark, Director of Home Publicity at the MOI, thought that '10 minutes for propaganda films were as much as people could stand'. The most famous, and most favoured by critics and public alike, was *Britain Can Take It* (1940), a reduced-length version of the film made originally as *London Can Take It*. This was intended to be a 'film despatch' for American audiences, in the hope that it would bolster US sympathy for Britain's plight. It was filmed in two weeks, and was showing in the United States by 15 October 1940.

The film sought to convey the bravery of Londoners at the height of the Blitz, combining footage with commentary by the US journalist Quentin Reynolds, who was the London correspondent of *Collier's Weekly* magazine. The polymath Humphrey Jennings, who had been one of the luminaries of the Mass Observation project, was one of the film's directors. He was clearly inspired by what he saw of the people of London, as he wrote to his wife Cicely in the United States during the making of the film:

Some of the damage in London is pretty heart-breaking – but what an effect it has had on the people! What warmth – what courage! What determination. People sternly encouraging each other by explaining that when you hear a bomb whistle it means it has missed you!... WVS girls serving hot drinks to firefighters during raids explaining that really they are 'terribly afraid all the time!' People going back to London for a night or two to remind themselves what it's like.

London Can Take It chronicles a period of about 18 hours during the Blitz, beginning one late afternoon, as Londoners return from work in the rush hour and then don their uniforms for the civilian services. In Reynolds' narration, they are 'the people's army', 'the greatest civilian army ever to be assembled'. As the sirens sound and air raids begin, vivid images and sounds of explosions and anti-aircraft guns are intercut with quiet images of people sleeping or playing darts in their private and public shelters, little oases of calm amid the storm. The work of the emergency services starts, followed by the cleaning-up operation afterwards. After the 'all clear' the next morning, Londoners return to work on time, and again the film impresses on its audience the idea that the nightly havoc of air raids cannot supplant the determination to maintain normality – even when, against an image

Opposite A still from the Crown Film Unit captures the tensions following a V1 incident in London, as a casualty is stretchered away (1941). Until 1940, the Crown Film Unit was outside direct government control (as the GPO Film Unit), but the pre-war approach to documentary filmmaking would continue within the embrace of the Ministry of Information.

The charismatic American journalist and war correspondent Quentin Reynolds (rear centre, facing front) at an American Division reception at the Ministry of Information. He provided memorably sonorous voiceovers for the MOI propaganda documentaries *London Can Take It* (1940) and *Christmas Under Fire* (1941). In 1941, he also published *A London Diary*, covering his experiences and observations during the first three months of the Blitz.

of shattered shop fronts, Reynolds observes: 'shops open as usual – in fact many of them are more open than usual'. Despite Reynolds' declaration that he is a neutral observer, his sympathies are never in doubt, for the film is a paean to Londoners' determination during the Blitz, symbolising the larger spirit of defiance and endurance in what Reynolds calls 'Churchill's island': 'The morale of the people is higher than ever before. They are fused together not by fear but by a surging spirit of courage that the world has never known.'

Humphrey Jennings went on to write and direct for the Crown Film Unit his much-admired full-length feature film *Fires Were Started* (1943). This blend of documentary and drama portrays a day in the life of London firefighters during the Blitz. There are eight central characters who, though fictional, were played by real firemen. The actors included Leading Fireman Fred Griffiths, a London taxi driver who joined the AFS before the war (playing Johnny Daniels), Leading Fireman Philip Wilson-Dickson who had worked in an advertising agency, Leading Fireman Loris Ray, a sculptor, Fireman T P Smith, who had been a waiter and Commanding Officer, and George Gravett, who was a regular in the London Fire Brigade. The new man in the unit, Bill Barrett, an advertising copywriter, was played by the writer- firefighter William Sansom.

The film revolves around the routine of Heavy Unit One in a London docklands fire station. Newcomer Barrett is integrated (with a sing-along) into the fire-crew, before the unit is portrayed in the thick of an air raid and its aftermath, ending with the funeral of one of the firemen. The film is perhaps unique in using real

Filmmaker Humphrey Jennings (left) suggests a shot to his cameraman in Westminster Abbey's Poets' Corner. He was directing one of the most highly rated wartime productions for the Crown Film Unit, *Words of Battle* (1941), in which Laurence Olivier voiced excerpts of English poetry and prose over evocative and symbolic scenes of British life and liberty, culminating in London. Jennings directed *London Can Take It* and *Fires Were Started* too.

firemen, real locations and drawing on real episodes. Sansom later said of it: 'As a practising fireman I could say this: the film was true to life in every respect. Not a false note – if you make the usual allowances for the absence of foul language which was in everybody's mouth all the time'. Caroline Lejeune, film critic of the *Observer*, found it:

... one of the finest documentaries we have ever made. I am quite sure it will bring prestige to the unit and to British films generally. I can guarantee that what I may call 'my' public will like it, and I have enough faith in the good heart of the wider public to believe that they will like it too. I have never known a film as honest and human as this one fail to get its message through. If it were my film, I should be very proud of it.

Historian Angus Calder, who would critique what he called the 'myth' of the Blitz, acknowledged that *Fires Were Started*, along with the MOI pamphlet *Front-Line*, both produced under the auspices of the Ministry of Information, epitomised the indomitable spirit of Londoners in the figures of the heroic firemen. It remains highly thought of.

Very shortly after *Fires Were Started*, Ealing Studios released a feature film about the Auxiliary Fire Service, entitled *The Bells Go Down*, which also drew on real locations and incidents for a drama that tracked the lives of a core of central characters from 1939 into the Blitz. In this case, conventional actors took on the main firemen's roles, with Tommy Trinder as Tommy Turk, James Mason as Ted Robbins and Mervyn Johns as Sam. As with *Fires Were Started*, heroism, sacrifice and

A vivid studio re-creation of the London Blitz for the 1942 film *Unpublished Story*, which combined a romantic plotline with a drama about the ethics of wartime journalism. In this scene, the male lead Richard Greene picks his way through the debris to get to the telephone box for an important call.

a sense of renewal are all on display, as Tommy falls to the flames and a newborn child is christened after him.

Journalist Quentin Reynolds provided further help to the Ministry of Information by contributing the voiceover for the Crown Film Unit's *Christmas Under Fire* (1941). This documentary depicted shelterers in Kensington and Leicester Square Underground stations on Christmas Eve. Christmas trees, Christmas puddings, children's war toys, along with bombed-out shops and theatres, and roof spotters, all feature, as Reynolds sombrely tells the viewer: 'No bells ring in England to celebrate the birth of the Saviour. No church bells are allowed to be rung in England.' The film went out to about a thousand cinemas in Britain, but again it was mainly intended for American consumption, and indeed would play in 16,000 US movie theatres.

With the Blitz over, the MOI's Film Division returned to presenting the nation's capital as the theme in the film *London 1942*, produced in 1943. Taking a day-in-the-life approach to the city, its narrator could claim that 'though scarred London still presents a smiling face'. The film unfolds from dawn to dusk, as a myriad of scenes evoke the dimensions of mid-war London life: Allied servicemen from many nations, including the first American contingents; *Goodbye Mr Chips* playing in Leicester Square; emergency water tanks; the 'citizen army' of the Home Guard; salvaged iron railings removed from London parks; picnickers eating, while anti-aircraft crews stand guard; food growing everywhere, from window boxes to allotments; customers buying groceries using ration points; British Restaurants and factory canteens; the National Gallery's lunchtime concerts; 'the mobilisation of women' and mothers handing children to the communal nurseries; the Royal Family; London as the 'hub of the Allied war effort', and No. 10 Downing Street as the centre of 'world strategy'; the 'warmth and comfort' of a pub interior contrasting with the blackout; night shifts at factories, for 'the machines must never stop', and the thousands of volunteer fire-watchers atop London roofs.

Returning to the Blitz era was the 1942 British feature film *Unpublished Story*. It starred Richard Greene and Valerie Hobson as Bob Randall and Carol Bennett, two journalists working for the fictional newspaper *The Gazette*. The film actually tackles the issue of wartime censorship, for Randall has been evacuated from Dunkirk but is unable to publish his experiences. As the Blitz unfolds, Randall's investigations discover a pro-Nazi organisation posing as a pacifist movement called the 'People for Peace Society', but again he cannot make anything public, for the group is being watched by Britain's intelligence services. Although together with Carol Bennett, the fashion correspondent, he obtains damaging information on the group, eventually leading to the Nazi-sympathisers' capture, the reporters have to accept that, because of MOI censorship, the story cannot be told. While delivering a message about the paramount nature of security in wartime, the film fully evokes the Blitz. The newspaper's offices suffer a direct hit, and there is much footage of the main characters in London's East End after one of the big raids.

Produced in the same year, *Salute John Citizen* heavily featured the Blitz. Its plot revolves around the trials and tribulations of the Buntings, a London family who live at 'Laburnum Villa'. After Mr Bunting returns to his former work at a department store, because of the wartime staff shortages, both he and his daughter Julie undertake dangerous ARP work. She later leaves home to work in a factory. As air raids destroy the city around them, one of Mr Bunting's sons, Chris, who is committed to the war effort, is married in a bombed-out church but is later killed; the other son, Ernest, is forced by his own experiences of the Blitz to reject his former pacifism. The film was based on novels by Robert Greenwood, and featured Edward Rigby and Mabel Constanduros (as Mr and Mrs Bunting), Jimmy Hanley (as Ernest), with other roles played by Dinah Sheridan, Stanley Holloway and George Robey. *Salute John Citizen* is a very good example of a propagandist feature film depicting an ordinary London family 'sticking it out' during the Blitz.

While all these films were British-produced, Hollywood too tackled the Blitz in 20th Century Fox's *Confirm or Deny* (1941), which, like *Unpublished Story*, concerned London-based journalists and the problem of censorship. Its male lead was Don Ameche in the role of 'Mitch' Mitchell, who works for the Consolidated Press of America in London, and who is determined to get a scoop on what seems to be the imminent German invasion of Britain. After his London offices are destroyed by a bombing raid, Mitchell decamps to the wine cellar of the Regency Hotel, where alongside him is Jennifer Carson (played by female lead Joan Bennett), a teletype operator working for the Ministry of Information. Another raid traps them both in the cellar just as Mitchell is trying to get his scoop out, and events conspire to make him abandon his selfish pursuit of a story, which Jennifer Carson opposes, in favour of supporting the war effort and winning her affections. It is a somewhat more glamorous and romantic depiction of life under the Blitz than *Unpublished Story*.

Each film, in its own way, addressed London's experience under the extreme pressures of bombing and wartime privations. Together with the many other films that the public flocked to during 1939–45, they contributed to a cinema culture that formed a very important element in the maintenance of morale, especially for Londoners. When Herbert Morrison wrote his Introduction to the 1948 book *Red Roses Every Night: An Account of London Cinemas Under Fire*, he spoke of the 'millions who, between long spells of war work and disturbed nights, turned to the cinema for relaxation'. And he was unstinting in his praise of those who made these films available, without whom they would have remained dusty reels on a storeroom's shelf:

The cinemas never let us down. When they were shut it was only because they were too badly damaged to open. Truly the men and women of the cinemas deserved and had the thanks of the public throughout those terrible years.

Londoners – the permanent and the transient ones, those in uniform and those without – throng around Piccadilly Circus and the still-boarded-up base of Eros's statue, to mark Victory in Europe Day, 8 May 1945. Union flags are on display, and so too is the Stars and Stripes along Rainbow Corner, on Shaftesbury Avenue; even the Soviet flag is on show. For some Londoners it was a day of remembrance and thoughtfulness. For many thousands, it was a time for exuberance.

EPILOGUE

WAR'S END, LONDON'S FUTURE

'What a scene for London!'

Leila Faithful's oil triptych *VE-Day Celebrations Outside Buckingham Palace* (1945) presents a vivid contrast to the sombre, sometimes mordant, palettes of so many paintings of London during the war. Now all is light and effervescent spring colour, matching the mood.

By the time the last V2 crashed to earth in Kent, the US and British armies under the overall control of General Eisenhower were across the Rhine, and Russian armies were bearing down on Berlin. In the wider context, the V2 had arrived too late to have any influence on the fortunes of war. However intimidating it was for London and its people, it was a sideshow in the war's outcome; and even Londoners could appreciate that the endgame was approaching. As early as the beginning of March 1945, Gwladys Cox had noticed that 'The Tobacconist in West End Lane has Union Jacks for sale, and says they are going like hot cakes, people buying them up before the final rush.' On 4 April, George Britton was trying to make sense of it all in a letter to his son-in-law Albert Elkus:

This morning's news gives instructions about a national holiday on the day the war with Germany ends and the day after for all Government employees. I am not quite clear in my own mind how we can have a definite day for the end of the war if the Germans are to carry on a guerrilla warfare indefinitely.

What concerns us more particularly at the present time is the fact that we have had no rocket bombs for six days. When the threat is definitely removed it will seem like heaven.

In April, Vivienne Hall was certainly enjoying 'no more rockets no more flying bombs – we hope – no more black-out', and adding the wish that 'soon – again we hope – no more fighting'. That month, the numbers of people sheltering in London's Underground stations and deep shelters shrank to 6,000 and 2,500 respectively. In Berlin, by the end of April, the Russians were in control and on the verge of capturing the *Reichstag*, and Hitler was dead.

On 2 May, the men and women of the Civil Defence services were stood down – there being no possibility of further attack on London or Britain. Two days later, London's Underground canteen facilities were stopped too, though the Underground shelters remained open for the homeless. By 7 May, Vivienne Hall's wish was finally granted, and she could exult:

> This week has been one of the weeks we have dreamed about, thought about, longed for for over six years – each day we thought peace would come, the German armies have surrendered all over Europe and we have felt sure it must end soon, but each day had not been given over to the final surrender!... Everyone is tensed up and waiting – expectant and almost in the same state of nervous anticipation as during the bombing – waiting and waiting – this so exciting, so very exciting....

The next day, 8 May, was designated Victory in Europe Day – VE Day. It was a day for explosions of a very different kind to those Londoners had got used to: of thankfulness, of patriotism, of colour, of fireworks, of relief, of joy. Mollie Panter-Downes described to her American readers the scenes she witnessed:

> The desire to assist in London's celebrations combusted spontaneously in the bosom of every member of every family, from the smallest babies, with their hair done up in red-white-and-blue ribbons, to beaming elderly couples who, utterly without self-consciousness, strolled up and down streets arm in arm in red-white-and-blue paper hats. Even the dogs wore immense tricolored bows. Rosettes sprouted from the slabs of pork in the butcher shops, which, like other food stores, were open for a couple of hours in the morning. With their customary practicality, housewives put bread before circuses. They waited in the long bakery queues, the string bags of the common round in one hand and the Union Jack of the glad occasion in the other. Even queues seemed tolerable this morning. The bells had begun to peal and, after the storm, London was having a perfect, hot, English summer's day.

Right and below VE Day crowds mass along Whitehall, past the Cenotaph, in front of the flags adorning the Ministry of Health. Come the evening, Churchill was addressing the people from the ministry's balcony, and receiving a victor's accolades in return. He had already waved to crowds from the Buckingham Palace balcony, a rare privilege afforded to a mere politician, but the times were exceptional.

In Battersea, South London, two young girls scarcely bigger than the Union flags they hold, join in the events of VE Day atop a pile of rubble. Sales of flags had boomed even as early as March, as people scented an approaching reason to celebrate.

At St Paul's, services were held throughout the day, as 35,000 people flooded to the cathedral, and by midday large crowds were gathering in the West End. In Piccadilly, US servicemen threw rolls of lavatory paper – their version of ticker tape – from the windows of their club. It was a time for Britain's leaders to show themselves. Winston Churchill was driven to Buckingham Palace to have lunch with King George VI. Later, at 3pm, the prime minister broadcast his victory speech before heading to the House of Commons. By evening, he was back at the palace, appearing on the balcony before the vast throngs, along with the King and Queen, and accompanied by princesses Elizabeth and Margaret. Then, Churchill returned to Whitehall to show himself before the people once more, on the balcony of the Ministry of Health.

Finally, at 9pm, the sovereign's address to the nation was broadcast. He began:

Across London, neighbourhoods erupted in celebration at war's end, each in its own way. Here, men and women dance the conga around a bonfire in East Acton on the evening of VE Day.

Today we give thanks to Almighty God for a great deliverance. Speaking from our empire's oldest capital city, war battered but never for one moment daunted or dismayed, speaking from London, I ask you to join with me in that act of thanksgiving. Germany, the enemy that drove all Europe into war, has been finally overcome.

For the Royal Family, there was yet another appearance on the palace balcony before the day was out – their eighth of the day, such was the appetite of the crowds for glimpses of them.

Eddie Lawrence, a civil servant in the Ministry of Agriculture, was just one of the thousands who, as he put it in a letter (to Henry Strong), 'joined the singing and shouting crowds in the West End'. Patriotic celebration was to the fore: 'We put a Union Jack on the top gable of our house and strung coloured lights round the edge of the roof.'

Nellie Carver had to combine work with pleasure on 8 May: 'Up at 7.30 – Breakfast then upstairs to hang out flags etc. We have two strips of gay ones from the Coronation & a new one I bought.' She then rushed off to collect rations, for the shops were only open for a few hours as it was a public holiday. She had to go to work but was allowed to leave early, in time to hear some of the special VE Day radio broadcasts. Later that evening, she and her mother wandered up and down their road, watching the fireworks and listening to the singing. The absence of street lighting made the special illuminations all the more effective. 'At last,' she wrote, 'we went in & to bed – absolutely happy, altho it still seemed dangerous to see lights everywhere & to hear bangs in the sky.' It had been, she thought, a wonderful scene.

The celebrations continued the next day, which was also a public holiday. Nellie Carver visited a nearby street party for 150 children. On her return home, she found four bonfires blazing:

> People were again rushing up with old chairs etc. (I do hope good ones were not sacrificed as nobody appeared to care!) The children – who looked so clean at the Party & not in bed yet were having the time of their lives – gloriously dirty with smoke & soot dancing round the fire singing – dogs were barking madly & more fireworks going off under one's feet. What a scene for London!

The following week, Vivienne Hall finished her own dairy with the words 'Two days holiday with roaring, happy crowds marked the end of this ghastly war… At any rate for this week all is happiness and the relief is terrific.'

For many, that sense of relief came not in a rush, but incrementally, as they gradually acclimatised to peace rather than war. During VE Day itself, diarist Robert Herrmann had thought 'the true Londoner of the 1940–45 vintage rejoiced in a spirit, not of riotous gaiety but of slightly awed and most profound thankfulness'. In the last entry of his diary, he wrote:

> Even a full month after the last siren, with firewatching over and the blackout ended, Londoners did not go about saying 'It's over'. The process of realization was so slow and the relaxation of the tension so gradual that the old precautions died hard. For instance it was

early May before I got out of the habit of leaving my best suit out at night so that in the event of being rendered homeless during the night one might at least have one decent suit left.

There was, in short, no definite day on which one passed from a state of subconscious apprehension to one of complete security. Slowly, as realization came, the sense of relief grew. One day it struck one that the stirrup-pump could be given away, another day one realizes that there was every chance of finding one's home in the same state as one left it in the morning. Women stopped taking ration cards, clothes coupons, favourite pieces of jewellery, with them wherever they went.

In all sorts of ways, London had to manage the transition from war to peace. The handful of recently built deep shelters found other uses: the one at Goodge Street housed US soldiers and acquired the name 'Eisenhower Tower'; the one at Clapham was taken over by the government, and the shelter at Chancery Lance became a telephone exchange. (Three years later, in 1948, the Caribbean immigrants who arrived aboard HMT *Empire Windrush* were temporarily accommodated in the shelter at Clapham.) On VE night, there were still 1,200 people sleeping in the Underground, but their bunks were removed the following week, and by July all public shelters were closed. Instructions were given out for Anderson and Morrison shelters to be dismantled and made ready for collection by local boroughs – unless householders wanted to hang on to them for £1 (Andersons) or £1 10s (Morrisons).

Parades continued throughout London in the days and weeks that followed VE Day, such as the farewell parade held by former Civil Defence workers on 10 June, in Hyde Park, which was addressed by the King. On VE Day, George VI had told his subjects 'We have come to the end of our tribulation', but he had not forgotten the continuing struggle against Japan. When that battle, too, was won, London broke out once more in celebration, for Victory over Japan – VJ Day – on 15 August 1945. For Nellie Carver, her day involved travelling up to Central London to see the King and Queen on the Buckingham Palace balcony, while back in West Norwood there were more flags, fireworks and bonfires. However, she thought that somehow the excitement she had experienced on VE Day was now lacking. It was true that although many Londoners had family and friends fighting in South-East Asia and the Pacific, the VJ Day celebrations were not quite on the scale of those for VE Day.

If Victory over Japan Day on 15 August 1945 seemed to diarist Nellie Carver more muted than VE Day, the message seems not to have got through to these revellers in Piccadilly Circus.

Perhaps nothing could ever have matched that first, cathartic eruption of relief. One year later, in London's Victory Parade of June 1946, marching columns would take two hours to pass the dais where George VI took the salute. Evelyn Waugh was already jaded; he thought it a masquerade, a 'procession of Brazilians, Mexicans, Egyptians, Naafi waitresses… claiming that they won the war' as they streamed behind Churchill and Attlee. At the same time, neither the Poles (for whom Britain had ostensibly gone to war) nor the erstwhile Russian allies were present in the 1946 parade. Politics was already moving on.

Indeed, even by September 1945 the post-war euphoria was beginning to pall in the eyes of some, overtaken by the urgencies of the present. Eddie Lawrence's brother-in-law, John King, was feeling that:

London is one solid mass of people, you can hardly walk along the pavements, one begins to wonder if anyone does any work at all, something seems wrong somewhere when the country is crying out for effort that so many people are able to mill aimlessly about town all day – they can't all be on holiday.

'Effort' was certainly demanded in all spheres of life. For London, there was the serious business of reconstructing the city, and of rehousing the thousands of people who had lost their homes.

The wartime coalition government had produced no White Paper on housing, as it had for education and health. The bombing and

Regimental Sergeant Major Stilwell is measured up for a 'demob suit' at the Clothing Depot in Olympia, West London (18 June 1945). War's end meant the return of thousands of Londoners from the armed services, faced now with the challenges of re-entry into civilian life, in a city altered by war.

V-weapons campaigns had destroyed 50,000 houses in Central London and a further 66,000 in Greater London. Another 1.3 million were in need of repair. It was estimated in January 1945 that 1 million new houses were needed immediately, and that a further 3–4 million would be required in the long term, so the challenge was immense. The ever-popular Lord Woolton had redirected his energies as Minister of Reconstruction from late 1943, but still there was much criticism that too little was being done. One problem was the sheer bureaucracy stemming from the number of ministries involved – Health, Works, Town and Country Planning, Labour, Supply, and the Board of Trade, all of them with fingers in the pie. There was a call for a new, dedicated Ministry of Housing.

At a local level, property damage first had to be assessed by local authorities. There was a sliding scale: 'A' (destroyed houses), 'B' (to be demolished), 'C' (uninhabitable but repairable) and 'D' (habitable but needing repair). It was then the role of the War Damage Commission, established in 1940 and headquartered in Piccadilly, to pay for the damage and to repair properties to their original state. By May 1945, a million claims had flooded in for damage wrought by the V-weapons alone, whose one-ton warheads had killed fewer people than anticipated but wrecked so many buildings. Finally, it was the responsibility of the Ministry of Works to tackle the damaged homes. A London Repairs Executive had been established (headed by Duncan Sandys) in November 1944, which had, by the end of that year, almost 130,000 men at work, a good number of them drawn from the Civil Defence services. Three thousand US service personnel with the right skills were also drafted in to help repair Londoners' homes, which endeared the 'Yanks' to grateful inhabitants. The huge task was not quick, and sometimes it was months before people were back in their homes. While they waited, storage facilities for their possessions began overflowing. Empty premises across the capital were used for the purpose, but still so much ended up being damaged, moth-eaten or stolen. By the end of 1944, just over 250,000 homes had been repaired. There was a long way to go.

If Londoners' homes were destroyed or the repairs took longer than six months, then they were re-housed. For this purpose, the government had given boroughs the authority to requisition houses for bombed-out families. The homeless could stay rent-free for the first couple of weeks, and then would have to pay what they could within their family budget. Sometimes the only housing available was out of the borough, in large houses in the West End, for instance, such as the houses in Gloucester Terrace, Hyde Park Gardens and Westbourne Terrace that were converted into flats for 1,000 people. The new accommodation tended to be unpopular with East Enders, and some people had to leave London altogether.

The billeting allowances were hardly generous, and sometimes the homeless would find themselves exploited, as Mrs Irene Byers, who lived in Somerset, had noticed during the war:

> I met a lovely young wife from Streatham. She had a six-month-old baby and was staying at Croydon and when her house was bombed she lost everything, furniture, wedding presents – the lot – and is now staying with friends at Bridgewater, who charge her 30s a week for one small room. Some friends! The Government only contributes 5s and the rest she has to find out of army pay. Her husband is fighting in France and she is very bitter about money-making opportunities in Somerset. It certainly gets under my skin the way some people are profiteering from other people's misery.

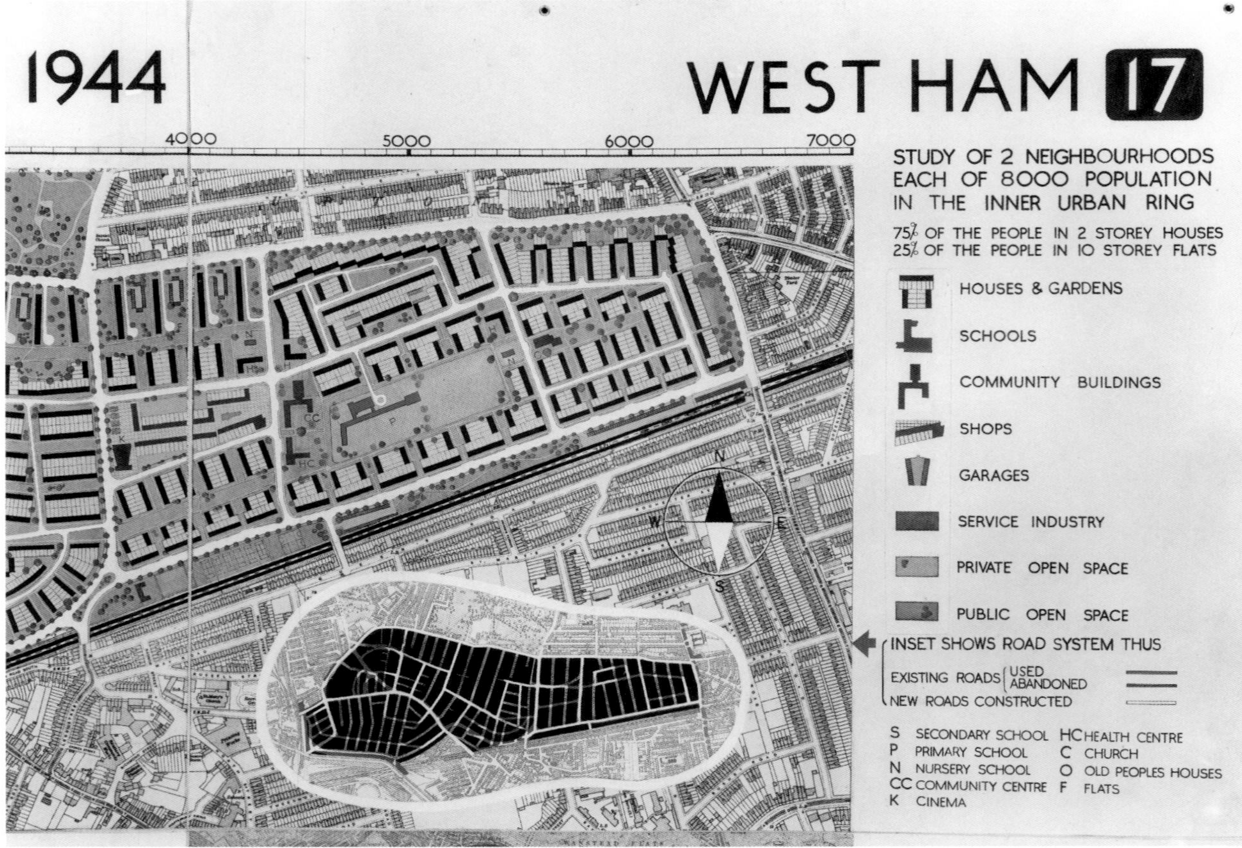

One portion of Professor Abercrombie's *Greater London Plan 1944* shows the existing streets of terraces (lower area) but also the newly envisaged, more spacious, homes and flats for two neighbourhoods of West Ham. This area of London had, after all, been badly mauled during the Blitz.

However, there was also in evidence a spirit of generosity towards Londoners. Some cities and towns adopted London boroughs and provided donations of furniture, kitchen utensils, cutlery and crockery for the new homes of those having to be rehoused. The people of Shropshire, for example, sent 45 loads of housewares, each weighing 5.5 tons, to be distributed by the WVS in Hackney. Donations also came from further afield, such as the thousands of Red Cross blankets and quilts sent over from the United States and Canada.

For London's reconstruction, at least there was a framework for thinking – the *Greater London Plan 1944*. It provided the foundations for rebuilding London, giving local authorities the power to compulsorily purchase bomb-damaged sites (at 1939 prices) and turn them into designated areas for construction. And the plans envisaged something better than what had gone before – for instance, in deprived and bomb-ravaged Stepney and Poplar, the goal was to improve Londoners' quality of life by allocating the living space previously occupied by ten inhabitants to a limit of four persons.

Construction work is underway on a Uni-Seco prefabricated 'emergency house' (1945). Part of the impetus behind the prefabs idea was to make the best of a shortage of skilled construction workers while at the same time providing sufficient accommodation for returning servicemen, newly married couples and the homeless. In March 1944, Churchill spoke of making 'up to half a million of these' homes. In the end, around 156,000 were built across the country by 1949.

A former bomb site in London is now filled with prefabs, cheek by jowl with the surviving terraces, presenting a stark contrast between old and new (1945). Boasting fitted kitchens (with fridge) and wardrobes, indoor bathrooms and heating systems, prefabs made up for their impermanent outer construction with desirable mod cons. Churchill thought them 'far superior to the ordinary cottage as it exists today'.

The London County Council also quickly took over bomb-damaged sites and made them ready for new 'prefabs' – the temporary, prefabricated homes that were quick to construct and which proved popular with Londoners. The buildings were compact but well designed, often with modern conveniences to which their inhabitants were unused. On balance, Mollie Panter-Downes seemed impressed with the novel structures – she had noted their arrival in May 1944:

> Londoners were last week introduced to an architectural blueprint of what large areas of Britain are going to look like after the war. The first of Mr Churchill's promised prefabricated steel houses for newlyweds has, like a squat mushroom, suddenly sprung up in the shadow of the Tate Gallery. While its aesthetic appeal is limited, lots of housewives who go to see it will think its labor-saving devices are much better-looking than anything in the Tate. It is being emphasized that such houses represent only a temporary solution of the postwar housing problem, which, on this bombed island, will

certainly be acute – a reassuring guarantee to those apprehensive lovers of rural England who were beginning to visualize bungaloid growths sprawling all over the green countryside.

Many people would go on to live happily in prefabs for decades afterwards, as the structures long outlived their 'temporary' purpose.

The housing shortage also meant rising house prices, and this unwelcome development most affected middle-class Londoners, as Mollie Panter-Downes explained in April 1945:

> Londoners whose war jobs took them out of the city or who could afford to move their children out of bombing range are now beginning to return to town, and, as a result, the prices of London property are starting to show the same alarming upward curve they developed after the First World War. Depressed couples in search of a small family house in which to settle down as Londoners once more are finding that the good things are prohibitive in price and that the moderately priced houses appear to have received a little too much attention from the bombers. The new government limit on house repairs is ten pounds, so the problem of getting a dirty, leaking house into habitable shape is a difficult one. However, some amateur house-decorating help is available. For example, the charwoman's husband, on leave from the Navy, may oblige with a little distempering, or a friendly air warden may come around in off-duty hours and do a bit of carpentering.
>
> The returning middle-class people, who normally could afford a neat little house in Kensington or Chelsea, are discovering that today's abnormal prices are beyond them and wondering whether it will turn out that they are a forgotten group for whose needs the government housing program will not provide. It is still not satisfactorily clear how fully or how soon the government will be able to provide for even its most important customers, the fighting men, many of whom may be freed before long to come home and ask tiresome questions about such matters. As in every European country, shelter and food will be the big primitive questions of the immediate future, and it will be against a background of the government's success or failure in answering them that the people will go to the polls to decide the color of the next chapter in England's political history.

Unsurprisingly, housing, along with employment and social security, became key issues in the General Election of 5 July 1945, the first for nearly ten years. Churchill formally resigned as prime minister of the coalition government on 23 May, before being reappointed to lead a pre-election caretaker government. He was seen as a statesman, the man who had led Britain to victory. However, the electorate wanted a government that would push through the plans for social legislation that had been formulated during the war. Not the least of these were the provisions for a National Health Service and social security as laid down in the Beveridge Report of 1942 – that 'two-shilling slab of involved economics,' as Mollie Panter-Downes called it, which 'Londoners queued up to buy… as though it was unrationed manna dropped from some heaven'. Even Vere Hodgson, an arch-Churchillian, had been a fan, declaring 'I'm all for Beveridge.' In short, while, in mid-1945, Churchill remained focused on global strategy, diplomacy and winning the war against Japan, many voters, including those in London, were turning their minds to winning the peace.

As the politicians took to campaigning, Nellie Carver and her mother went to see Churchill give a speech at West Norwood's tram terminus, in support of his son-in-law Duncan Sandys, the local MP:

> He chucked his daughter (Mrs Sandys) under the chin, shook hands with our Member & climbed up on a platform. Someone from the Thurlow Arms handed him a pint of ale in a tankard – & with every appearance of enjoyment & a most wicked schoolboy smile [he] held it up & drank it in full view of the delighted crowd. How wonderful to be so lacking in self-consciousness & so absolutely natural! He made a fine fighting speech & in spite of a few interruptions you could feel the grip he has on the crowd – it was worth the heat & squashing to be there – one could understand it all – just to hear him.

Others were unsettled by what they saw as a rush for change. Gwladys Cox, for one, could not 'see why we could not continue with a National Government, this would check the hotheads on both sides'. She found it 'distressing, too, to hear the disparaging remarks the candidates themselves addressed to each other. Coming so soon after the team spirit in the war years, once again the bickering began. Surely we are not going to fight among ourselves.'

However, the tide of change was unstoppable. In London, large areas, such as the East End, drew massive Labour Party support, not least on account of the people's experiences during the economic privations of the 1930s. Moreover, the war itself – with its dissolving of class barriers as people from all walks of life entered the military and civilian services, and endured the hazards of bombing – had whittled away at natural deference towards social 'superiors' and the idea of the governing classes, a trend that particularly affected the Conservative Party. In truth, Conservatives had adopted many of the prevailing social-reform goals (even if with different means to achieve them), but their electoral prospects were very much identified with their leader. And in the end, even Churchill the war hero could not save the fortunes of a party that had finally come to love him.

Much to Nellie Carver's disgust, Britain gave the Labour Party a landslide victory when the votes, including those of servicemen and women abroad, were finally tallied. On 27 July she was 'simply furious at the unthinking ingratitude of the Public' and wrote a letter of support to Churchill, thinking it was the least she could do. In the London suburbs, Eddie Lawrence and others were equally appalled: 'the happiness and exuberance of spirits was brought to an abrupt end by the results of the General Election. The gloom and despondency that prevailed in Hinchley Wood could not have been greater if we had lost the war.' His sister-in-law Doris King felt 'staggered by the election result especially as I live and work in a very Conservative atmosphere – the end of the world would have occasioned only a little more alarm.'

In Whitehall, the new Cabinet took shape within 24 hours of the result. Within it were many experienced war ministers, including Ernest Bevin (former Minister of Labour and National Service) as Foreign Secretary, Aneurin Bevan at the Ministry of Housing, Hugh Dalton as Chancellor of the Exchequer and Ellen Wilkinson at Education. The great Londoner Herbert Morrison became Lord President of the Council and Leader of the House of Commons. The Labour Party went on to triumph also in the local elections in November 1945, including winning council seats in Westminster for the first time in forty years.

The world did not end, and other Londoners felt that things were looking up. George Britton assessed the situation on 2 August:

> Now the final figures are out it appears the Liberal party is as good as dead, the Conservative party more or less moribund and the Labour party with a workable majority left to clear up the mess. I do hope that a Brighter Britain emerges.

For London there was just one task left: to rebuild a city.

SOURCES

IWM DOCUMENTS © IWM unless otherwise stated

Private Papers of Harry Atterbury (Documents.133520)
Private Papers of Viola Bawtree (Documents.18070), © Estate of Viola Bawtree
Private Papers of Mrs Winnie Bowman (Documents.37690)
Private Papers of Mrs Brinton-Lee (Documents.9761), courtesy the Estate of Mrs Brinton-Lee
Private Papers of Mr and Mrs Britton (Documents.4735), courtesy the Estate of Mr and Mrs Britton
Private Papers of Mrs Irene Byers (Documents.526)
Private Papers of Nellie Carver (Documents.379)
Private Papers of Kathleen Church-Bliss (Documents.1354), courtesy of Alison Speirs
Private Papers of Mrs Gwladys Cox (Documents.2769)
Private Papers of Jack Edwards (Documents.25976)
Private Papers of Elizabeth Elkus (Documents.1177), courtesy the Estate of Elizabeth Elkus
Private Papers of Vivienne Hall (Documents.3989)
Private Papers of Mrs Ruth Harris (Documents.25174), © Estate of Ruth Harris
Private Papers of William Haslam (Documents.7735)
Private Papers of Robert Herrmann (Documents.19644)
Private Papers of Vere Hodgson (Documents.4767)
Private Papers of Joseph Jackson (Documents.13207)
Private Papers of Reverend James Mackay (Documents.7737)
Private Papers of Mrs Violet Marsden (Documents.14525)
Private Papers of Ms Hilda Neal (Documents.11987), © Estate of Ms Hilda Neal
Private Papers of Henry Penny (Documents.20563)
Private Papers of William Regan (Documents.781), © Estate of William Regan
Private Papers of Miss Vera Reid (Documents.12001)
Private Papers of Mrs Ingeborg Samson (Documents.13008), courtesy Inge Samson
Private Papers of Mrs Valerie Shoulder (Documents.5429)
Private Papers of John Simonson (Documents.8488), © IWM, courtesy the Estate of John Simonson
Private Papers of Henry Strong (Documents.5632)
Private Papers of Mrs Joan Veazey (Documents.11458)
Recollections of the Evacuation of Dulwich College Prep School (Documents.4902)

IWM SOUND ARCHIVE © IWM

Oliver Bernard (11481)
George Frankland (19041)
Stanley Parker Bird (7375)
Sherwood Philip Piratin (10210)
Alda Ravera (28357)
Stephen Spender (11627)
Teresa Wilkinson (21596)

PUBLICATIONS

Anthony Aldgate and Jeffrey Richards, *Britain Can Take It: British Cinema in the Second World War*, I.B. Tauris, 2007. Reproduced with permission of the Licensor through PLSclear.
Anonymous, *Fire Over London: The Story of the London Fire Service 1940–41*, Hutchinson, 1941
Arthur Askey, *Before Your Very Eyes*, Woburn Press, 1975
Geoffrey Best, *Churchill: A Study in Greatness*, Penguin, 2002
John Bew, *Citizen Clem: A Biography of Attlee*, Quercus, 2016
Suzanne Bosman, *The National Gallery in Wartime*, National Gallery, 2008
Angus Calder, *People's War*, Jonathan Cape, 1969
—, *Myth of the Blitz*, Jonathan Cape, 1991
Ritchie Calder, *Carry on London*, English Universities Press, 1941
Sir Henry Channing, *Chips: The Diaries of Sir Henry Channon*, Weidenfeld & Nicolson, 1967
Terry Charman, *The Day We Went to War*, Virgin Books, 2009
John Conen, *The Little Blitz*, Fonthill, 2014
Cyril Connolly, *The Golden Horizon*, Weidenfeld & Nicolson, 1953
Mark Connelly, *We Can Take It! Britain and the Memory of the Second World War*, Pearson, 2004
Noël Coward, *Future Indefinite*, William Heinemann, 1954
Michael Davie (editor), *The Diaries of Evelyn Waugh*, Phoenix, 2009 (originally Weidenfeld & Nicolson, 1976)
Bernard Donoughue and G.W. Jones, *Herbert Morrison: Portrait of a Politician*, Phoenix Press, 2001 (originally Weidenfeld & Nicolson, 1973)
Richard Farmer, *The Food Companions: Cinema and Consumption in Wartime Britain, 1939–45*, Manchester University Press, 2011
Geoffrey G. Field, *Blood, Sweat, and Toil: Remaking the British Working Class*, 1939–1945, Oxford University Press, 2011
Constantine FitzGibbon, *The Blitz*, Corgi, 1974 (originally Macdonald, 1970)
Theodora FitzGibbon, *With Love*, Century Publishing, 1982
Juliet Gardiner, *'Over Here': The GIs in Wartime Britain*, Collins & Brown, 1982
—, *The Blitz*, HarperPress, 2010
Charles Graves, *London Transport at War 1939–1945*, Almark, 1974 (originally as *London Transport Carried On: Being an Account of London at War 1939–1945*, London Passenger Transport Board, 1947)
—, *Off the Record*, Hutchinson, no date
Henry Green, *Caught*, Hogarth Press, 1978 (originally Harvill Press, 1943)
Toby Haggith, '*"Castles in the Air": British Film and the Reconstruction of the Built Environment, 1939–51*', University of Warwick PhD thesis, 1998
James Harding, *Ivor Novello*, W.H. Allen, 1987
—, *Emlyn Williams: A Life*, Weidenfeld & Nicolson, 1993
Meirion Harries and Susie Harries, *The War Artists*, Michael Joseph, 1983
Tom Harrisson, *Living Through the Blitz*, Collins, 1976

Nick Hayes and Jeff Hill, *'Millions Like Us'? British Culture in the Second World War*, Liverpool University Press, 1999
Robert Hewison, *Under Siege: Literary Life in London 1939–45*, Weidenfeld & Nicolson, 1977
Richard Holmes, *Churchill's Bunker*, Profile Books, 2009
Ashley Jackson, *Churchill*, Quercus, 2011
Ted Kavanagh, *Tommy Handley*, Hodder & Stoughton, 1949
Pat Kirkham and David Thoms (editors), *War Culture: Social Change and Changing Experience in World War Two*, Lawrence & Wishart, 1995
James Lees-Milne, *Prophesying Peace*, Faber & Faber, 1977
John Lehmann, *I Am My Brother*, Longmans, 1960
— and Roy Fuller (editors), *The Penguin New Writing 1940–1950*, Penguin, 1985
Norman Longmate, *The Doodlebugs*, Hutchinson, 1981
—, *Hitler's Rockets: The Story of the V-2s*, Hutchinson, 1985
—, *How We Lived Then: A History of Everyday Life During the Second World War*, Arrow, 1988 (originally Hutchinson, 1971)
Rose Macaulay, *Letters to a Sister*, Collins, 1964
Ian McLaine, *Ministry of Morale*, Allen & Unwin, 1979
Mass Observation, *War Begins at Home*, edited by Tom Harrison and Charles Madge, Chatto & Windus, 1940
Ministry of Information, *Front Line 1940–41: The Official Story of the Civil Defence of Britain*, His Majesty's Stationery Office, 1942
Guy Morgan, *Red Roses Every Night: An Account of London Cinemas Under Fire*, Quality Press, 1948
Leonard Mosley, *Backs to the Wall: London Under Fire 1939–45*, Weidenfeld & Nicolson, 1971
Harold Nicolson, *Diaries & Letters 1939–45*, Collins, 1967
Lucy Noakes and Juliette Pattinson, *British Cultural Memory and the Second World War*, Bloomsbury, 2014
Mollie Panter-Downes, *London War Notes, Persephone Books*, 2014 (originally Farrar, Straus & Giroux, 1971)
Frederick Pile, *Ack-Ack: Britain's Defence Against Air Attack During the Second World War*, Harrap,1949
Anthony Powell, *The Soldier's Art*, William Heinemann, 1966
—, *The Military Philosophers*, William Heinemann, 1968
Winston G. Ramsey, *The Blitz: Then and Now*, 3 vols, Battle of Britain Prints International, 1987–90
Rachel Reckitt, *Stepney Letters*, privately printed (Mimthorpe, Cumbria), 1991
Sonya Rose, *Which People's War? National Identity and Citizenship in Wartime Britain* 1939–1945, Oxford University Press, 2003
William Sansom, *The Blitz: Westminster at War*, Oxford University Press, 1990 (originally as *Westminster in War*, Faber, 1947)
Jonathan Schneer, *Ministers at War: Winston Churchill and His War Cabinet*, Oneworld, 2015
Andrew Sinclair, *War Like a Wasp: The Lost Decade of the Forties*, Hamish Hamilton, 1989
William Sitwell, *Eggs or Anarchy*, Simon & Schuster, 2016
Peter Stansky, *The First Day of the Blitz*, Yale University Press, 2007
Andrew Stewart, 'The Battle for Britain', *History Today*, Vol. 65, No. 6, 2015
Matthew Sweet, *The West End Front: The Wartime Secrets of London's Grand Hotels*, Faber & Faber, 2011
James Taylor, *Careless Talk Costs Lives*, Conway, 2010
Donald Thomas, *An Underworld at War: Spivs, Deserters and Civilians in the Second World War*, John Murray, 2003
Joseph Vecchi, *The Tavern is My Drum*, Odhams, 1948
Maureen Waller, *London 1945*, John Murray, 2004
David Welch, *Persuading the People: British Propaganda in World War II*, British Library, 2016
Jerry White, *London in the Twentieth Century*, Bodley Head, 2008
Paul Willetts, *Fear and Loathing in Fitzrovia*, Dewi Lewis, 2005
Robin Woolven, 'London and the V Weapons 1943–1945', *Journal of Royal United Services Institution for Defence Studies*, Vol. 147, No. 1, 2002
—, 'Munich, London and ARP', *Journal of Royal United Services Institution for Defence Studies*, Vol. 143, No. 5, 1998
Lord Woolton, *The Memoirs of the Rt. Hon. The Earl of Woolton*, Cassell, 1959
Philip Ziegler, *London at War 1939–1945*, Mandarin, 1996 (originally Sinclair-Stevenson, 1995)

IMAGE LIST

Prologue
D 2239, HU 36171, HU 36202, Art.IWM PST 15282, Art.IWM PST 15445, HU 36217, D 73, D 1052, D 997, LN 6194, D 140, HU 63736

Chapter One
C 5422, HU 73115, D 712, Art.IWM PST 6229, HU 131375, C 5424, HU 131496, Art.IWM ART LD 2276

In Focus: Sheltering London's People
HU 63827A, HU 131482, D 1503, D 1571, D 1675, Art.IWM ART LD 759

Chapter Two
HU 36220A, HU 131381, Art.IWM ART LD 4977, HU 131413, HU 131455, D 1093, D 1091, HU 131459, Art.IWM ART LD 1376, HU 136883, HU 131378, HU 131495, D 20990, Art.IWM ART LD 1076, HU 131452, D 2055, HU 97330, HU 131469

In Focus: London's Defenders
HU 36168, TR 450, TR 474, Art.IWM ART LD 2905, D 4603, Art.IWM ART LD 371, D 2617, HU 64317, D 2154

Chapter Three
D 6573, Art.IWM ART LD 632, HU 131409, D 3161, D 14248, D 2369, D 12595, D 25037, D 10727, D 8338, D 2373, EPH 10126, Art.IWM PST 6080, Art.IWM PST 0059, D 1498, D 10681, D 10506, HU 48187, D 5923, D 10405

In Focus: Lawbreaking in London
Art.IWM PST 14426, Art.IWM PST 14610, FRE 10543, HU 131427, A 25390, HU 90524

Chapter Four
HU 63234, D 4712, H 2646A, CH 5701, A 11593, D 3950, D 5140, EPH 10982

In Focus: Churchill's London
H 20446, HU 58256, MH 27623, HU 45913

Chapter Five
D 2974, D 16392, Art.IWM ART 16438, D 5648, D 17925, D 17180, TR 1147, D 5210, Art.IWM ART LD 893, Art.IWM ART LD 1353, Art.IWM ART LD 939, HU 36154, Art.IWM ART LD 1879, D 2412, OWIL 54492, D 2973, HU 36268, EPH 673

In Focus: Literary London
HU 131395, D 21910, D 9562, D 7799, The Lyre Bird reproduced by permission of the Henry Moore Foundation

Chapter Six
HU 131386, Art.IWM ART LD 2798, HU 131448, HU 131468, HU 131479, D 21215, HU 87304, HU 131488, HU 131366, Art.IWM ART LD 4719, HU 44273, HU 638, C 5736, MUN 3854, HU 137060, MUN 3853, HU 66194, CL 3407, Art.IWM ART LD 4807, HU 131433

In Focus: London on Film
MH 24293, D 1777, D 1861, D 4229,

Epilogue
EA 65879, Art.IWM ART LD 5202, TR 2876, H 41849, HU 49414, EA 65881, D 25636, D 26324, (MOW) T 4750B, D 24183, D 24187

AUTHOR'S ACKNOWLEDGEMENTS

I am very grateful to Terry Charman, the former Senior Historian at the Imperial War Museum, London, who is now enjoying retirement. Terry gave me a large number of books about Second World War London and the home front, which have proved invaluable, went through the D-series photographs with me, helped me with his particular expertise on music and films of the era, and read the manuscript. I am also grateful to Tony Richards, Simon Offord and Jane McArthur for their help with documents and photographs respectively. Finally, I'd like to thank Mark Hawkins-Dady for his careful and considerate editing, and Madeleine James and Stephen Long for bringing it all together.

INDEX

Page references in italics refer to illustration captions